DISCARD

WESTERN INTEGRATION
and the
FUTURE OF EASTERN EUROPE

WESTERN INTEGRATION
and the
FUTURE OF EASTERN EUROPE

Edited by
DAVID S. COLLIER
and
KURT GLASER

Published in cooperation with
Foundation for Foreign Affairs, Inc.

HENRY REGNERY COMPANY
CHICAGO · 1964

FOUNDATION FOR FOREIGN AFFAIRS SERIES, NUMBER 9

The Foundation for Foreign Affairs, 154 East Superior Street, Chicago 11, Illinois, is a non-profit corporation devoted to the promotion of a wider understanding of international relations—political, economic, and cultural. Books in the Foundation for Foreign Affairs Series are published in the interest of public information and debate. They represent the free expression of their authors and do not necessarily indicate the judgment and opinions of the Foundation.

Contents

Part One

ECONOMIC PROBLEMS OF EUROPEAN UNITY

Part Two

POLITICAL AND MILITARY PROBLEMS OF EUROPEAN UNITY

Part Three

TOWARDS EUROPEAN-AMERICAN PARTNERSHIP

Introduction

As THIS VOLUME is being readied for publication, we are approaching the end of the second decade since the close of hostilities in World War II, when Soviet and Western troops drew up along a supposedly temporary occupation boundary which soon crystallized into the Iron Curtain that today truncates Germany and Europe. Since this dividing line has remained geographically stable, except for a minor shift eastward in Austria in 1955, the historically myopic are tempted to regard it as a permanent institution. Realism, they declare, consists in accepting the status quo, in "learning to live with" unsatisfactory situations, as the popular slogan goes, and in hoping that in the long run the problem of the Iron Curtain will be solved through a "mellowing" of the adversary, through a "meeting half-way," or perhaps through the superimposition of universal formulae such as total disarmament or world government.

Yet the political balance across the Iron Curtain has by no means been as stable as would appear at first glance. The Soviet Russians, on their side, have never been able to consolidate their new colonial empire, the tenuousness of which was demonstrated in 1953 in the Soviet Zone of Germany and in 1956 in Poland and Hungary. Western Europe has simultaneously experienced a phenomenal economic recovery followed and extended by measures of integration, limited initially to the economic and military spheres, but pointing increasingly toward a Political Europe capable of exercising power as a coherent entity.

One of the significant results of World War II was that the United States, unintentionally and to some extent unwillingly, became for all practical purposes a European power. Since American defense begins at the Elbe, if not in Berlin, Americans share with Europeans an overriding interest in the security and prosperity of the old continent, including the recovery of *Europa irredenta*, that part of the European Community now suffering under the yoke of Communist domination.

vii

Common aims can best be realized through common policy; this in turn demands a common understanding of problems. It is for this reason that a group of German and other European students of international affairs and a group of Americans with European interests have met in a series of conferences on the future of Eastern Europe. The first, held in Chicago in March, 1962, considered the topic "Berlin and the Future of Eastern Europe," and provided the basis for a book with the same title.[1] The papers given at the second conference in Wiesbaden in September, 1963, around the theme of "Western European Integration and the Future of Eastern Europe," have been revised to form the articles constituting the present volume. A third conference has already been scheduled to take place in the near future.

The sponsors of the Wiesbaden conference were the Foundation for Foreign Affairs of Chicago, and the Studiengesellschaft für Fragen mittel-und osteuropäischer Partnerschaft of Wiesbaden. As in the earlier conference at Chicago, the scholars and public figures who participated spoke as individuals; their opinions as expressed in the articles that follow do not necessarily reflect the views of the Foundation, the Studiengesellschaft, or the editors.

Since the organizers of the conference made a deliberate and successful effort to secure a wide spectrum of views, a few comments by the editors may be helpful in bringing the contributions into meaningful relationship. The discussions following the papers at the conference showed fundamental agreement—far more than is evident from the papers themselves—on three important points. The first is that in spite of Communist military threats and aggressive infiltration, the political, social, and economic systems of the free world have proved their superior viability. Secondly, it was evident to all that the integration of Western Europe is exercising an increasingly magnetic force on the European peoples behind the Iron Curtain, who are becoming under the circumstances more painfully aware of their ties with the West. Finally, there was no dissent from the conviction that the demand for social, intellectual, and political freedom is a universal human trait, which no amount of totalitarian indoctrination can ever really extinguish.

So far as the specific political situation is concerned, there is a wide range of interpretation and an even wider choice of suggested policies.

[1] David S. Collier and Kurt Glaser, eds., *Berlin and the Future of Eastern Europe* (Chicago: Henry Regnery Company, 1963).

We find on the one hand a tendency to reduce the entire conflict symbolized by the Iron Curtain to a matter of conventional power politics and economic utility. This interpretation is formulated most clearly in the contribution of Professor Carrington, who observes that while the American approach to the East-West struggle is ideological, the British, which he represents, is political. Applying the criteria of traditional political and economic rivalry to East-West competition in the developing countries, Carrington notes with satisfaction that "in spite of all the trade missions, the amount of genuine commerce between the Communist countries and the African Commonwealth countries is very small indeed." The validity of this traditional approach depends on the extent to which Soviet foreign policy represents a political rather than an ideological force, and to which promotion of trade is actually the purpose of Soviet trade missions.

Although Professor Epstein assigns a much higher importance to the ideological side of the East-West struggle than does Carrington, his policy recommendations may also be classified as essentially traditional. Epstein rejects categorically the "liberation" policy proclaimed by the late John Foster Dulles in the 1952 election campaign, a policy which he declares to have been a complete failure. He supports American leaders who advocate seeking a *détente* through negotiations with the Soviets, and considers it unrealistic to make the self-determination of peoples east of the Iron Curtain a precondition for relaxation. In view of the gradual metamorphosis of Communist political and social institutions, Professor Epstein suggests a *détente* designed to head off nuclear warfare should not bar the way to eventual freedom for a re-united Europe.

At the other end of our intellectual spectrum we find analysts such as Baron von Guttenberg, who states categorically that Communist ideology backed by Soviet power is the basic cause of the Cold War. Guttenberg recognizes fully that military and political (including economic and propaganda) weapons are interchangeable in Communist strategy, and therefore approaches East-West relations in the non-conventional frame of reference of a single though variegated continum of struggle. A policy of accommodation, representing a retreat on the political front, would in his opinion produce not relaxation but aggravated Communist aggression. General Howley, in his article on Berlin, likewise indicates that the East-West struggle is strategically a war and demands the same kind of strategic thinking.

Substantive support for Baron von Guttenberg's analysis is provided in the parts of Professor Meissner's article dealing with the ideological side of Soviet foreign policy. Meissner points out that the Kremlin was able to achieve the division of Germany in three parts and the sovietization of East Central Europe without regard for the then-existing American nuclear monopoly, because it knew that ideological disorientation would paralyze the United States from making effective use of its resources. He emphasizes that both Moscow and Peking remain solidly committed to world revolution, though they differ as to means for achieving it.

Suggestions for non-conventional ways of exploiting the economic strength of the West are offered by Dr. Jaksch, who has borne a share of responsibility in developing policies for German relations with the Eastern bloc. Since Communist governments are inclined to accept Western trade and aid granted on a "no strings" basis, and then use the goods for their own political purposes, including the support of aggressive satellites and subversive movements, the only feasible procedure is to reward measures of evolution in the direction of freedom and democracy. Dr. Jaksch proposes that trade with the Communist bloc should be in exchange for political concessions, such as the freeing of political prisoners and families of exiles, the de-collectivization of farms, and permission for opposition parties to operate. The West, he urges, needs the concept of a constructive anti-communism, rather than letting the Kremlin dictate the subjects of international discussion.

Those authors who have touched on military affairs, including Professors Mosely and Possony, and Colonel Miksche, are agreed that NATO should be strengthened, but have variant proposals for bringing this about. As the reader will see, there are two sides to the question of "proliferation" of atomic weapons among states that do not already possess them.

It may be that for many readers, this book will raise questions as well as answer them. Among those which occurred to the editors after reading the manuscripts and noting the assumptions made by the various authors, are the following, which seem basic to any serious consideration of American strategy:

1. It has been stated that the policy of liberation has "failed"— but has it ever really been tried? While there may be some truth in the criticism that the Eisenhower-Dulles version of "liberation" alternated between brinkmanship and empty verbiage, serious advocates of liberation such as James Burnham and the Kersten Committee of 1954 had in mind a definite policy of action, spelled out in consider-

able detail in Kersten's Summary Report.[2] This policy is based on the premise that political warfare is an *alternative* to military warfare. A properly conceived policy of liberation, using political, economic, diplomatic, and propaganda weapons with maximum effectiveness, is held by its advocates to *reduce* the danger of total war.

2. It has been alleged by numerous "experts" that since the so-called "German Democratic Republic" which the Kremlin has installed in its occupation zone of Germany is "exercising the powers of a sovereign state," we cannot avoid the ultimate necessity of recognizing it. Is not the uniform worn by the police that guard the zonal borders and control travelers on the Autobahn less important than the ultimate control of these forces? Border control may be delegated to police forces of subordinate authorities, as U.S. Military Government delegated control functions to the West German border police before the Federal Republic regained its sovereignty. The true criterion of sovereignty is the ability of a state to exist on the basis of its own power. We must, therefore, ask the crucial question: If Soviet troops were withdrawn, could the "German Democratic Republic" continue to exist?

3. More than once, our authors expressed the thought that the natural allies of the West in the satellite area are the oppressed peoples, not the governments that Moscow has imposed upon them. This idea has been developed further by Mr. Brutus Coste, secretary-general of the Assembly of Captive European Nations, who points out that the unreliability of the satellite armies, from a Soviet point of view, is a part of the system of deterrents which prevent further Communist aggression.[3] We must therefore ask ourselves: Might not a policy of "accommodation" with Communist governments, by undermining the morale and hence the deterrent value of the satellite peoples, actually increase the danger of military war?

4. Finally, two of our authors have assumed that American action during the Cuban missile crisis of October 1962 was an unqualified success, and one of them suggests that the Kremlin was faced with "a clear choice between withdrawing from an over-exposed position or making the decision for an all-out nuclear exchange." Aside from the

[2] United States House of Representatives, 83d Congress, 2d Session, Select Committee on Communist Aggression, *Summary Report* (Washington: United States Government Printing Office, 1954).

[3] Assembly of Captive European Nations, Report of Secretary General Brutus Coste, "East–Central Europe—Factor of Western Security," presented at meeting of May 6, 1963, in Strasbourg. ACEN News, No. 97-99, pp. 12-16 (New York, May-July, 1963).

more obvious question of the facts concerning shipments of rockets (as distinguished from their casings) to and from Cuba, we may be inclined to ask whether the Soviets did not have a third alternative: to take their chances in a limited engagement, which might well have occurred had the Soviets neither withdrawn nor initiated nuclear hostilities. It might indeed be argued that the Soviets made a variety of that third choice, by combining an ostentatious withdrawal with the leaving of substantial "technical" forces in Cuba.

Comparison of all the facts and points of view brought out by the various authors suggests that effective Western policy in the struggle for human freedom must be eclectic, combining political, diplomatic, economic, and ideological factors with an adequacy of military power and with sophisticated forms of non-military struggle. Such a policy, representing true flexibility, would be best equipped to deal with the alternation of "peaceful" and violent tactics envisaged by communist strategists. Rather than rest on the laurels of spectacular treaties and "disengagements," we should heed the Communist theorist who confirms the continuum of struggle in these words:

> "It remains the truth that peaceful coexistence is the inevitable condition for the further development of the proletarian revolution today . . . While peaceful coexistence is an absolute necessity in the progress of human society, a peaceful road to socialism is not an exclusive method, it is only one of the possibilities; in no way does it exclude the need for a flexible alternation of armed and peaceful forms of fight."[4]

The editors hope that the ideas contained in this volume will be of some help in strengthening both American and European policy to master whatever forms of peaceful or less-than-peaceful competition that may ensue in coming phases of the East-West encounter.

David S. Collier
Foundation for Foreign Affairs, Inc.

Kurt Glaser
Southern Illinois University

June, 1964

4 *Pravda*, Bratislava (organ of the Slovak Communist Party, not to be confused with the Moscow *Pravda*), August 7, 1963.

WESTERN INTEGRATION
and the
FUTURE OF EASTERN EUROPE

CHAPTER I

The New Western Europe and the World Strategy of Democracy

PHILIP E. MOSELY

IF WE LOOK BACK eighteen years to the European nadir of 1945, and then at the Europe of today, we and all citizens of free countries cannot but be deeply gratified at the profound transformation that has taken place in the fortunes and prospects of Western Europe. In the wake of a second European civil war, which was also the most devastating and exhausting world war ever known, even the future existence of this great center of modern civilization was in question. Europe's dismembered limbs seemed to be twitching aimlessly, while its remaining chimneys stood out gaunt and smokeless above mountains of useless rubble. And the self-inflicted wounds of destruction, hate, and hopelessness were then being compounded by the crude severing of Europe in half as stooge parties and Moscow-trained police forces consolidated Soviet control over ancient European territories that Hitler's blind ambitions had made a prey to Stalin's armies.

Today non-Communist Europe faces many problems, but, fortunately, they are problems of strength, of future achievement, not of helpless waiting. Western Europe, though still disunited politically, is more closely knit in its economic and cultural life than it has been at any time since 1913. Rebuilding its capacity as a workshop of the world, free Europe is once again the biggest single factor of international trade, and it enjoys a higher and more broadly based standard of living than at any time in its long history. Some Europeans even ask whether their continent is not sinking into a passive attitude of "getting-and-spending," without thought for the political and cultural creativity that has radiated from Europe over so many centuries. This self-depreciating doubt seems to me misplaced. Surely, it is not surpris-

1

ing if Europeans wish to postpone some of the burdens of responsibility, to enjoy their newly gained productivity and prosperity, and to
relax while feelings and hopes of a common European destiny grow
sufficiently strong and stable to support a new effort of European imag-
ination and initiative.

If we now look to the future, instead of to 1945, a similar span of
eighteen years brings us to the year 1981. That date has, by coincidence, been set as the culminating year of the twenty-year Party Program which was adopted by the Communist Party of the Soviet Union
in October, 1961. By comparison with the creative possibilities that
are being brooded over and argued over with passion in Western Europe, the Soviet picture of life in 1981 is a dull and colorless one. More
and better clothing, a two-room apartment as a minimum for all, more
busses and trains but few automobiles, the same intellectual and artistic conformity for all. No wonder the Soviet Party Program has
aroused so little genuine enthusiasm at home, and so little envy abroad!

But enough of self-congratulation and complacency. In the dangerous world of today we must ask ourselves several difficult questions.
What are the main dangers that face a renascent Western Europe?
What are the risks that must be defined before they can be overcome?
And what are the unique opportunities that await a Europe reawak-
ened to its historic role of creativity? These stirring and complex
questions can be dealt with here only briefly and in broad outline.

Changes Since Stalin's Death

Basic to Europe's role in the world is the ability of the West to assure
its survival with as much certainty as may humanly be possible. The
achieving of that ability, in turn, depends in large measure on how
we define the nature of the Soviet challenge. Is the Soviet system going
to remain a threat to Europe and the West? Or is it changing so rapidly
from within that its persistent hopes of incorporating all Europe into
the Soviet empire are now nothing but an automatic and monotonous
repetition of the messianic claims of Communist dogma? And is the
Chinese Communist challenge to Moscow's hegemony within the
Communist part of the world likely to distract the Soviet rulers from
the temptation to take on new risks in order to make new gains?

Much has changed in Soviet society since Stalin's death, and these
changes, especially in the material sphere, have been for the marked

benefit of the Soviet people. After several decades of intense privation and exploitation, the people of the Soviet Union have begun to enjoy some of the fruits of their sacrifices. A rapid expansion of housing, a somewhat improved supply of food and clothing, a steady flow of television sets, refrigerators, washing machines, and other consumer durables, an adequate system of old-age pensions for the urban population, a reduction in the working day—these and other benefits make Soviet life more rewarding and provide stronger incentives for more efficient work. Despite the recent tightening of party controls, Soviet literature and the theater now have more leeway to present some of the real problems of post-Stalin Russia. In proclaiming the goal of replacing the "dictatorship of the proletariat" by an "all-people's state," the leaders invite a wider range of participation by loyal activists in running cultural life and supervising local administration, housing, recreation, and justice, while always preserving and strengthening the "leading role" of the Communist party.

A careful reading of Soviet programs and statements makes it clear, nevertheless, that all these changes, real and proposed, are intended to be changes within the basic system of Communist dictatorship. We have no grounds for assuming that the party, which led or drove the country through almost unimaginable crises of civil war, collectivization, and invasion, will not maintain its supreme and exclusive control behind the more flexible forms of rule it is now preaching. For one thing, these methods are mild only in comparison with Stalin's; the controls that the party exerts over individual lives and careers are stern and comprehensive, compared with anything people in the West have known. In the second place, the party's controls over all forms of knowledge, literature, the arts, and information are active and rigorous. As Khrushchev has emphasized over and over, he will not tolerate any "co-existence of ideologies." Indeed, he cannot, for the leader's right to rule rests on an "ideocracy," on the claim to possess the sole correct view and understanding of past, present and future. Other regimes base their legitimacy on popular vote, on hereditary monarchy, on support by a military establishment. The Soviet regime, as in Lenin's and Stalin's times, bases its rule on the claim that it alone has the ideological key to the future of all mankind.

The revolutionary romanticism of the early years of Bolshevism has long since died down, but it has been replaced by other and perhaps more durable emotions. The thrilling picture of Russia as one of the world's two greatest powers has compelling force for all those "activist" strata of Soviet society on which the leaders rely to move this powerful system forward. After more than a century of feeling relatively weak, backward and threatened, Russians have responded enthusiastically to Khrushchev's frequent reminders that today no question, anywhere in the world, can be decided without the Soviet Union having its say. And the messianic claim that the Soviet revolution has not only led Russia to an unprecedented peak of power but has also laid down the only valid pattern for reconstructing the entire world now evokes a more confident and more energizing response among Soviet people than it ever did before.

The dispute between Moscow and Peking for leadership over the Communist part of the world presents the Kremlin with unforeseen and baffling problems. The conflict has deep roots and may have far-reaching consequences, but it is not at all clear that it seriously limits the Kremlin's ability to pursue its own goals by its own means and in its own time. Communist China is so far inferior to Soviet Russia in strategic power and economic strength that it can raise this challenge only in the perspective of far-distant goals. Even the acquisition of a modest nuclear force would leave Peking vastly and increasingly inferior to either Soviet or American power. A nuclear leap-forward might have some political impact within Asia, but its effect would in turn depend on whether both America and Russia remained impassive and inactive in the face of that development. Meanwhile, in some parts of Asia, particularly in Southeast Asia, India, and Indonesia, the split leaves China free to pursue its own militant goals without regard to Soviet interests and advice. By the same token, it also leaves the Kremlin free to apply its far wider range of policy instruments without regard to Peking's interests and hopes.

The prediction has often been made that a falling out with Peking would force the Soviet leadership to relax its pressure on Europe. Indeed, some soothsayers foretell a time when the Kremlin will appeal to Europe to come to its defense against a militant China! Actually, Soviet Russia is so strong today in the essential sinews of power that it can cope with China's challenge within the Communist part of the world, while at the same time maintaining an active pressure against America and a renascent Western Europe. Khrushchev has apparently decided to seek a period of somewhat relaxed relations with the West; this may have resulted from his reappraisal of the perilous climax of the Cuban missile crisis. If this is so, the reasons for it lie in his new estimate of the present balance of strategic power, and in his hope of delaying the emergence of a consolidated Europe as a third great power, not in any limitations on Soviet ability to cope with Communist China's restless militancy.

For almost fifteen years Soviet leaders have striven, even if by clumsy and self-defeating means, to forestall the emergence of a more or less united Western Europe. They have seen, perhaps even more clearly than most Europeans, that this is the one great potentiality for shifting the balance of power to the disadvantage of communism. To accomplish their aim, they have made extravagant use of domestic Communist parties; except in Italy this effort has either eroded or isolated local Communist strengths. They have offered blandishments, the attraction of which they over-estimated, to each European nation. More often they have uttered dire threats of nuclear destruction, until Europeans have learned to treat these threats almost too casually.

Now, having admitted that a nuclear war would destroy not only the West but also the painfully accumulated gains of Soviet well-being and power, Khrushchev may hope to forestall the consolidation of Western Europe, not by real concessions to its legitimate interests, but rather by a protracted period of negotiations. Past experience has shown that the willingness of the Soviet leadership to negotiate with the West, and the degree of that willingness, are determined primarily by its estimate of the actual or potential strength of its opponents. I know of no case in which a nation has successfully negotiated with the Kremlin from a position of weakness. If the West hopes to emerge from a prolonged period of negotiation with its positions and prospects strengthened, it must not be distracted by the mere process of negotiation, with its ups and downs of hope, from the further building up of those factors of strength that brought the Kremlin to the negotiating table in the first place. And a major part of that strength is the spirit of understanding and mutual trust that, despite some minor contrary currents of policy, activates the nations of the Atlantic world.

The European Contribution to Western Strategy

The ultimate guarantee of survival for the free nations rests today in the American nuclear deterrent, but this does not mean that the strategic arrangements that were inevitable and acceptable in the 1950's will remain so to the end of the 1960's or to the mid-1970's. A united Western Europe can become, over the world, an active partner rather than a strategic dependent. To be an active partner, however, Europe is going to require either the possession of a nuclear deterrent of its own, or else a substantial sharing in the control and the costs of an Atlantic deterrent. If Europe is to achieve a truly independent nuclear deterrent, outside any partnership with the United States, European statesmen and public opinion will have to give very careful thought to all the factors involved. Or, if it is to share in the management of a common Atlantic deterrent, much more must be done to envisage the handling of this great responsibility. Only a few of these factors can be suggested here.

One basic fact, which French official thinking seems to ignore, is that a small or token deterrent will not guarantee Western Europe against a sudden nuclear attack, or against nuclear blackmail, exerted by the massive nuclear-missile power of the Soviet Union. The idea that a retaliatory force of modest power can deter an attack, or a threat of attack, overlooks a number of serious obstacles. For one thing, the nuclear attacker has vast advantages over the attacked, and we do not know when, if ever, adequate means of active defense will be available to blunt the effects of a first-strike attack. And, for all we now know, anti-missile defenses, if and when they become available, may be even more expensive than the largest nuclear-missile force of today. Furthermore, despite the partial ban on testing nuclear bombs, the research effort to develop more effective weapons and invent means of anti-missile defense will go on, and these programs entail very large costs of scientific manpower, engineering and money. Today the United States is spending on defense research and development almost as much as the other partners in NATO are spending on their entire defense effort. It would be unwise, and for a long time to come, impossible for Western Europe to replicate the vast American and Soviet effort. On the other hand, a small European-NATO deterrent could be created at a relatively smaller, though still substantial, cost if the United States provided the research, the training, the weapons, and much of the supporting systems for its operation. But the United States could hardly take this risk unless the European deterrent were closely integrated, politically and strategically, with the main U.S. deterrent. Nor would a small but independent European deterrent establish any new security for Europe beyond the guarantee already provided by the U.S. deterrent.

In order for the European members of NATO to have a clearer understanding both of the tremendous striking power and of the serious political inhibitions that are inherent in a nuclear strategy, it is important for them to participate much more fully than in the past in a joint responsibility for strategic planning and decisions, and in the actual operation of a multilateral nuclear force. An Atlantic deterrent, which would enlarge substantially the range of points from which deterrence can be exercised and Soviet blackmail faced down, can be more effective than a single U.S. deterrent. A systematic program of joint study would make it possible for those leaders who believe that separate national deterrents within individual European countries can stand up to the massive threat of Soviet nuclear power to think out the alternatives more carefully. They would, I believe, become more aware of the concrete limitations that are imposed by geographical, strategic, political and economic factors. The answer to the problem of assuring the long-range survival of both Western Europe and North America is not to move apart in many separate directions, but to build a stronger political foundation of unity, so as to manage effectively the new and massive factors that now enter into the strategic equation.

Within that equation there are other factors besides that of strategic deterrence, but there is great confusion and uncertainty over the role, both strategic and political, of conventional forces. Within NATO–Europe many strong supporters of Atlantic interdependence are puzzled by the American insistence on the need for building more powerful conventional forces in Western Europe. Does this mean, they ask, that NATO and America would tolerate the sudden occupation by Soviet forces of even a narrow band of NATO-defended territory without going to nuclear war? Would not a stronger conventional posture in the West lead or mislead Soviet planners into assuming that they could carry out such an incursion without fear of nuclear retaliation?

The course and aftermath of the Cuban missile crisis should have helped clarify the reasons that lie behind the American pressure to strengthen the forces of NATO. The existence of a somewhat superior U.S. strategic deterrent did not prevent the Kremlin from "trying its luck" by secretly installing intermediate-range missiles in Cuba. On the other hand, because the United States naval, air, and land forces also held a superiority in conventional forces around and over Cuba, the United States could have destroyed the Soviet forces on Cuba without using nuclear weapons. The prospect confronted the Soviet leaders with a clear choice between withdrawing from an over-exposed position or making the decision for an all-out nuclear exchange. The U.S. local conventional superiority would have been ineffective without the possession of a powerful nuclear-missile force or without the clear determination, in extreme necessity, to use it. At the same time the U.S. possession of conventional superiority was a decisive factor both in achieving the immediate American objective and in enabling both sides to avoid unleashing a nuclear holocaust.

To some extent, this lesson can be applied to the situation of Western Europe and the unequivocal U.S. commitment to come to its defense. In the future, as now, both sides to the conflict over the future of Europe will have a strong desire to make gains or avoid losses without going to all-out nuclear war. If the Soviet Union continues to have a clear preponderance of conventional power located within close range of its objectives, it may at some time be tempted into a new adventure in the expectation that it can make local gains on the ground and still maneuver to escape a nuclear engagement. Turning the scenario around, we can say that it is dangerous for NATO to rely exclusively on the threat of nuclear holocaust as the sole means of saving West Berlin from a variety of imaginable Soviet moves. It would be much wiser, and conceivably much less costly in the long run, to build up NATO's conventional strength so that Soviet strategic planners would have to envisage a broad and flexible spectrum of possible NATO responses to any of their moves against Berlin. And, finally, the possession by NATO of conventional preponderance would give much more bargaining strength to the captive peoples of East Central Europe to help them resist Soviet demands for greater subordination to Soviet policy and oppose Soviet exploitation of their real and potential assets.

The present situation of NATO's conventional forces presents a number of serious risks, both strategic and political. If, after a more or less prolonged period of *détente,* the Soviet leaders should decide to make one of those sudden and secret shifts for which they are famous, it would be essential to have NATO's strength available in being, not on paper. A coalition army is no stronger than its weakest sector, and it is dangerous, in a test of political will-power, to have to rely on a force that is not actually prepared to go into action promptly and effectually.

Finally, there are certain political risks that cannot be overlooked when we consider NATO's present capabilities. The United States has stationed in Europe and under NATO command larger forces than any European ally except the Federal Republic of Germany, and it has contributed a very large share of the costs. These continuing expenditures weaken its balance of payments and thereby strain its ability to support other equally essential parts of its foreign policy. The United States is, of course, helping to defend Western Europe, not only because of a close feeling of common fate, but also because of its direct national interest. However, many Americans wonder whether it is not at least as much an interest of their European allies to remain strong and free, and whether the defense of a common vital interest does not require some readjustment of the common burden. In addition to its major sacrifices for the common defense of Western Europe, the United States is also devoting great efforts to defense purposes in other parts of the world and to foreign military and economic aid; from these the nations of Western Europe gain many indirect benefits while making, except for Great Britain and France, relatively minor contributions.

In this brief survey it is not possible to do more than suggest some of the problem areas of Western military strategy. What is clear is that all the NATO allies need to examine more closely the changing context of their strategic security and the means required to assure their common defense into the 1970's. They will discover that a united Western Europe can and will do more than it is now doing to transform its potentially great weight into a decisive factor in the world balance of power.

The Perspectives Opened by European Economic Unification

The exact form and content of Europe's contributions to the creation of a more favorable strategic balance in the world are, and will remain, the focus of many disagreements and uncertainties. The same, fortunately, is not true, at least not in the same degree, of its role in the world economy. Europe's own efforts and its industrial genius, backed by timely and large-scale assistance from the United States and Canada, launched the free half of the continent into a new stage of dynamic economic progress. Indeed, Europe is again a pace-setter in many fields of industrial advance. At the same time, the acceptance of new responsibilities for raising productivity and for sharing the enlarged national income more broadly has begun to reshape Europe's social and psychological structures in ways that are gradually rendering obsolete many of the traditional class, religious, and ideological conflicts it has inherited from the past.

A relatively small number of farsighted Europeans and Americans foresaw at war's end that Europe's postwar upswing could achieve its full momentum only through creating a larger European market, with all the advantages of a continent-wide scale of production and competition. From the Schuman Plan of 1950, to the Rome Treaty of 1957, and thus to the launching of the European Economic Community in 1958, France and Germany have led the way in overcoming many formidable obstacles in order to move along the path traced out by Jean Monnet and Paul-Henri Spaak, statesmen of a truly European scale. Now an operating reality, the Community faces a whole series of decisive choices, choices that will go far to set the pattern of the world economy in the next decade and beyond.

In shaping the channels and rules of world trade, especially through the 1963-64 negotiations in GATT, the Community has an unparalleled opportunity to knit together the interests of the free world by promoting the continuing liberalization of tariffs and the gradual removal of other restraints on the movement of goods and on competition. Both the United States and the European Free Trade Association (EFTA) are equipped to go far in this direction. The expansion of the U.S. economy that has occurred during 1963 can also facilitate the transition to greater liberalism in trading conditions.

Through adopting a liberal approach the Community can go far toward overcoming the negative political effects of President de Gualle's veto, in January, 1963, on further negotiations for the assimilation of Britain and other EFTA members into the Common Market of the Six. The United States will also have to make numerous and difficult adjustments in its tariff and other restrictions on trade. Because of the Trade Expansion Act of 1962, it is in a better position to do so than at any time since World War I. One basic question that the Community will have to face is whether its future trade policy is going to represent an arithmetic highest denominator of protection for the weakest sectors and weakest producers within sectors, arrived at through the familiar process of special-interest log-rolling, or whether it will help open still wider world markets for the most progressive and efficient sectors and producers everywhere. There is no need to point out which course, broadly applied, will accomplish more both for the expansion of world trade and for the steady growth of the European economy.

In the new round of GATT negotiations the Community has a special opportunity to help knit some of the "special cases" into a liberal trading pattern. Switzerland and Sweden will, of course, be able to look out for their own interests even in very tough bargaining situations. Austria is in a more vulnerable situation, and here an element of Community generosity can have important political implications. Yugoslavia should be attracted toward the Community and Austria by extensive and stable trade agreements. The recent establishment of closer trade relations between the Federal Republic of Germany and Poland, and the prospect of similar trade arrangements with Czechoslovakia and Hungary, and perhaps with Rumania, can have important long-range repercussions on the ability of the satellite regimes to pursue their own economic ambitions. The hothouse development of industry in the satellites, much of it inefficient in terms of real costs, and the continued serious lag in agriculture, have, it is true, combined to make their ties with the Soviet Union a decisive factor. Nevertheless, closer economic ties with the West can help introduce an important element of flexibility into their over-rigid planning and management and can give them some additional bargaining power in their negotiations with the Soviet Union.

Finally, while it is utopian to suppose that economic factors offer a leverage sufficient to change their political dependence on Soviet policy, it is desirable for the satellites to multiply their contacts with the West. Looking at Western Europe through a wider window, they will be better able to form their own judgments on such issues as the defensive attitude of NATO, the risks that can arise from new Soviet pressures on West Berlin, or the myth of German "revanchism" as an active political force. These and other political interests of the new Europe point to the need for an increasingly liberal and open policy on the part of Western Europe, and away from too much concern with satisfying the special interests of its less productive and less venturesome sectors.

In contradiction to the generally liberalizing trend of U.S. foreign economic policy, the Kennedy administration proposed, in July, 1963, the enactment of a tax penalty to discourage new U.S. investment abroad, except for certain exemptions established for Canada, which, in this as in many other respects, seems to prosper best when treated as part of a single North American entity. This new policy, which may or may not have much effect on the U.S. balance of payments, can have some useful side effects in the European capital market. For one thing, if it can be enforced, which is not certain, it will tend to short-circuit the postwar habit of placing European private funds in New York, for re-investment in American disguise within Europe. It should likewise intensify the search for ways of broadening investment channels within Europe. It should, on balance, not hinder the trend toward technical and production agreements between American and European firms with their beneficial effects on European productivity; such agreements, which have become increasingly frequent in recent years, do not necessarily involve large-scale transfers of capital.

The flow of U.S. capital to advanced industrial countries, including Western Europe, is, however, only one of many factors that have resulted in a persistently unfavorable U.S. balance of payments. It is to be hoped that the positive responses of U.S. and European investors, as well as stronger efforts to adjust the burdens of military and development costs, will make it possible before long to abandon this policy, which runs counter to the longer-range U.S. efforts to promote nondiscriminatory trade and investment. Fortunately, the advanced countries are now better equipped institutionally than at any time since 1914, especially through the World Bank, the Monetary Fund, and the OECD, to consult closely on the adjustment of their policies, and thus to avoid the older pattern of blind national action and retaliation.

The Challenge to European Leadership

One of the main challenges to Western Europe is to use its great and growing accumulation of resources in trade, investment and technical skills to knit the developing countries into the free-world pattern of economic and political cooperation. The political de-colonialization of Asia and most of Africa has released a tremendous upsurge of new ambitions, which far outrun the capacity of any but a few of the new governments to satisfy. On the other hand, the needs of Europe for food, fiber, fuels, and minerals are growing rapidly, and these requirements can best be met, in most cases, through the cooperative expansion of production in the newly independent countries.

The European Economic Community has shown a strong awareness that it has a very important role to play in this area of endeavor. Through the agreement associating most of the former French colonies in Africa with the Common Market, it has opened its growing outlets to their raw materials. It has also made provision for discrimination in favor of African infant industries, so as to weaken the charge that Europe wants to keep the former colonies from replacing industrial imports with their own production. It has likewise enlarged somewhat the Community's contribution to African development programs in education, transportation, and administrative and technical training. All this, added to the large contributions that France has been making to help its former dependencies, provides a firm though still modest basis for a greater European effort to assist much of Africa to make better use of its resources for its development.

One especially useful device, applied increasingly, is the consortium financing of large-scale new enterprises. This has the beneficial effect of assuring to the participating firms a future sharing of access to bauxite, iron ore, and other raw materials. It also dilutes the one-to-one relationship between metropole and former colony. It does not entirely remove the emotional impact of left-wing charges of "collective colonialism," but even the more radical regimes in Guinea and Ghana seem satisfied with the economic effects of the consortium approach.

A proposal widely discussed in recent years is that Western Europe should concentrate its development efforts in Africa, while the United States should do the same in Latin America. This suggestion smacks too much of an allocation of "spheres of influence" to please either Africans or Latin Americans. While European mineral interests and needs will undoubtedly look mainly toward Africa over the next decade, U.S. firms also have a constructive role to play there. Over the past decade their influence has helped to blunt the colony-metropole antagonism and has stimulated the placing of a stronger emphasis on educational and social welfare contributions that outside investors can make to the development of independent countries.

Within Latin America, Europeans and European business interests have played an important role, both economic and cultural, for over a century. In some countries the European participation in national development has provided a stronger cultural bridge to a modern way of life than many U.S. development efforts. The Latin American elite often assimilates new social ideas and new economic techniques more rapidly from the smaller-scale European initiatives. Finally, as demonstrated in the recent Coffee Agreement, there are numerous commodities in which competition between Latin America and Africa can be destructive to the interests of either or both. Western Europe and America have a common interest in avoiding such a direct confrontation and clash of interests between the two great developing continents.

In helping the developing countries organize the use of their raw materials and move on to self-sustaining economic growth, the European approach has certain advantages over direct U.S. and Soviet aid programs. With its habitual and intimate mixture of governmental and private responsibilities and resources, Western Europe can be more flexible than the more doctrinaire free-enterprise approach favored by the U.S. Congress, or the even more dogmatic Soviet insistence on building up the public sector exclusively. Finally, Europe offers the newly independent countries something that the Soviet Union, with its continuing emphasis on autarchy, cannot offer: a large, growing and stable market for their raw materials. The prospects for a strong West European and Community role in economic development are excellent. But Europe will discover that it must act even more boldly and imaginatively if it is to meet both its needs and its opportunities through the rest of the century.

Even before it was fully enjoying the fruits of its economic revival, Europe was again demonstrating the vitality of its leadership in culture and the arts. For a variety of reasons the creative initiative in film-making has shifted to European centers. Similarly, while European painters and composers now seek the final accolade in recognition by New York, many American artists and musicians are again turning to the more intimate atmosphere of European milieus to give their talents time to ripen and to test their creative thinking. The smaller scale of publicity and the diversity of tastes in Europe, together with the more intimate participation of audiences and viewers in making reputations or leaving them unmade, continue to weigh heavily in the development of new talents. The contrast between massive success and artistic oblivion is still too great in America to provide a satisfactory ladder of artistic maturation.

Despite the shocks that war and economic disruption administered to the structure of taste-making, Western Europe has shown a remarkable continuity and vitality as a center of artistic and musical judgment. Only in the field of the novel have American creativity and inventiveness kept a distinct lead over their European counterparts, but that lead is now diminishing. The cultural achievements of Western Europe continue to support and strengthen its leading and stimulating role throughout the world, even in the Communist-ruled countries of Western Europe.

Many Europeans wonder whether their continent can maintain the tradition of an elitist and innovating culture in the face of the many changes that are taking place in its social structure. The spread of mass consumption will, they fear, dilute the traditional role of highly cultivated strata as patrons and recognizers of new artistic and literary talents. The rapid expansion of secondary and higher education may, they suggest, weaken the continuity of the taste-making elite, by swamping its special role in a "middle-brow" culture. These risks exist, of course, but they seem exaggerated. The decisive groups of *arbîtres du goût* have always been small, and the traditionally well educated and prosperous strata have usually lagged a generation or more behind the pace-setters. The spread of education should not lead to a vulgarization of taste, especially in a continent which has so many examples of past artistic and intellectual creativity ever present in so many of its centers.

The broadening of the European educational ladder has advantages as well as risks. A certain degree of simplification of learning is needed in order to fill Europe's neglected requirements for well-trained middle ranks of technicians and sub-managers. The process of adapting systems of education to the needs of wider strata within European societies can also make these resources more accessible and more useful to the developing nations of Africa and Asia. So, the slow and partial "Americanization" of educational processes within Europe can, on the whole, be beneficial to Europe's own evolution and also to its role in the developing countries.

As Europeans and Americans together look to the great achievements of the new Europe, several major opportunities stand out. Western Europe is again becoming a factor of great weight in the world balance. By developing its full economic and technological potentials, it can set up permanent obstacles to the doctrinaire ideological claims and expansionist ambitions to the Soviet leadership. By harmonizing its initiatives with those of North America, it can help rebuild the world economy on a stable foundation of active and imaginative expansion. It has at present perhaps its final and greatest opportunity to knit the developing continents into a compatible system of economic expansion. In all these spheres America's co-responsibilities in seeking workable adjustments are also very great.

In order to gain a larger measure of control over their strategic security, Western Europeans, together with Americans, must give intensive thought, both official and private, to problems of survival in an age of nuclear power and continental-size powers. In one way or another, an increasingly powerful Western Europe must be enabled to share in the fundamental decisions and responsibilities of strategy. Perhaps none of the currently fashionable formulas will prove acceptable over time, but the search for the more effective political organization of survival has only now begun. Whether this in the end will be a European or an Atlantic formula remains uncertain, and perhaps this decision can be left open for a few more years.

Finally, behind this crisis of growth is the problem of the political role of the new Europe. Political inventiveness has thus far lagged behind both economic initiative and the strategic revolution. The effort of political invention, if it is to succeed, must be pursued more or less simultaneously at three levels: the European, the Atlantic, and the free-world level. For Europe eventually to exert its full political weight in the Atlantic community and, more broadly, in the free world, it may have to give priority to the effort of political invention within the European setting. In doing so, however, it should give constant thought to shaping and stiffening its political framework in ways that will knit the new Europe even more closely into the wider framework of the opportunities and needs of a strengthened and well-ordered free-world system.

Part One

ECONOMIC PROBLEMS
OF EUROPEAN UNITY

CHAPTER II

The Nature and Prospects of the Common Market

ALFRED MOZER*

THE PURPOSE OF THE TREATY establishing the European Economic Community, which includes France, the Federal Republic, Italy and the Benelux countries—Belgium, the Netherlands and Luxembourg—is to merge, in a transition period of 12 to 15 years, the six national economies into a single economic community with the characteristics of a national economy. By the end of this year we shall be halfway through the twelve years which constitute the minimum transitional period. This is enough to permit an appraisal, not only of the intentions with which the Common Market, as the Community is popularly called, was established, but also of results achieved in a number of fields.

A significant fact which becomes immediately evident is that the Community, against the background of a generally favorable world business situation, has developed faster than the average of the world's industrial countries. This is true whether the criterion is that of expansion in productive capacity, intra-Community trade, or trade with non-member countries. It does not seem unreasonable to draw the conclusion that this *additional* growth is attributable to integration.

This gratifying development has been achieved despite the difficult tasks encountered by the national economies in the process of adaptation. A body of officials corresponding in number to the establishment of an Economics Ministry in one of the larger member countries has

* The author of this article is the Chief Executive Assistant to the Vice-President of the E.E.C. Commission. He wishes to emphasize, however, that he is writing on his own responsibility and not on behalf of the Commission or any of its members.

been set up, not to oversee the traditional and routine course of economic activities, but to carry out the experiment of adaptation in many fields. The aim is mutual harmonization of economic activities in economies which have been developed for a long while—and in many cases developed along wrong lines—within the national frontiers. There is hardly any order of priority for dealing with the problems. Every measure in one sector has multiple repercussions in other fields. It is as though you tugged at the corner of a table-cloth. The whole cloth moves with great danger for the dishes served on it.

The problem can best be illustrated with examples of the tasks accomplished. We have, for instance, reduced by about half the tariff walls separating member countries, and the reduction has been made more rapidly than provided for in the Treaty. This unquestionably impressive achievement has, however, made it obvious that measures at the frontier are not the sole, perhaps not even the most important, obstacles to trade. The elimination of these obstacles and consequent development of a common internal market brings the Community institutions up against a multiplicity of existing rules, regulations, ordinances and manipulations within the individual national economies, whose existence was often known only to the experts dealing with them. In the jungle of these protective rules and regulations, which were in many cases fully justified at the time they were introduced, the notion of economic freedom and of a market economy often takes on an ironic note. Those who look askance at the fact that approximately one thousand international meetings of various groups of experts take place every year in Brussels should recognize that they are being held with a view to unifying, simplifying, and reducing to the necessary minimum the national rules and regulations. Without the clearing of this primeval forest, the full development of the Common Market is impossible.

In addition to these rules and regulations issued by public authorities, there are the overt or concealed arrangements, including cartels, between individual firms and economic groups in the private sector. Here, too, the fact cannot be disputed that in many cases and in particular circumstances these arrangements do not serve mainly selfish group interests but can be of general importance and useful to the national economy. The following experience may show you that the work of the Community organs in this field is important: in the few years since the Treaty began to run the representatives of individual branches of production from the six member countries have been establishing contacts at Community level, and nearly three hundred branches now have secretariats in Brussels. It is probably not completely unreasonable to suppose that the competitors of yesterday did not unite so rapidly in the interest of consumers. The danger, as some see it, that the market which has long been shared under cartel arrangements will be replaced, in theory at least, by a free market at the end of the transitional period is by no means hypothetical. The Treaty imposes on the Community the obligation to serve the citizens of our countries, improve their standard of living, and ensure them the advantages of a large-scale economy based on division of labor. The attainment of this aim lays great tasks upon those responsible for dealing with distortions of competition and with cartel policy. These tasks are not made any easier by the fact that some member countries have no cartel policy, while in others the ideas on such policy differ widely.

To align public and private rules and regulations in the six countries, and to abolish distortions and prevent agreements in the private sector which would be contrary to the general interest, requires an approximation process which leaves untouched practically no field of economic or governmental activity: fiscal systems, cost determination, economic policy, or monetary measures.

An area requiring constant and specific policy consideration is that of transport. Agreement in this field is hampered by contradictory ideas as to how a transport system should be related to the economy as a whole. There is general agreement that transport is a service sector, or in American parlance a public utility. In some countries, however, public transport is expected to pay for itself, in others it is subsidized, while in still others it is used as a means of distorting competition.

Agriculture is another sector posing special problems, the nature of which is suggested by the text of the E.E.C. Treaty. Whereas a timetable was worked out for the mutual adjustment of other branches of the national economies, the contracting governments saddled the E.E.C. Commission with the difficulties involved in a Community agricultural policy. The Treaty laid down certain conditions and left it to the Commission to elaborate such a policy. What has so far been developed is a system, a set of instruments, in itself neither liberal nor protectionist, which will have to be built into a common agricultural policy—and this policy will be primarily concerned with prices. It must concern itself with prices because they will be decisive for the three essential elements: the incomes of producers, the relation between output and consumption—with due regard to our external relations—and consequently the satisfaction of requirements at reasonable prices. Again without going into details it is desirable, as an indication of the scope of this task, to point out that so far no international or supranational organization has had the courage and the will really to get to grips with the question of agriculture. And yet there is no branch of the economy for which it is more necessary to draw the conclusions from the changed political situation in the world.

In past times, states have gone to extreme lengths to support the agricultural sector of the economy—which is more conservative than most because many of its production factors are unchangeable. They were motivated by the strategic desire for self-sufficiency in foodstuffs. This consideration of wartime supply has lost much of its urgency in a world which makes wars between relatively small nation-states seem out of date. In the agricultural field as well as elsewhere, it is necessary to think in terms of larger areas. If this leads to thoroughgoing structural change, there is justification for the demand that the consequences of outdated national agricultural policies of past decades shall not be borne entirely and exclusively by the particular generation of farmers alive today.

A further important area of common planning and action is that of social policy. The expansion of six national economies into a larger economy leads to a harmonization of social benefits (a development which must not be confused with a leveling down: as we know, the existing national economies also have their social gradations). The Treaty requires that, like goods, capital, and services, workers too shall move freely throughout the Community. This freedom would, however, remain an empty formula in the absence of the necessary technical conditions, particularly in the field of social insurance and the other social benefits.

One of the major tools of social policy is the Social Fund. This mutual assistance Fund provides from a Community chest half the costs of re-education for workers changing their trade as a result of changes in the economic structure of the Community.

The same spirit of solidarity is reflected in our association with eighteen countries in the continent of Africa; through this the Community is providing $800 million within five years to improve infrastructure in these countries.

While other equally important fields of work could be mentioned, this choice of examples should be sufficient to show that nearly six years ago an experiment was launched, the beneficial effects of which are beginning to be seen, but which is facing problems of undeniable complexity.

A detailed discussion of the European Economic Community's external relations lies beyond the scope of the present article. A Community external policy in the field of trade began to take shape in the working out of a common external tariff, to which some desirable downward adjustments were made in the Dillon round of negotiations. The projected further talks with American representatives are, of course, to cover much more than an adjustment of duty rates. They will bring agriculture into the purview of discussion, and will provide an opportunity to prove that this Community does not wish to stand apart from the world but, being deeply aware of the share of responsibility that rests upon it, desires to be part of the free world.

The Institutional Structure of European Integration

Turning to the organizational structure of the European Economic Community that has set itself the tasks to which we have alluded, we find that the Community organ empowered to make *proposals* for decisive measures is the Commission. The institution with *power of decision* is the Council of Ministers which, like Janus, has two faces: it is on the one hand an integral organ of the Community and on the other a conference of national ministers, responsible for representing national interests. Besides these stands a Parliament which so far consists of representatives from the national parliaments and is vested with modest powers of recommendation. Finally there is the Court of Justice which decides when conduct is contrary to the Treaty. It should not be claimed that in drawing up the Treaty the best possible balance was found between legitimate national interests and what ought to be done in the interests of the Community. As the transitional period proceeds, the Community element becomes stronger and the right of veto by individual countries disappears in more and more fields. With this shrinking right of veto the influence of the national parliaments over measures taken by the no longer completely sovereign governments also diminishes. Unless a dangerous shift in the distribution of powers is to occur, the European Parliament will have to be endowed with powers corresponding to those withdrawn from the control of national parliaments. More instances of this sort could doubtless be mentioned in which the Treaty falls short of the ideal division of powers. Be that as it may, we have a democratic structure for the wider Community conceived with the intention of doing justice to the democratic structure of our national communities. This point is decisive for our Community; it *can* live and deserves to live only in a democratic form which is able to ensure an honorable balance between national and Community interests and to ensure the equality of all members without subjecting any one of them to the dictates of another. In this, integration differs from coalition and from the modern exploitation of national economies—the new form of the old colonial policy—practiced in the COMECON.

It may perhaps cause astonishment that questions of political principle are injected into a discussion of the character and prospects of the Common Market. This cannot be avoided: it reflects the truth that, although the E.E.C. has an economic aim, it is nevertheless a political fact.

This reality, with its radical consequences, becomes even clearer when it is remembered that the economic problem of integration is in no way an isolated or unrelated phenomenon. It has a history and, all evidence would indicate, a future. One fact in its history was an awareness during the early postwar years that our Western Europe had to achieve a close union in order to survive in a world of powers of continental dimensions. Marshall aid provided the initial impetus for our reconstruction. The first European attempt at a merger which was to be more than a coalition ended in the European facade: the Council of Europe. Of its fifteen member states, only six had the courage in 1950 to begin the experiment of partial integration, in the sphere of coal and steel. An attempt at military integration in the European Defense Community came to nothing, and with it the concurrent experiment of a political community. It was only then that a further attempt was made, in the economic field. There is no logical sequence in this succession of experiments. Different projects were tackled because they offered chances of success or corresponded to the imperative needs of a given situation. The lodestar throughout was the conviction that there must be comprehensive integration with a democratic structure. Consequently, integration in those fields where success has not yet been achieved remains on the agenda.

On the political plane, it is necessary to guard against integration being twisted in the direction of individual hegemony masquerading under a pan-"European" label. Attempts to tread this evil and disastrous road jeopardize all parties concerned and end in that competition between nationalisms with which we are all too familiar.

The need to be alive to the danger that integration might be twisted and betrayed is coupled with the problem of extending the Community. This Community of the Six is not coterminous with the concept of Europe, not even of the Europe which is today free and master in its own house.

Unfinished Tasks of European Integration

The veto pronounced on January 14, 1963, at a Paris press conference against extending the Community—and the regrets at its casting felt by many continental Europeans—do not alter the fact that it is Great Britain, the spokesman for a group of countries that in the last analysis were as interested in the widening of the Community as we ourselves, which must be charged with having for many years refused all co-operation, indeed with deliberate efforts to prevent integration, and this even though one of its great statesmen was among the first who saw in European union a question of life and death for this continent.

It may indeed be seen as an indirect recognition of the success of E.E.C. that Great Britain and certain other countries finally decided on that change of course to which, as a result of the Paris veto, we have not been able to respond.

The task remains. The objective remains. Integration must be completed, in depth and in breadth, socially and geographically. And this must be done with a structure corresponding to the free and democratic principles of the West. What is threatening us today is a political hegemony which seeks to use economic integration as an instrument of political domination. How far such a concept is from democracy and how close it comes to dictatorial systems of various colors is shown if we remember the slogan of a German dictator which ran, "With Hitler for a new Europe"; it also has similarities with the COMECON. When in 1948 a Bulgarian Communist leader, who had won his international spurs before the former Reich Court in Leipzig, expressed the idea of a federation of East European satellites, he was sent on sick leave to the Crimea—and never recovered. Today the members of that enforced community, built up under the leadership of one country, are fighting for the first modest rights of self-determination.

They are striving towards that democratic structure which we are being advised to abandon for the trappings of sovereignty in the Europe of the Fatherlands. If our political concept aims at something more than an expansion of trade with the authorities of these state-trading countries, to liquidate the structure of democracy in our efforts towards integration is less acceptable than ever, for it would mean that we had renounced these aims. What justification would there then be for our way of life, for the principles of our social order when compared with a social order which has no respect for the individual, if even we are prepared to reduce by our dialectics the power of the idea to the idea of power? What happens to the lessons of history, even of very recent history? Visionaries whose eyes are fixed on the landmarks of yesteryear are, when all is said and done, men without a sense of history, men for whom mimicry must replace the task of thinking about what matters here and now.

The specific internal tasks facing the Community can be mastered, though not without effort, not without friction and temporary setbacks. A remark to our American friends may be in order at this point. Conversations with Americans indicate that most people in the United States think that European integration is a *fait accompli*. This it is not. It is a process which is ongoing, which has prospects of success, but which still calls for much work and great patience.

The aim cannot be satisfied merely by the implementation of the Rome Treaty. It can be finally fulfilled only if integration continues in other fields—such as the field of politics and that of defense—while economic adjustment proceeds. Such integration need not duplicate the pattern of the E.E.C. Treaty. Different aims require different means, but the democratic structure is not negotiable.

The tasks facing us in the world at large provide incentives for the solution of internal problems. The idea of European integration is not a product of fear and a consequence of the threat from the East. Even without this threat it would still be a necessity if we are to hold our own in a changed world. Hence the tasks which only a united Europe can solve. The nature of these tasks, whether economic, political, or military, is of secondary importance. The decisive point is that they are there to be solved. When the "Europe or Commonwealth" dilemma that the British are supposedly facing is advanced as an objection to widening of the Community, the appropriate reply is that the Commonwealth today is primarily a matter of cultural links, because the economic market of the former Motherland has long since ceased to meet the needs of these countries. Thus the Commonwealth will not become an alternative to Europe, but Europe a real necessity for the Commonwealth. The loss of Commonwealth political and cultural links with Great Britain would be a heavy blow not only for that country but for all Europe, and for this reason alone a Europe enlarged to include Great Britain has a lively interest in the maintenance of the latter's links with the Commonwealth.

A further and stronger incentive to making a reality of European unity is the fact that it is probably the only way to establish an effective Atlantic partnership. World-wide tasks face this partnership. I have in mind, for instance, the whole gigantic complex of problems involved in the negotiations on the basis of the Trade Expansion Act. Here lies the possibility of a policy of attack, a chance for the West to adopt an offensive economic policy to defend the future of its social order. Here is an opportunity for a link-up in the Atlantic setting to embody Europe's need to assert itself and to make its voice heard in decisions within the Atlantic alliance—something vastly more important than the present (purely defensive) quarrel about an independent nuclear force.

Either we shall succeed in so interweaving and engaging the Atlantic partners politically and economically that the military consequence—comparable security for every part of this Atlantic area—follows ineluctably, or there will be no security for us. Having your own bomb does not give it. Above all when it is recommended to us with the disarmingly naive argument that every country, for instance America, uses it purely in its own national interests, while at the same time we are supposed to consider it doubtful protection in the hands of an American partner but an extraordinarily reliable protection when in those of *one* European country.

The importance of military security is not, of course, to be underrated. There could be little disagreement that not a less but a more integrated NATO structure is needed. But at a stage of development when Communism, the dominating party of which has lost something of its monolithic attribute, is adopting the tactics of expansion by political and economic means, our reaction with this internal quarrel about the power of decision over defensive military action no longer corresponds to the existing situation. In this world today more is at stake than a hand on the button which releases the atomic bomb.

It seems to me that anyone who forgets this fact and leaves it out of his calculations is suspiciously near a concept which ends with the prospect of a next world war.

It remains, of course, a fact that only determined readiness to act by the West, in the military as well as in other spheres, has held back the leaders of Communism from aggressive conquest of further parts of the world and will do so in the future. But this recognition is no blueprint for the future. The situation today offers great openings for a political and economic offensive by the Western world on the political and economic plane. Exploiting them in common will afford the Atlantic partnership possibilities of weaving its members together for all time. But before this can happen there must be unity in Europe, we must have economic and, in the end, political integration. Reason cries out for such action.

Faith can be placed in the young generation of Europeans. Our generation has completely destroyed for them the vainglorious ideal of a nation-state claiming leadership over other nations. These young people will not be content with efforts to patch up the old system—unless, of course, they decide to repeat the catastrophic policies of their fathers. The conclusion is therefore justified that the prospects for the Community, for integration, for the Atlantic partnership, and finally for the further development and consolidation of the free world are quite promising.

CHAPTER III

The Commonwealth and European Integration

C. E. CARRINGTON

ABOVE AND BEYOND the policies of the Foreign Office in London and the Department of State in Washington, there is a fundamental distinction between the attitudes of the British and American peoples toward the problem of the Iron Curtain in Europe. This difference is reflected in the assumptions underlying the presentation of news by the popular press and in the prejudices at the backs of the minds of ordinary citizens. The British, throughout the whole of their imperial epoch, regarded the Russian Empire as a potential enemy. The English word "jingoism" (which corresponds to the French term "chauvinisme") became a popular slogan in nineteenth-century London, describing the views of those anxious to fight the Russians on almost any issue. Though the British in general do not brood over their past history, all of them remember the Crimean War of 1854-6. Our foreign policy over two or three generations was obsessed with the "Eastern Question," that is, with resisting Russian penetration into those parts of the East that we regarded as the British sphere of influence. We were most disturbed by Russian designs upon the North-West Frontier of British India. Our alliances with Russia in the two World Wars were uneasy, and we have not forgotten that for a part of each war the governments which held power in Russia gave aid to our enemies. In short, we have a long tradition of resistance against Russian diplomatic and military aggression which is not shared by our American allies. Accordingly, enlightened and pacific opinion in Britain is disposed to consider the possibility of a *détente* with Russia in purely political terms. We see no great difficulty in peaceful coexistence, if only—and it is a formidable "if"—immediate problems can be solved.

American popular opinion, on the other hand, tends to look on the problem of the Iron Curtain as a phase in the crusade against Communism. The American approach is ideological, while ours is political. While the Americans have less traditional hostility to the Russian state, the British have less anxiety over the Communist menace. The pragmatic British mentality is strongly resistant against Marxian dogma, indeed against any dogmatism in practical affairs. Communism is too formal a creed to make an easy conquest of English minds, either at the intellectual level or as a spell-binding formula for the half-educated. Thus the Communist party in Britain has enlisted few adherents with any influence among thinking people or with any power to sway the masses. Negligible in numbers and feeble in its intellectual appeal, the British Communist party counts for almost nothing in the public estimation. This contempt is not shared, of course, by those who are better informed, and the technique employed by the Communists of infiltrating and occupying key positions, especially in the trade unions, may be as dangerous in Britain as elsewhere.

So far as Eastern Europe is concerned, we have no innate hostility towards those European countries which are now described as satellite-states of Soviet Russia. If it were not for the Warsaw Pact we should be prepared for terms of complete friendship with them.

The schism in Europe is thus regarded by the British—generally speaking—as a local problem to be solved, finally, by those nations which have to live with it, and our adherence to the North Atlantic Treaty implies that we, the inhabitants of Great Britain, are involved only so far as we are committed to the defense of Western Europe and no further. If the strategic necessity of NATO should disappear at some future date, our political involvement in Europe would lose much of its purpose.

Common Market vs. Commonwealth

The belief that Mr. Macmillan's proposal to enter the European Economic Union was dictated by strategic rather than by commercial pressures caused deep misgivings in the minds of many of the British during the Brussels negotiations of 1962. It was felt by many that we were being urged to support a political union in order to strengthen a strategic bloc, while the supposed economic advantages were put forward as a pretext. This seems to be the real dilemma in British politics at the present time. Though no responsible leader of any of the three parties proposes a withdrawal from NATO so long as the cold war persists in its present form, there is a real difference of opinion, cutting across all three parties, between those who wish to see Western Europe integrated into a permanent superstate and those who regard our military commitments and our commercial tariffs as temporary measures adapted to the present situation. To the latter group the hope for the future lies not in regionalism but in the eroding of national barriers and in the growth of worldwide rather than regional organisms.

During the Common Market negotiations, Mr. Macmillan asserted that our adherence to the E.E.C. would, in the long run, prove to the advantage of the Commonwealth, a coherent proposition which could be supported by some good arguments but which a large section of the British people did not accept as convincing. Long before General de Gaulle's rupture of the negotiations, Dr. Adenauer had warned the British, in speech after speech, that they were confronted with a straight choice—Europe or the Commonwealth. Still earlier, at the conference held at Accra, in October of 1961, the assembled finance ministers of all the other Commonwealth countries had warned the British in plain terms that in their opinion the Commonwealth would be weakened by British entrance to the Common Market. Furthermore, they stated very plainly that not one of the Asian or African Commonwealth countries regarded association with the E.E.C. under Part IV of the Treaty of Rome as anything but a derogation of the status they enjoyed as full Commonwealth members.[1] While this was well known when the Brussels negotiations began, no pressure was brought by the other countries to prevent Mr. Macmillan from negotiating, because it was not customary for Commonwealth members to act in that way. On the other hand, the propaganda employed to justify the negotiations created a general belief in the other Commonwealth countries as well as in Britain that there was no alternative. The British, it was contended, must get into Europe at almost any cost and the other countries must make the best of it. This was the

[1] These views were repeated very strongly in interviews given to the London press by the leading statesmen from Ghana, Nigeria, and Tanganyika, when they attended the Prime Ministers' Conference in September, 1962. (Summarized in the *Guardian*, London, Sept. 18, 1962.)

reaction to be read in the press, especially in that of the "old loyal dominions," Canada, Australia, and New Zealand; but no one should suppose that they enjoyed the prospect.

Commonwealth Attitudes in the East-West Conflict

Alone among the Commonwealth countries, Britain, Canada and Cyprus are directly involved in the issue of the Iron Curtain in Europe: Canada as a prominent member of NATO, Cyprus as a very small state in which the British occupy military bases by treaty. Though Australia and New Zealand can be counted upon to stand by Britain in a crisis (as they did even over Suez), they are not committed to the defense of Berlin or of Western Europe.

The Asian and African Commonwealth countries present a different set of factors. No one can appreciate British policy without giving weight to the continuing British relation with India and Pakistan and to India's policy of non-alignment, often inaccurately described as neutralism. Indian political leaders have indignantly denied that they are neutralists. Their stated aim is to assert their own policies, to hold aloof from the entanglements in which their former colonial rulers had involved them, to resist the tendency which drives them into one or another of the power blocs, because "all members of blocs are sometimes committed to action against their own wishes." Such a policy, it is alleged, constitutes not isolationism but the determination to take each issue on its merits without prior commitment and with no limitation but the principles of the United Nations Charter.[2]

The Indian doctrine of non-alignment has been adopted by every one of the African Commonwealth territories which has proceeded to independence since 1957; and this marks one of the clearest distinctions between de-colonization in French and in British Africa, since several of the former French colonies have retained their military dispositions and their *cadres* of French officers with little change. This may be ascribed partly to the fact that the former British colonies

[2] Summarized from *The Commonwealth in Africa*, by C. E. Carrington (R.I.I.A., Oxford University Press, 1962). When Mr. Nehru had to face hostile criticism in the parliament at Delhi, after the Chinese invasion, he strongly asserted his continuing faith in positive non-alignment even though he had received military aid only from the democratic countries—actually from the United States, the United Kingdom, and Australia. His words were not well reported in the British press, but fully in the Indian press. See *The Hindu*, March 20, 1963.

were larger, more socially advanced, and more able to provide for their own security than the French colonies; partly to the fact that the British Empire never created—or attempted to create—a centralized administration like that of the French Union. Long before political independence all British colonies enjoyed a large measure of administrative autonomy. Each colonial administration managed its own finances, its own customs regulations, even its own defense forces under the very lightest control from London, rarely exercised and not enforced without consultation. When a British colony proceeded by the well-trodden path to self-government and independence, the transfer of power required no administrative rupture. The already autonomous systems and cadres were merely placed under new political chiefs.

Before independence, many African leaders gave notice that they would follow Mr. Nehru's example. No one could assert that non-alignment was inconsistent with Commonwealth membership, since the Commonwealth had no stouter champion than Mr. Nehru. The Commonwealth as an institution is not committed to the defensive treaties against Communist aggression, and the ambivalent position of Britain, involved in Europe but with prior commitments to the Commonwealth, is nowhere more evident than in the field of strategy.[3] Britain and Canada are members of NATO while Australia and New Zealand are not; Britain and Australia are members of SEATO while Canada is not; Australia and New Zealand are members of ANZUS while Britain is not. Each of these strategic groupings is regional, and the worldwide character of the Commonwealth does not preclude regional arrangements. The plain fact that all the Commonwealth countries do not cooperate for each of these particular ends does not discourage them from co-operating for many other ends.

The majority of the Commonwealth countries tend to be neutral with regard to the problem of the Iron Curtain in Europe, since they regard it as a regional problem which is no concern of theirs. This political attitude, rooted like so many of their political principles in a British colonial past, is much strengthened by what may be called the psychosis of de-colonization. Access to independence releases a flood of political enthusiasms which were damped down by the administering power in colonial days. Like the adolescent on reaching

[3] The Malaysia Agreement of July, 1963, permits the U.K. to maintain bases for "assisting in the defense of Malaysia and for Commonwealth defense." (London, Stationery Office, Cmnd. 2094.)

manhood, every young nation shows a tendency to taste forbidden delights. It had been warned against the Communists, had been taught to regard Soviet imperialism as a danger, and had been screened from contacts with the dwellers behind the Iron Curtain. Now set free, like a young man who has been given a latchkey and can spend his own money at will, the young nation asserts itself by opening the forbidden door and by entering into relations with the dangerous people. All new nations tend towards the left in politics. To initiate is to be radical, and every radical engaged in asserting independent status will be dull-witted if he does not study radical planning in other merging countries. We may well think that the industrial progress of Germany or of Japan in the last twenty years is the social phenomenon most worthy of study, but the independent African, reacting against the guidance of his colonial mentors, will inevitably be fascinated by the stories told of progress in Russia and China, the revolutionary states from which he has been debarred. No wonder that Guinea and even Ghana should turn with interest towards Soviet Russia.

It is an error to suppose that this implies an increase of Communist influence in Africa. Such an influence is indeed being promoted by the subtle myth of "neocolonialism" and by infiltration of the trade unions, but not by direct Soviet aggression. The common saying in Africa is that having rid themselves of British (or French) colonialism they are not so foolish as to admit Russian colonialism. Whether they are blind to the dangers of Communist infiltration is another question, outside the scope of this paper. Even M. Sekou-Touré of Guinea, for all his Marxist training and technique, made it clear to the Soviet embassy that the Russians were not to attempt domination in his country. It would be easy to say, though an overstatement, that Communism has lost much ground in Africa during the last two years, since Mr. Khrushchev's egregious blunders over the Congo. But this analysis would not take into account the growth of diplomatic contacts between the new African states and the Communist countries, the negotiation of commercial treaties, and particularly the appearance of China as a diplomatic factor in Africa.

How is this to be related to the theme of the relation between Eastern and Western Europe? Two or three years ago, when there was much talk of Eur-Africa, the possibility that Britain would join the E.E.C. led to the fantasy that under the aegis of the Common Market there might be a further union with English-speaking and French-speaking Africa. It was never near to practical politics and it was sure to fail because none of the ex-British colonies and only a few of the ex-French colonies were ready to adopt the strategic implications of NATO. One point on which they are agreed is to "keep the cold war out of Africa," because they regard it as none of their business.

On strictly strategic grounds this determination may well prove to the advantage of the Western European powers. If we cannot yet bring the cold war to an end it will be advantageous to limit its territorial extent. But more than that, it may prove to the advantage of mankind. There is evidence that after burning his fingers in 1959-1961, Mr. Khrushchev, too, is willing to keep the cold war out of Africa and to pursue his aims in that continent by other techniques.

Political non-alignment in Asian and African countries, so long as they retain their numerous contacts with the West in other fields of public life, works to the advantage of the West by limiting the scope of the cold war and by forming bridges between the free countries and the Communist countries.

The Problem of Diplomatic Representation

Part of the problem of independence for a new country is to create a diplomatic service. With the multiplication of small nations it is necessary for a great power to maintain more than a hundred diplomatic stations, that is to say a foreign service quite beyond the capacity of a country with a small educated class. To some extent the new nations in Africa overcome their shortage of trained diplomats by conducting their foreign affairs in the lobbies of the United Nations building, which again adds to the importance of the meetings of the Assembly. Otherwise these new nations are poorly represented abroad and not many of the older nations send missions to them. Part of the system which holds the ex-French colonies in special relation with France is the good offices of French diplomats in countries where their ex-colonies are not represented; similarly, the Commonwealth serves its own members. Since Britain has more than one hundred missions overseas it is usually the British Embassy that fills the gap but it is important that any Commonwealth country may perform auxiliary services for another in the absence of full representation.

India and Canada, as well as Britain, are well-represented by diplomatic missions in all parts of the world, India even in Albania and

Mongolia where Britain is not represented.[4] India, Pakistan, and Ceylon, and one African Commonwealth member, Ghana, have full diplomatic relations with China; and on its side China has recently sent missions to Tanganyika and Uganda in Commonwealth East Africa. Soviet Russia maintains diplomatic missions in twelve Commonwealth countries, including all those in Asia except Malaya, and all in Africa except Uganda; but Sierra Leone and Tanganyika among the Africans, and New Zealand among the old Commonwealth countries, have no embassies in the U.S.S.R. Czechoslovakia has eight diplomatic missions in Commonwealth countries, but only four of these countries have sent missions to Prague. Poland has seven missions in the Commonwealth and receives four. Yugoslavia, also, has nine diplomatic missions in Commonwealth countries and has received four from them. The reason why each of the Communist countries sends out more missions to the new nations in Asia and Africa than it receives from them is not so much a greater desire for diplomatic relations as the difficulty and the expense to a new country of maintaining a diplomatic service. Only Ghana, the most advanced and the least impoverished of the African Commonwealth countries, is fully represented by its own diplomats in the Communist half of the world.

Imperial Preference and Its Significance

The Brussels negotiations, and still more the failure of these negotiations, led to a widespread effort by all overseas Commonwealth countries to open new markets, often through commercial negotiation with Communist states. In considering this trend in relation to European integration it is necessary to draw another distinction between French and British colonial policy during the last years of empire. That France should carry her colonies with her into association with the E.E.C. was natural and reasonable. They were already integrated into a single comprehensive trading-system—almost a customs-union—which ensured that more than half of their external trade was with France, while the whole of their financial arrangements, like their military systems, was already integrated with that of France. When the Treaty of Rome was signed and the first steps were taken

---

[4] The following particulars give the position as it was in April 1963. Since that date there has been much bilateral negotiation between Commonwealth countries and Communist countries.

towards forming the E.E.C., the de-colonization of French Africa was also proceeding according to a plan which implied no change in their commercial and financial systems. Their adherence to the E.E.C. as associated territories opened new markets to them and held out a promise of still larger capital investment. Having been members of a small customs-union they became members of a larger customs-union. It was a release.

The de-colonization of British Africa took another form and, to appreciate the distinction, it will be necessary to look back into British imperial history. It has never been the policy of Britain to weld its empire into a customs-union. Not only has every dominion on advancing to self-government resisted any such tendency, as Canada did more than a hundred years ago, but British governments, of the right and of the left, in generation after generation, have rejected proposals for an imperial tariff. The so-called "imperial preferences" set up by the Conference at Ottawa in 1932 have been generally misunderstood, and it is only too plain that recent discussions about them in the press (even the British press) have largely been conducted by people who don't know what they are. The British Prime Minister at Ottawa, thirty years ago, began by announcing that the British Empire could not possibly be a self-contained economic unit, that the colonies ought to diversify their trading patterns and that the agreements to be made were a first step to similar agreements with other nations. "Let us aim," he said, "at lowering, not raising barriers."[5] Accordingly, no general tariff system was admitted and there is no general Ottawa Treaty. Twelve distinct bilateral agreements were made between pairs of Commonwealth countries to promote their trade. All were variable at six months' notice; most have been amended in the course of thirty years; all can be amended again if the Common Market negotiations should require it. Those of the agreements to which Britain was a party vary according to the circumstances of the colony concerned, but all have two common features: Britain undertook to maintain the "Commonwealth right of free entry" for raw materials from the colony, and she admitted the right of the colony to protect its infant industries by a tariff, even by a tariff directed against the mother-country.

In return, the colony granted specific preferences to British merchandise, which have often been the subject of negotiation since. The right of free entry is on quite another footing, since it is our pledge

[5] Report of the Ottawa Conference, 1932. (London, Stationery Office, Cmnd. 4175.)

to the countries for which we have been responsible to ensure steady markets for their foodstuffs and raw materials. Half the food on British dinner-tables comes from the Commonwealth under the right of free entry. The factor which was never squarely faced in the Brussels conversations was the necessity of an economic revolution in Britain and throughout the Commonwealth if we rejected the principle. It was very well understood in the Dominions, where their search for new markets at once became more urgent.

The Commonwealth trading pattern had another limb, which has become important during the last few weeks. At the GATT negotiations in May 1963, Canada, Australia, and New Zealand fought for their right to protect their industries by a tariff and Mr. Erroll, the British Minister of Trade, strongly championed their cause.[6] This too is a memory of the Ottawa Agreements of 1932. British policy with regard to protective tariffs shows signs of reverting to its historic principles, to the belief that affluent nations should lower their tariffs to admit raw materials from the emergent countries, that the necessity to take shelter behind a common external tariff is a sign of weakness, and that the proper use of protective tariffs is to foster new industries, especially in new countries.

The stand for the Commonwealth made by the British at the GATT negotiations is a reminder that the Sterling system and the Commonwealth trading pattern are not to be written off as declining assets. It is not true to say that Commonwealth trade is diminishing. After a high peak in 1958, the rate of progress in countries which live by exporting raw materials was slowed down by a weakening in world prices. Accordingly, such well-established trades as those between India, Australia, and South Africa on the one hand and Britain on the other showed a temporary slackening. The monthly averages[7] of British exports to these countries dropped about five per cent below the peak of 1958 to a low point at the end of 1961 and have now returned almost to the peak figure. The upward trend in the early months of 1963 shows a curve with the same function as the curve of our expanding trade with Western Europe. This temporary fluctuation in world trade at a time when our regional trade with Europe was expanding was very loosely used by propagandists to suggest that the Commonwealth was on the decline, and the subsequent attempts

6 See the London press, especially *Daily Telegraph*, May 17, 1963.
7 *Board of Trade Journal*, June 1963, p. 1442.

by the Commonwealth countries to open new markets were wrongly represented as additional evidence of this decline. Refer back to British imperial history and you will see that the foundation of our policy since the Ottawa Agreements of 1932 has been that Britain should maintain the market for the emerging Commonwealth countries and that they should diversify their trading pattern "by similar agreements with other nations." The Sterling system has always been a free and outward-looking pattern of trade.

The year of the Brussels negotiations, when all the endeavors of the British government were concentrated on coming to terms with the E.E.C., and when the Commonwealth countries were warned that they might lose their preferential position in the British Market, was inevitably a good year for our trade with Europe and a bad year for our Commonwealth trade. Adjusted and final figures are not yet available at the time of writing, but the statistics provisionally issued by the British Government[8] show that in 1962 exports of merchandise from Great Britain were worth £3792 millions, of which £1208 millions were taken by the Commonwealth countries and a further £281 millions by the two ex-Commonwealth countries, Ireland and South Africa, which still adhere to the Sterling Area and enjoy the benefit of the Ottawa agreements, making a total of £1489 millions or 39 per cent of our total export trade. In the same year exports to the "Six" have risen to the very satisfactory figure of £719 millions, 18 per cent of our total, even though we were not members of the E.E.C. Our trade with the countries of EFTA has risen on about the same scale.

Note that even in that year, when our European trade flourished and our Commonwealth trade languished, the ten million Australians bought more British goods than the fifty million West Germans. Even the three million New Zealanders bought almost as much as the forty million Frenchmen.[9] And the fact that the trade with Australia and New Zealand was financed by British banks and carried in British ships provided a further advantage to Britain in this branch of our trade over our trade with France and Germany. Though Commonwealth trade was more profitable to Britain and much more extensive than European trade, nevertheless the other Commonwealth countries applauded the fact that we were diversifying our trade and we applauded the fact that they were diversifying theirs, since both

[8] *Trade and Navigation Accounts, 1962.*
[9] See Appendix III.

modes of expansion strengthened the Sterling-Commonwealth system as a whole.

Trade Patterns of Commonwealth Countries

The export of Canadian hard wheat from the three prairie Provinces to Britain, with its gigantic and permanent system for storage, finance, and transportation by land and sea, has been remarkably steady in volume for fifty years. Though Canadian wheat production has long outgrown the British market, this staple trade with Britain, protected by the right of free entry, is still fundamental to the Canadian economy, even though Canada is a fully industrialized state. The nervousness which Canada displays over dominance by the United States is stimulated by fears that the American wheat surplus will be dumped on the world market to the detriment of hers, and hence the interest that Canada displays in selling wheat to Communist China at the rate of about a million tons a year for the last three years.

Australia, also a fully industrialized country, also bases its economy upon a staple export trade which was built upon the Commonwealth infra-structure of shipping and finance. Long ago, Australia outgrew the British market for wool though it still depends upon it, and for thirty or forty years, at least, Australia has been searching for new outlets. Here there is no tariff to consider and Australia, which already sells as much wool to continental Europe as to Britain, has nothing to fear in this respect if Britain should enter the Common Market. That Australia should also sell wool to Japan in great quantities implies no loss to Commonwealth trade, indeed the contrary as it adds to the strength of Sterling. The new factor is the export of Australian wheat to China, nearly two million tons a year.

The difficulty of these new lines of trade is that China has so little to export that advanced countries wish to buy. In 1961, the peak year, Australia's exports to China were worth £57 millions, her imports from China £2 millions; Canada's exports were worth £40 millions; her imports £1 million. When considering Commonwealth contacts with Communist China, the peculiar case of Hong Kong should not be overlooked. So long a free port, the last of the *entrepôts* which Imperial Britain threw open with liberality to the trade of the world,

Hong Kong is still a loophole into China, from which it imports goods to the value of £60 or £70 millions a year. Its exports to China are about one-tenth as great.

The special case of New Zealand, which lives by supplying mutton and butter to the British market, was widely discussed during the Brussels negotiations. New Zealand already sells some meat to Soviet Russia and is now negotiating to sell more.

The place of India and Pakistan in this movement of trade has been given prominence by Dr. Hallstein's visit to Delhi in April 1963. In his humane and outward-looking speech he pointed out that the Common Market countries had an export surplus with Asia and desired Indian imports whether India became an Associated Territory or not. The response in the Indian press and the immediate reaction in the Pakistani press was to urge on the trade negotiations, not only with the E.E.C. but no less with the Communist countries. Pakistan, which has made good progress with its development plan in the last two years, has this year opened trade talks with China, with Soviet Russia, with the E.E.C., and most urgently with Czechoslovakia, which can supply what Pakistan needs for its growing heavy industry. No sensible person in Britain looks with disfavor on the growth of trade with Western Europe and the influx of Western European capital into India and Pakistan. Our own pattern of trade, the gigantic investment we have made in these countries, and the cultural links (more Indian students come to Britain than ever before) will be secured—not weakened—by other European contacts.

So far as Africa is concerned, the proliferation of Communist trade missions has produced little genuine commerce between the Communist countries and the African members of the Commonwealth. Taking Ghana as the most advanced, we find that in 1962 only seven per cent of Ghanaian exports went to the Communist countries and only five per cent of imports came from them. Communist trade with Nigeria and with the East African territories is negligible. The interesting factor here is not trade but aid,[10] and in this respect Ghana has been the recipient of technicians, promises, and allotments of money to the amount of £76 millions from the U.S.S.R., East Germany, and China. There are about five hundred Russian technicians working in Ghana. No visitor to Ghana will be as aware of this as of the universal use of the English language, the hundreds of British teachers, the

[10] See Appendix IV.

Ghanaian professional men trained in British universities, and the evidences in every direction of the Commonwealth infra-structure. Ghana is the most divergent of the African Commonwealth states, yet it is still associated with the other Commonwealth countries by a thousand social ties.

Guidelines for Future Policy

It has been the bitter experience of several great nations that efforts to win friends among the emergent countries by grants of aid produce little gratitude, and Russia in Africa has reached this stage. It is when aid, trade, and investment go together that they create a solid foundation for a lasting association.

My conclusion is to recommend to students of world affairs that they should not underrate the significance of the Commonwealth, even in 1963 when it has suffered and is suffering some severe shocks. Do not overlook the permanent structure of trade, finance, transportation, and communications which still carries more than a quarter of the seaborne trade of the world, which extends into every region, and which, therefore, involves the Commonwealth in every regional problem, which is integrated, not by any constitutional charter, but by a common language, culture, and system of education.

When considering Britain's place in Europe, think of a Britain that has no quarrel with the Communist countries of Eastern Europe and no quarrel with Soviet Russia, except that we shall resist the Russians if they quarrel with us; a Britain that has no fears of corruption by Communist propaganda; a Britain that lives on world-wide trade and that can never commit itself to an inward-looking regional group; a Britain that is affiliated with nations in all parts of the world to whom it has guaranteed a market for their produce and with whom it retains a complex network of cultural links; a Britain whose commercial policy, for a hundred years, has been founded on free imports from these emergent countries because their prosperity is our prosperity and their liberty our pride. If such a Britain can take its place in a free association of all—not six only—of the European countries, if they are prepared to share their affluence with less fortunate countries then, on these conditions, the British can be good Europeans.

Appendix I

COMMONWEALTH TRADE WITH EASTERN EUROPE AND THE U.S.S.R.
(three-year averages in £ millions)

	Imports from E. Europe		Exports to E. Europe	
	1956-8	1959-61	1956-8	1959-61
Total C'wealth .	£150m.	£203m.	£157m.	£240m.
U.K.	103	137	77	92
India	24	32	18	35 (jute, tea, hides)
Canada . . .	3	5	15	17 (wheat)
Australia . . .	3	4	15	22 (wool)
Malaya and Singapore . .	2	3	17	44 (rubber)
Rhodesian Federation . .	0.5	0.6	0.4	5 (copper)

No other Commonwealth country's export to Eastern Europe reaches £5 million.

Appendix II

COMMONWEALTH TRADE WITH CHINA
(three-year averages in £ millions)

	Imports from China		Exports to China	
	1956-8	1959-61	1956-8	1959-61
Total C'wealth .	£134m.	£135m.	£60m.	£97m.
U.K.	15	25	17	23
Hong Kong . .	74	68	9	7
Malaya and Singapore . .	19	19	9	9
Ceylon	9	8	10	7
Australia . . .	2	3	7	25
Canada	2	2	1	14

No other Commonwealth country's export to China reaches £5 million. In 1961 the Australian wheat export touched £57 million, the Canadian £40 million. The Hong Kong trade is *entrepôt* trade.

Appendix III

THE PATTERN OF BRITISH EXPORT TRADE
(Trade and Navigation Accounts, 1962)

Britain's Best Customers in 1962

Exports of merchandise to:

U.S.A.	£327 millions
Australia	229
West Germany	199
Canada	188
Sweden	154
Netherlands	151
South Africa	146
Italy	139
France	138
Ireland	135
India	116
New Zealand	107
Denmark	103

Total exports:	£3792
to Commonwealth countries	£1208
to the E.E.C.	£ 719

The ten best customers in 1938 were: South Africa, India (undivided), Australia, U.S.A., Canada, Ireland (undivided), Germany (undivided), France, New Zealand, Denmark.

Appendix IV

AGREEMENTS FOR ECONOMIC AID FROM COMMUNIST COUNTRIES
TO COMMONWEALTH COUNTRIES, 1954-1962

Note that the signing of an agreement does not imply an immediate transfer of funds to the recipient.

Amounts allocated in $ U. S. millions. An asterisk (*) means that the figures are not yet available.

from U.S.S.R.	to Ceylon	$ 30 m.
	India	804.3
	Pakistan	30
	Ghana	105

from Czecho-Slovakia	Ceylon	*
	India	82.5
	Ghana	28
	Nigeria	*
from Poland	Ceylon	8
	India	64
	Cyprus	1.4
	Ghana	28
from Hungary	India	16.8
	Ghana	14
from E. Germany	India	*
	Ghana	*
from Rumania	India	13.5
	Ghana	*
from Bulgaria	Ghana	*
from Albania	Ghana	*
from China	Ceylon	26.2
	Ghana	19.6

CHAPTER IV

NATO and the Need for a New Policy

BARON K. T. VON UND ZU GUTTENBERG

Since walter lippmann coined the expression "cold war," thereby providing a definition of the East-West conflict which has remained standard, there has been no lack of regularly recurrent assertions that this cold war has already come to an end or will terminate in the near future. Both past and present statements to this effect are traceable to Western "coexistence propaganda," which becomes particularly evident whenever the waves of the cold war are temporarily calmed.

It is thus entirely proper that an exchange of views by Western scholars and politicians concerning the future of Europe should include a discussion of the nature of this conflict, which is at the root of the partition of Europe and has galvanized the politics of the entire world far beyond the boundaries of Europe. For only those who understand the true character of the struggle will be able to face it successfully. In politics as in medicine, therapy depends on correct diagnosis.

No objective observer can seriously question that the essential source of the cold war is the Communist expansionism underlying Soviet international policy, which is backed by the entire military and economic strength of the Soviet bloc. The "cold war" thus begins with a militant ideology. This perception may be a platitude, but it cannot be repeated often enough. For we are constantly subjected to an unlimited flood of assertions and proposals by Western politicians, thinkers, and scientists which make sense only if the basic ideological character of the cold war is consciously or unconsciously denied, and the conflict between East and West reduced to a mere struggle of power politics among competing nations.

Strange as it seems, those who recognize Communist ideology as the root of Soviet policy, and thus as the evil force motivating the cold war, are often themselves accused of being unrealistic ideologists. It is even contended that anti-Communism rather than Communism is the political disease of our day. Through a trick of intellectual sleight-of-hand, defense against an anti-libertarian ideology is denounced as an ideology in itself.

Although the cold war is ideological in nature, it is not a collision of two ideologies—for a Western or free ideology does not exist. The idea of freedom is better expressed in the statement that freedom and ideology are mutually exclusive. The cold war is consequently nothing other than the result of the incessantly asserted claim of an ideology to universal rule—both over those already subjected to it and over all others whose subjection is to come.

If this definition is correct, certain conclusions are inescapable. The first is that an end of the cold war can be expected only as the result of a decisive change in the Communist ideology which determines the direction of Soviet Policy, or in the power which is used to support this policy. Until such a change occurs, the free world has only the choice of resisting the Communist drive to achieve total rule or else surrendering its freedom bit by bit to the "salami tactics" of the enemy.

Up to now the West has decided in favor of resistance. Such resistance has assumed two forms: that of the accumulation and coordination of economic and military strength for the defense of the existing frontiers of freedom, and that of the intelletual commitment without which the greatest miliary and economic efforts would make no sense—commitment to the truth that freedom is indivisible. Freedom is indivisible because the desire for it is universal; it cannot be limited to particular peoples or territories without compromising its own essence.

This means that the basic policy of the West in its confrontation with Soviet Communism has had two components. One of these is uncompromising defense of the territory of freedom. The other consists in upholding and advocating the demand that freedom be restored wherever it has fallen victim to Soviet-Communist oppression. To put it briefly, the Western will to defend the status quo with military means has been coupled with the intention to change that status quo by political means.

We cannot, however, realistically ignore the fact that the Western will to realize the demand of the oppressed peoples of Eastern and Central Europe for freedom has manifested a constantly dwindling intensity in recent years. American efforts to make the fate of these peoples the subject of international discussion and negotiations have long since tapered off. The annual arguments in the so-called Hungary debate in the United Nations symbolize the last miserable remainder of the once burning indignation of the Western world against the breaches of treaty and law with which Soviet Russia subjugated the Eastern half of Europe.

It cannot be denied that various degrees of relaxation have occurred in certain countries of the satellite area since Stalin's death. All these developments together do not, however, alter the fundamental fact that this half of Europe must continue to live and suffer under foreign colonial rule and ideological compulsion. Consideration of the attitude of the Western world toward these unhappy Polish, Czech, Magyar, Bulgarian, and other enslaved peoples must therefore include the question whether we have not begun to indulge in simple hypocrisy. It seems to me in any case that fashionable slogans such as "contacts," "politics of flexibility," "making holes in the Iron Curtain," or "realism" are all too often used merely to cloak indifference, resignation, and not infrequently brutal selfishness. One fact remains incontrovertible: whatever the apparent brilliance of plans advanced for exploiting the existing tensions between Eastern capitals and other phenomena of the so-called "thaw," the governments in Warsaw, Prague, and Budapest are tied to Moscow by the fact that their continued existence depends on Soviet power—a consideration far stronger than any inducement which the West might offer.

The natural allies of the West in the satellite area are the oppressed peoples, not the governments that Moscow has imposed upon them. It is, therefore, to be feared that a Western policy of cooperation with these governments would necessarily have primarily negative effects. First of all, such a policy would mean the loss of valuable friends for the West, for the East European peoples continue to stake their hopes, not on the Kadars, Novotnys, and Gomulkas, but—in spite of everything—on the West. Secondly, no development could so effectively advance Mr. Khrushchev's plans as Western abandonment of its refusal to accept his colonial empire. Events in 1953 and 1956 showed that Soviet Russia's European conquests are also its Achilles' heel, insofar as the oppressed peoples have not given up their will for freedom and resigned themselves to their fate.

There is evidence to support the impression that the predominant position in the West has been gained by that school of thought which considers a stable order in Eastern Europe under Soviet hegemony more promising than a continuation of the instability which has existed until now. In other words, acceptance seems to have been achieved for the thesis that it is possible to count on evolutionary developments in Eastern Europe, and that this process can most effectively be promoted through better relationships with satellite governments.

This theory rests upon fallacious reasoning. Any Western policy of tacit or explicit recognition of Soviet war booty in Eastern Europe must necessarily lead to discouragement of the peoples in that area and hence to a reduction of tension between the oppressors and the oppressed—the tension which is the actual driving force behind whatever evolution has been observed. Any such Western toleration of Soviet colonialism cannot fail, furthermore, to expand Moscow's freedom of action. Any consolidation of Soviet rule in the satellite area— and a stabilization of the existing situation in that region through a Western policy of "normalization" could have no other effect—would be regarded by the Kremlin as a confirmation of its imperialist policy and would thus lead in the long run to intensified Communist aggressiveness.

Evaluation of the contemporary political situation must start with the fact that the West seems less and less inclined to make the cause of East European freedom its own. The Western concept of things has to this extent changed. Its first aspect, commitment of the West to the military defense of its own freedom, remains unimpaired. Its second aspect, however, championship of the cause of freedom beyond the status quo, has already been considerably restricted. The colonial status of Eastern Europe is today mentioned only in replying to verbal attacks by the Soviet Union, if not ignored altogether. For practical purposes, we are moving steadily toward unqualified acceptance of a status quo under which the East Europeans are enslaved, while slowly but steadily "normalizing" our relations with the quisling governments in that area.

There is only one point at which the West has upheld its demands up to now: it has, throughout the long years which have elapsed since

World War II, refused consistently to accept the partition of Germany into two sovereign states—the European objective to which the Soviet Union accords the highest priority. The status quo in Germany has remained an objective of contention—but only for the following reasons:

First, because Germany, itself a member of the Western alliance, is able to speak in its own cause;

Secondly, because this alliance is obligated by treaty not to recognize the partition of Germany; and,

Thirdly, because the dangers of a Western status-quo policy for Germany are more clear and obvious than in the case of Poland or Hungary.

These three reasons—partly of formal and partly of opportunist character—seem a flimsy obstacle to adoption by the West of the same so-called "realism" with respect to Germany which it has already manifested in its relations with the non-German satellite states. For the truth of the matter is that there is no longer any substanial reason of principle why the West should concede Mr. Khrushchev the status quo throughout Eastern Europe but make a single exception in the case of Ulbricht's pseudo-state—once the idea has taken root that the policy of the status quo as a whole is the correct prescription for further treatment of the East-West conflict.

It is, of course, a gross oversimplification to speak without further qualification of "the West," of "Western policy," of the "Western attitude," or the "Western alliance." It would be desirable, in this connection, to take account of the many variations within the alliance in judging the international situation and in recommending policies to deal with it. The limits of this brief presentation do not, however, permit us to follow the trail of all those forces, the cumulative effect of which determines the limits within which what might be called a common Western policy is realized. It seems important to point out, however, that the expression "Western policy" will continue to be almost a synonym for "American policy" for as long as the NATO continues to be less a true alliance than a protective system which mighty America provides for the many small European states, and America's position and power permit it to act as the only qualified spokesman for the West.

To repeat: so far as Eastern Europe is concerned, the Western position has shifted. During the early part of the cold war, it was never doubted that true relaxation was impossible without realization of the right of self-determination for the states of Eastern Europe. Today, however, greater popularity is enjoyed by the reverse formula: relaxation is needed as an initial step to prepare the ground for the final and gradual return of freedom to the satellite states. Pursuant to the same logic, the receipt for this relaxation is no longer alteration but acceptance of the status quo.

That this change in the Western attitude would one day necessarily touch the German problem was to be expected. As soon as the slogan "change through rapprochement" achieved influence over Western policy and aroused the hope that persistent negotiation and patient advocacy of common interests would change enemy objectives, the partition of Germany was bound to appear in a new light. There is no reason whatever for hoping that Khrushchev, Gomulka, Kadar, Novotny and Company may respond favorably to such "rapprochement" and then excluding Herr Ulbricht from the same category. And it is just as difficult to explain to someone why a policy of accommodation and mutual understanding should be useful at every point where West encounters East, but not along the line where free Germans and German Communists confront each other.

It is thus by no means surprising that for a considerable time Western tendencies have been observed that would extend "relaxation through acceptance of the status quo" to Germany. Under the pressure of the Soviet threats against Berlin, these assumed the form of concrete American proposals during the spring of 1962. The essence of these proposals was to achieve an armistice in the cold war by offering the Soviets, in addition to other measures of East-West accommodation, admission of the Soviet-Zone pseudo-state to international bodies. These proposals met with German objections, so that they were not presented to the Soviets at that time.

It was clear, however, that German rejection of these proposals did not in any way mean the end of the policy of "relaxation through acceptance of the status quo." It is true that the Cuba conflict gave rise to the initial impression that the West had generally returned to the previously accepted insight that the Soviet Union is really interested neither in the status quo nor in relaxation. Even at the height of the crisis, however, there was no lack of critical voices which warned against drawing dangerous and false conclusions from the Cuba affair.

These warnings unfortunately turned out to be largely correct. It cannot be denied that in the aftermath of the Cuba crisis, Soviet policy was far less condemned for its obvious recklessness in undertaking the installation of rocket bases in Cuba than praised for its "reasonableness" in dismantling the launching pads under American pressure. It was thus no wonder that widespread expectations were aroused that Moscow would show the same "reasonableness" in other matters. It is, furthermore, not an exaggeration to say that the experiences of the Americans during the course of the Cuba crisis were such as to strengthen already existing tendencies toward American-Soviet bilateralism.

With the formalization and conclusion of the Moscow atom treaty by Great Britain and the United States, the policy of "relaxation through acceptance of the status quo" entered a new stage. The fact that the signatories did not consult the Federal Republic sufficiently before seeking and agreeing to a formula for the participation of Ulbricht's pseudo-state shows clearly that unqualified continuation of the traditional Western "one-Germany policy" is now being challenged by the expectations of relaxation which gave rise to the Moscow treaty. It is only logical that the hope for "change through rapprochement," or—as Kennedy put it in St. Paul's Church in Frankfurt—for "the day on which we can live in peace with the Communists," cannot reasonably exclude Herr Ulbricht. The Communist with whom the Germans would have to deal in this case is precisely the same Herr Ulbricht. It is indeed hard to see how the demand that we should one day live in peace with Herr Ulbricht can be reconciled with the hitherto common policy of seeking reunification of a free Germany— that is, with the announced intention of telling Herr Ulbricht to go to the devil.

German criticism of this new policy has been downgraded with warnings that the Germans could easily fall into the role of eternal disturbers, who spoil every relaxation with dogmatic and legalistic obstructionism. Such twistings of the truth are to be roundly condemned. I am myself a critic of the new policy—not because I am opposed to relaxation, but because the policy promises to produce the exact opposite.

This brings us back to our point of departure—the simple truth that the cold war has only one basic cause: Communist ideology backed by Soviet power. This being the case, the relaxation which we all desire, abatement of the cold war, and agreement between East and West will come no sooner than the day on which the Soviet Union abandons its interests in expansion and in exporting the world revolution. That this day is not yet in sight, seems to me an irrefutable fact. It is impossible to point to a single sign that such a fundamental change in Soviet policy is in process.

It is particularly hard to see any indication of a true reform in Soviet policy in the Moscow treaty for a partial suspension of atomic tests. The rapprochement contained in the treaty is very one-sided. It consists—insofar as the actual substance of the treaty is concerned—essentially in the fact that the West constantly reduced its demands, while the East stood pat on its initial position. In wording the formal and procedural clauses of the treaty, Soviet obstinacy succeeded in forcing the American and British negotiators into accepting a formula which would hardly have found the concurrence of the German federal government, had that government been duly consulted in a manner befitting its role as an ally.

The Western alliance today faces a basic decision. Do we continue to follow the time-tested principles which have shaped NATO policy until now, or do we really need to develop new ones? This writer sees no need for a violent change of course. The enemy has not changed his goals. The cold war will continue to be our lot for a long time to come.

But let me close with a warning: the craft and cunning of the enemy are less dangerous than impatience and wishful thinking within our own camp. Nothing is more dangerous than drawing an image of the enemy based not on reality but on our own wishes.

CHAPTER V

Neo-Imperialism Versus European Partnership

WENZEL JAKSCH

T HE LIFE OF OUR GENERATION has been shaped by great historic events. We have experienced them from different sides, have seen them in different lights, and have felt different consequences in our personal fortunes. It is only through intercontinental sharing of points of view and experience that we are able to see this complicated world in its proper proportions.

Most of our contemporaries experience current history as echoed by publicity or as mirrored by television. Important elements of the contemporary situation are thus often neglected: *the silent facts,* the apparently undramatic happenings of everyday life. An astronaut, for instance, enjoys many times as much publicity as the 10,000 political prisoners in the dungeons of an Ulbricht or a Kadar. *The spirit of resistance in the dictatorships is, however, no less important for the free world than the exploration of space.* It is altogether impossible to conceive of the entire instrumentation of modern technology apart from the human impulses that produce it. The material superiority of the West will be of little use to us as long as the manipulators of the Eastern bloc understand better how to harness human impulses for their goals—whether impulses of love or hate, of lust for power, of humanitarianism or of destruction. For this reason, our present concern is less with economic statistics than with the radiation of Western policy as it reaches the peoples of Eastern Europe.

In an era of "accommodation," it is more necessary than ever to remind the peoples of the free world of the *fundamental fact of the splitting of Europe.* The wall running through the middle of Berlin is no isolated phenomenon. It is also a symbol for the fact that a bloody frontier has been drawn across Europe, on which shooting is a daily occurrence, and along which the deaths of innocent people in mine fields and barbed-wire entanglements never come to an end. Along this artificial border, the *encounter of two economic systems takes place*.

Three broad fronts of encounter between East and West must be kept in mind. The *encounter of military power* reached a dramatic climax in the Cuba crisis. Recently we experienced the negotiations in Moscow for a ban on atomic testing. The protagonists in this *encounter on the diplomatic front* likewise have no reason to complain of lack of publicity. The third front of encounter, that of the *daily contact of the two economic systems,* one on each side of the Iron Curtain, produces the fewest sensations. We ourselves pay too little attention to it, although it is precisely in this sector that the West enjoys the most favorable position.

Observation of the continuing encounter between the Common Market and the so-called "Council for Mutual Economic Aid" (COMECON), as it has developed during the last two years, brings into evidence the following facts, which are important for Western policy makers:

1. The Common Market tends to unfreeze economic thought throughout Eastern Europe. It is the most effective refutation of Marxism-Leninism which the West has yet produced.
2. The success of the Common Market has demonstrated the absurdity of the economic theses in the Party Program of the CPSU.
3. As an instrument of supra-national economic cooperation, the European Economic Community has demonstrated unchallengeable superiority over the "Council for Mutual Economic Aid." The methods and accomplishments of the E.E.C. have served to make clear the inadequacy of the COMECON.
4. Rumania's objections to subordinating its national economic interests to the wishes of the Soviet planning bureaucracy has forced the Soviet Union to yield. This may be regarded as a painful defeat for Russia's European policy, since it established a precedent for the entire area of the satellites.

This daily encounter between an economic partnership of free peoples and the threatening amalgamation of the East European economies into a Soviet Russian economic empire promises to have far-reaching consequences. It has become a topic of conversation among Communist functionaries in the satellite countries that little Luxembourg with its 300,000 inhabitants is a partner with full rights in the Community of the six E.E.C. states, and that Belguim and the Netherlands play important roles alongside the German Federal Republic, France, and Italy.[1] Contrasted with this equality is the endless list of discriminations, injuries, and indignities which the non-Russian members of COMECON are forced to endure. Such comparisons, which are drawn daily in Eastern Europe, serve to build bridges of the mind across the Iron Curtain.

Let us consider the ideological defeat of Soviet Communism in the area of European unification. The Communist theoreticians took as a point of departure for their appraisal of this question a prophecy made by Lenin in 1915. While still in exile in Switzerland, Lenin made a study of plans for the "United States of Europe," and came to the conclusion that such a solution would be "impossible or reactionary." Lenin classified efforts to unify Europe in the category of "inter-imperialist alliances," of which he predicted that, in view of the realities of capitalism, they would "necessarily represent only short intermissions between wars." In terms of the contemporary world situation, this judgment of Lenin's fits better into the Chinese concept of things than that of the Russians.

It is interesting to note that for a while the judgments of politicians and economic specialists of the Eastern bloc with regard to the Com-

---

[1] Representation of the individual member states in the organs of the Community is provided for in the E.E.C. treaty as follows:

	Population (millions)	NUMBER OF REPRESENTATIVES in the European Parliament	in the Council of Ministers
Belgium	9.350	14	2
German Federal Republic (w/o W. Berlin)	55.073	36	4
France	47.600	36	4
Italy	51.114	36	4
Luxembourg	.320	6	1
Netherlands	11.889	14	2

The Commission, the actual executive organ of the E.E.C., consists of nine members. This assures that the smaller members have at least one representative each in the executive. Considering the population and relative economic potential of the member states, this allocation of influence may be regarded as extremely generous.

For a detailed comparison of the Common Market and COMECON, see Hermann Gross, "The Common Market and Eastern Bloc Integration," in *Berlin and the Future of Eastern Europe*, David S. Collier and Kurt Glaser, eds. (Chicago: Henry Regnery Company, 1963), pp. 183-204.

mon Market were quite contradictory, until finally the weight of facts could no longer be ignored. Khrushchev at first followed the path of Lenin's false prophecies. The young European Economic Community was for him a "bogey man"—on another occasion he called it an "unnatural union." The Moscow Institute for World Economy and International Relations, however, took the opposite point of view from the beginning. In a discussion sponsored by this Institute early in 1959, two years before the 22d Party Congress, the Soviet economist, A. Kirzanov, declared that the Soviet Union must base its policies on the fact that the Common Market had already begun to function. This opinion seems to have exercised a considerable influence in the discussions of the 1961 Party Program of the CPSU. In this statement of principles adopted by the 22d Party Congress, Lenin's dire predictions about "inter-imperialist alliances" are greatly watered down. Concerning the E.E.C., the Program has this to say:

"The international organizations of state monopoly which have been established ostensibly as measures of 'integration' and of ameliorating the market problem, are in reality new forms for the partition of the capitalist world market, and as such will become the focal points of severe friction and conflicts."

In his speech explaining the rationale of the new Program, Khrushchev attempted to reconcile the old economic wishful thinking of the Communists as best he could with the new reality. On October 18, 1961, he told the 22d Party Congress of the CPSU:

"The house of imperialism has been seized by an acute and deepseated crisis from its cellar to its roof. This naturally does not mean that imperialism has been brought entirely to a standstill or that its productive forces have been lamed by obsolence. *At certain periods of time and in certain countries, as a consequence of temporary influences, a more rapid economic growth is possible than is the case in other capitalist countries.* In general, however, the capitalist pattern of production inhibits to an increasing degree the development of modern productive forces" [emphasis added].

The limited influence of Khrushchev's skepticism is evident from an article by Lemin published a year later in the Soviet journal *World Economy and International Relations*, where we find the statement:

"The 'integration of Europe' is an economic reality that must be reckoned with."

As of mid-1962, Khrushchev was still embroiled in desperate struggle against this reality, and cursing the E.E.C. in picturesque language: "The tree will wither before it brings forth proper fruit." It is significant how much freedom of opinion the Soviet experts managed to exercise in this issue. The publication of the aforementioned article in *World Economy and International Relations* was followed by a conference of Communist economists from all parts of the world, devoted exclusively to the position to be taken by Communists with regard to the Common Market.[2] This conference, which took place from August 27 to September 3, 1962, in Moscow, ended with the adoption of 32 theses. According to the voluminous report of the conference published in the Communist journal *Problems of Peace and Socialism*, it was stated during the sessions that "the process of economic 'integration' now taking place in the countries of Western Europe . . . is without doubt the most important phenomenon in the economic development of capitalism during recent years." The Belgian Communist P. Joye emphasized.

"The Common Market is a reality which we must take into account, and to a certain degree a reality which is no longer to be reversed."

It is noteworthy that the delegates of West European Communist parties went furthest in describing the importance and the accomplishments of the E.E.C. They were the direct witnesses of the successes of the E.E.C., especially in France and Italy. In view of the absorption of millions of hard-core unemployed in Italy, they could not bemuse their followers with theories about the "aggravation of mass unemployment" through the E.E.C. The Italian Communists who attended the Moscow conference had prepared a memorandum, which contained the following statement:

"The E.E.C. has exhibited a remarkable vitality, and has created objective situations which cannot be abolished without serious results. The E.E.C. has arisen in response to real needs which arose from the development of productive forces."

2 This account is based on a report of this conference in *Die Kommunisten und die EWG* [The Communists and the E.E.C.], published by the Social-Democratic Party of Germany in April, 1963.

The phrase *"theoretical bankruptcy of Soviet Communism"* has been used with justification in discussing these contradictions, since the 1962 Party Program of the CPSU continues to describe the situation in capitalist countries in conventional Communist terms:

> "The working class continues to suffer mass unemployment and fear of tomorrow."

In reality, the territory of the Common Market is the scene of unprecented full employment. Individual countries within the E.E.C. are competing to mop up the last European labor reserves in Greece, Italy, Spain, and Turkey. Let us not praise the day of this E.E.C.-boom before evening falls. It is, however, impossible to doubt that the Common Market has aroused new economic impulses that are highly anti-depressive in their effects, wheseas economic life in the Eastern bloc is beset by increasingly acute difficulties.

The indecision of Communist rulers in the face of the successful consolidation of the Common Market is further expressed in a number of contradictory statements. Tito declared in a speech at Split in May, 1962, that the Yugoslav economy would have to *"arm itself against the storm of the E.E.C."* This wording makes it evident that the Common Market exerts an offensive attractive force toward Eastern Europe. The same feeling seems to be shared by the Communist Premier of Czechoslovakia, Vilem Široky, who on September 9, 1962, declared gruffly:

> "The Government of the Czechoslovak Socialist Republic considers the so-called Common Market a most harmful institution which is at variance with the interests of peace in the world, and with the principles of good mutual relations between nations; its substance and meaning is to disorganize international economic cooperation, to impair the interests and needs of nations and peace, and to serve the interests of war." (Rudé Právo, Prague, September 9, 1962)

We thus hear from Prague unmistakable echoes of Lenin's prognosis of 1915. A more friendly voice, however, comes from Budapest. The central organ of the Hungarian Communists, *Nepszabadsag*, admitted in early summer, 1963, that West European integration would have to be accepted as a reality, and then added: "... the socialist countries continue as before to regard East-West trade as an important instrument for the achievement of coexistence." The central organ of the Hungarian Communist Party thus indicated the conclusions which the country would have to draw from the achievements of the E.E.C.

This brief review makes clear the extent to which the Common Market has undermined the self-confidence of the Communist Party oligarchies in the Eastern bloc. From the very beginning, Soviet Communism had adopted the favorite thesis of Pan-Slavism, that of a "rotting of the West." For more than one hundred years, Russian messianism has fed upon the self-deception that Western Europe has grown too old and decadent, and will sooner or later be overrun by the youthful Great Russians. The progressive consolidation of Western Europe and the results of its economic integration must, therefore, force the adoption of new perspectives for the entire Russian policy with respect to Europe.

A further aspect, often neglected in international discussions, is the fact that when the peoples of Eastern Europe (and beyond them the peoples of the Soviet Union) look toward the West, they are not confronted with the system of classical capitalism, such as is described in Communist textbooks. *Western Europe is demonstrating to the Eastern bloc the accomplishments of a mixed economic system,* in which the privileges of ownership are forced to yield step-by-step to social equalization. Feudalism, a favorite object of Communist attack, has been practically liquidated in Western Europe. Monopoly capitalism too no longer enjoys the unrestricted mastery which the Kremlin would like to see. Not only Austria but Gaullist France as well has nationalized its raw-materials industries. These are historic facts, whether one approves of them or not. In West Germany, works councils of the employees and with them the trade unions exercise an appreciable degree of co-determination in mining and in other large enterprises. This does not mean that people do not have to work as hard; it does mean that plant organization has been democratized.

The advances of *welfare policy* since the war constitute an additional factor. Austria leads in the field of *social tourism.* During the pleasant weeks of summer the boats on the Grand Canal, the Rialto Bridge, and St. Mark's Square in Venice are crowded with workers and their families from the Vienna suburbs; both the Italian Adriatic coast and the Dalmatian coast of Yugoslavia are additional targets of an Austrian invasion every summer. At the same time, the shipyard workers of Hamburg pitch their tents on the shores of the Carinthian lakes, insofar as they do not spend their vacations in the Bavarian Alps or on the short stretch of Baltic coast that remains to us. The Alemanni from South Germany and Switzerland cross through the Alpine passes to the South; on the camping grounds along the Italian west coast one often does not know whether one's neighbor in the next tent is a school teacher from Freiburg or a metal worker from Zürich who studies botany in his spare time. France leads Europe with its legislation on child allowances—a fact demonstrated by its rising birth rate. We in West Germany have introduced a system of dynamic old-age pensions for employees. These pensions are adjusted every two years to the rising national income, so that the creeping devaluation of the currency cannot reduce the income of senior citizens. Great Britain has its nationalized health service, Sweden its "people's pension."

We must ask our American friends to look at all these achievements (certain of which are objects of controversy in the West) from the viewpoint of the so-called socialist camp in Eastern Europe. The fact is that there is ten times more social justice in Western Europe than in Eastern Europe. This is talked about behind the Iron Curtain however meagre the opportunities to communicate. The standard question that inhabitants of Eastern bloc countries ask visitors from the West is: how many hours must be worked for a suit or a pair of shoes, or how many work days a skilled worker must invest for a small auto.[3]

---

[3] The *Deutsche Industrieinstitut* of Cologne published in 1961 a detailed study of the purchasing power of average wages in the Soviet Union and in the German Federal Republic. Large differences in purchasing power were apparent even in various foodstuffs. A worker in West Germany must, for instance, work 13 minutes for a liter of milk; the Soviet worker must work 31 minutes for the same. The comparable figures for one kilogram of butter are: West Germany 2.27 work hours, Soviet Union 6.40. The West German worker earns a kilogram of margarine in 50 minutes, while his Soviet colleague must work 3 hours and 20 minutes to make the same purchase. The discrepancies are enormous —quite apart from quality—in articles representing an advanced standard of living.

	COST IN WORK HOURS (AT AVERAGE WAGES)	
	West Germany	*Soviet Union*
Vacuum cleaner	47	154
Refrigerator	156	476
Television with 53 cm picture screen	238	916
Automobile	2100	5952

The comparison for automobiles was based on the Soviet Moskovich and a West German 1.2-liter car. The Moscow sociologist Professor Mazlov *attempted* to discount this comparison by pointing to cheaper rents and various social services in the Soviet Union. The *Industrieinstitut* in Cologne was, however, able to support its comparison convincingly with references to Soviet social statistics. This confrontation of facts ended disastrously for Professor Mazlov. (See the Hamburg newspaper *Die Welt*, September 18, 1961, and January 6, 1962.)

The conversation usually ends with a shaking of heads by those who enjoy the blessings of Communism. The historic fact is, however, that social differences are disappearing in Western Europe—where the concept of the proletariat is no longer in our vocabulary—while in the Eastern bloc a new class of managers lords it over majorities deprived of rights. Tito is probably well aware why he sentenced Milovan Djilas to years of silence because of his book, *The New Class*.

These are the reasons why the Eastern bloc has to barricade itself against the magnetism of the West—why it has to build Berlin walls or lay mine fields along the Iron Curtain. This is, however, not the last word of European history. *The time has come when the West should no longer base its dealings with the Eastern bloc on a feeling of inferiority*. We have seen the contrast between the receptions for Kennedy in West Berlin and for Khrushchev in East Berlin. What room is still left for doubt? The decisive question is whether the weight of the West is greater than that of the East in the incorruptible scales of the world situation. This question has been answered since Cuba. What is needed now is to take advantage of the growing self-confidence of the West.

In this connection, I have a special request to make of our American friends. In view of our common higher objectives, the representatives of political science in particular should devote more attention to the phenomenon of *Western European democratic socialism*. By democratic socialism (sometimes known as social-democratism) is meant the ideology and practice of those European workers' parties that fight Communism as a variety of totalitarianism and reject every compromise with it. As Americans see things, the idea of the existence and effectiveness of an anti-Communist left is a little hard to fit into the pattern. And of course it is true that, as long as Social Democrats and Communists regarded the teachings of Marx and Engels as a common point of departure, there was always the danger that certain Leftists might wander off into the Communist camp. But it can be said on the other hand that conservatism alone is an insufficient weapon against Communist messianism. The world is moving forward, however much Communists may abuse the idea of progress.

A fact which is certainly important for the political strategy of the free world is that the strongest positions of European democratic socialism are precisely in the areas of contact with the Eastern bloc. In the North, we have the workers' parties of Scandinavia with their many years of governmental experience; we have the Social-Democratic

Party of Germany with a hundred-year tradition of freedom, and the strong parties of democratic socialism in the Netherlands, Belgium, and Switzerland. The front is extended to the southeast by the strongly based democratic-socialist labor movement in Austria, with its traditional influence throughout the Danube region, as far as Bulgaria. (In Finland the brunt of Russian pressure is directed against the right wing of an already divided Social Democracy; in Italy and France it is impossible to overlook the strength of the Communist Parties or the weakness of social-democracy.) In the ideological encounter between Western Europe and the Eastern bloc, it is important that *east* of the Iron Curtain there are old and still vital traditions of European democratic socialism—in Central Germany, in Bohemia and Moravia, in Upper Silesia, in the Polish, Hungarian, and Rumanian industrial areas, and particularly in and around Budapest. The uprisings in Central Germany in 1953 and in Hungary in 1956 demonstrated this fact.

Apart from the ideological ties which bind the older generation of East Europeans to the West, the younger generation also finds Western Europe attractive in terms of social organization. There is actually no longer any area of societal life in which the West European states need shun comparison with the "achievements" of Communist regimes. Even in welfare policies, the rigidity of the Eastern bloc stands in contrast to the dynamic of the West. The Stockholm correspondent of the Hamburg *Welt* wrote not long ago that a "quiet social-liberal revolution" was taking place in Sweden. This is true of Western Europe as a whole and under different conditions—even for North America. In Western Europe, the urge for social security is now accompanied by a striving for personal freedom. It is to be hoped that this trend will not halt at the Iron Curtain.

It should be remembered that the basic conditions for autonomous intellectual development are present in the satellite states, since they—in contrast to the Soviet Union—retain extensive and living memories of the rule of law, of religious freedom, and of the activity of free labor and peasant movements. In the Soviet Union Communism has already ruled for 46 years, in Eastern Europe for only 18 years. We can therefore safely assume that the mental disposition of the peoples is favorable for a fruitful dialogue between Western and Eastern Europe.

An additional factor is the *attraction that the idea of Europe exerts on East European youth.* That there is much evidence of this is known to everyone who has talked with young people from the satellite countries. We therefore cite only one voice, which is particularly interest-

ing since it refers to the encounter between the Common Market and
COMECON. The London Polish weekly *Wiadomosći* reported in
early April, 1963, on a conversation with a Warsaw student who expressed himself as follows:

"I will now explain why the idea of a united Europe is so attractive to me and many in my age group from a practical point of
view. First, because the emergence of a new economic, political,
and not least of all military power would create a new situation,
which would shift the balance decisively in favor of the West.
This might make possible certain pro-Western initiatives in Poland itself. From the economic point of view two facts are obvious:
the failure of COMECON so far, and the dynamic economic development of the Common Market. *This must make an impression on our technocrats.* Furthermore, the existence of a European economic power comparable to the Soviet could make at
least a partial economic independence from Russia possible."[4]

These statements were rebroadcast to Poland by Radio Free Europe.
They are supplemented by the remarks which Ambassador George
F. Kennan made to the press in Washington on August 23, 1963, after
the end of his assignment in Belgrade. It is Kennan's opinion that
". . . the conflict between Moscow and Peking has created a new international situation for the East European states. A reexamination of
relationships, particularly with the Western states, is therefore taking
place in Eastern Europe." A further element in this encounter is found
in the disappointments of the East European peoples and even of their
Communist elites with *Soviet trade methods.* The descriptions of Gomulka and the admissions of Khrushchev tell us something of the nature of Russian-Polish relations up to October, 1956. If it is true that
Stalin's ambassador in Warsaw behaved like the Czar's governor in a
Russian satrapy, one can easily imagine how the satellites were treated
in Bucharest, Sofia, Budapest, and Prague. Anyone who attempted
to represent the interests of his own country in dealing with Soviet
emisssaries disappeared as an "enemy of the Soviet Union" to some
torture chamber or to Siberia.

We know from Czech sources that the great Czechoslovak industrial concerns have passed through very unpleasant experiences with

4 German text in the journal *Europäische Begegnung* [European Encounter], Han-
nover, June, 1963.

their Soviet trade partners. The Bata works in Zlin (now Gott-waldov), one of the most modern shoe factories of the continent, groaned under the complaints of the Soviet customers concerning the quality of the product. The objections were entirely unfounded and were made because the Soviet buyers did not even wish to pay the Czech production costs. When the Bata works refused in one case to grant the discount demanded, they received back an entire shipment of boots, but with the uppers sliced apart. . . . The Skoda works of Pilsen delivered locomotives to the Soviet Union. Shortly before the agreed delivery date, a Soviet commission appeared and requested a number of minor changes, such as, for instance, a larger Soviet star on the front of the engines. The carrying out of these changes delayed the delivery for a few days beyond the date specified in the contract, whereupon the Soviet partner adamantly deducted the penalties provided in that document.

Practices of this sort were continued in somewhat subtle form after the official end of the Stalin era. It is not always easy for the West to discover what is involved in the measures referred to in COMECON jargon as "specialization," "coordination," or "equalization of levels." The workers of Central Germany usually bear the brunt of these policies. During the winter months of 1962, bitterness against obvious discriminations in the Soviet Zone had reached such proportions that even the kept press of Herr Ulbricht had to report that the workers of various plants had adopted a "hostile attitude toward the socialist countries, the Soviet Union in particular." One of these papers, the *Märkische Volksstimme,* let the cat out of the bag and reported the protest of the workers of the electric locomotive plant at Hennigsdorf near East Berlin against the *organized larceny of patents* by the Soviet partner under the pretext of *"equalization of levels."* An article in the paper indicated that in a plant meeting the workers argued as follows: "We have spent years here in developing an electric locomotive. Now the Soviet Union is receiving free of charge the technical information to build the locomotive itself."[5] Similar discussions took place in the "people-owned" plants of Saxony. The Communist newspapers were forced to admit this. Finally, the SED found itself obliged to circulate

[5] Communist Poland had the same experience in a different form with Communist China. The Polish exile press published detailed accounts of an episode in which the Chinese, in 1962 and 1963, ordered the equipment for five artificial fertilizer plants from their then Polish friends. Poland submitted the plans, whereupon Peking demanded exact detailed plans. When the Chinese were finally in possession of the detailed plans, they proceeded to build and equip the plants themselves.

a so-called "pedagogical letter" on the delicate subject of "international socialist division of labor." By way of justifying the "equalization of levels," this circular contended that the Soviet Union had "unselfishly made progressive activist methods available."

The "unselfishness" of the Soviet Union in its economic relations with the satellites is most dramatically evident in the field of price-setting. It is an open secret that the Soviet Union collects *political prices*, higher than those of the world markets, for its deliveries to the satellites, whereas it only pays *world market prices* for its imports from the same countries. "This profit from exploitation amounted to 6.3 billion marks during 1960." (*Der Spiegel*, No. 32, 1963.) The Soviet Union engages in clear-cut discrimination against its COMECON partners in setting the prices for its petroleum products, depending on whether the customers belong to the "socialist camp" or that of capitalism. It was determined in a study conducted by West German economic experts in 1962 (sponsored by the Research Council for Questions of Reunification) that while the Soviet Zone was charged $20 per ton of Soviet petroleum, the Federal Republic of Germany paid only $10. Italy and South American customers likewise purchase Soviet petroleum at prices 30 to 50 per cent cheaper than those paid by the satellites.[6]

There is a long list of complaints to the effect that the Soviet Union, misusing the pretext of "socialist division of labor," monopolizes lucrative branches of production for itself and degrades the satellites to the status of captive plants and forced consumers. The following cases in point were made public after the most recent COMECON conference:

[6] An expert analysis by Radio Free Europe determined, on the basis of Soviet foreign trade statistics, that the Soviet Union also operates with differential oil prices inside the "socialist camp." The following summary gives significant details: The average price per ton for Soviet crude oil in (new) rubles was 15.94 in 1959, 13.92 in 1960, and 12.37 in 1961. At the fictitious official exchange rate, 1 ruble equals 1.11 dollars U.S. But the prices paid by the German Federal Republic and the Soviet Zone were, respectively: 11.13 and 17.72 rubles in 1959, 9.13 and 17.71 rubles in 1960, and 8.38 and 17.20 rubles in 1961.

The price paid by the German Soviet Zone was, however, the most favorable crude oil price inside COMECON. In 1961, Pankow, at the price of 17.20 rubles, paid "only" 139% of the average price for Soviet crude oil, while Hungary paid 20.02 rubles (162%), Czechoslovakia 20.82 rubles (168%), and Poland 20.87 rubles (169%). Among the (then) non-COMECON countries, Mongolia was treated as a member of the bloc: it was forced to pay the highest price of all—22.96 rubles (186% of the average Soviet price) for one ton of crude oil. Yugoslavia, also outside the bloc, paid 12.64 rubles (102%) for one ton of crude oil, far less than the COMECON countries but nevertheless considerably more than the capitalist states. (E. T. in the *Ost-West-Kurier*, Frankfurt/M., No. 34/1963.)

The airplane construction of the GDR, which had been revived at great expense, had to be abandoned.

After the Soviet-Zone automobile industry had gone to considerable expense to make its *2.4-liter passenger auto, the "Sachsenring,"* ready for mass production, manufacture of this vehicle had to be discontinued.

Hungary was forced to limit severely its *production of motorcycles,* but succeeded in resisting a demand that it stop *production of tractors. (Der Spiegel,* No. 32, 1963.)

In cases where "socialist division of labor" would work to the advantage of the non-Russian partner, the principle is not followed. It is apparent that the Soviet Zone hoped to exchange certain special industries which it relinquished (airplane and motor-vehicle manufacture) for a leading position in the production of plastics. In the meantime, however, other COMECON states have entered the latter field. The specialist of the Soviet Zone for plastics, Professor Thinius, has in the meantime complained bitterly in the SED press about the "egotistical behavior" of unnamed brother countries.

The explosion of pent-up resentment against these practices took place at a meeting of the executive committee of COMECON in February, 1963, when the Russians attempted to block Rumania's industrialization plans. The official version is that they desired to degrade this partner country to a "poorly paid source of foodstuffs and raw materials." The history of the Rumanian rebellion is well known. In objecting to the Soviet demand, the Rumanians made skillful use of the phraseology of earlier COMECON resolutions dating from 1960, which promised the coordination of national economies ". . . on the basis of voluntary consent and mutual benefit" and assured "consideration of the concrete situation and distinctive national requirements." Peking seconded the Rumanians and injected the biting epithet of *"Soviet neo-imperialism"* into the debate. The ensuing COMECON conference of July 24-26, 1963, witnessed the capitulation of the Soviet Russians to the Rumanians. The latter are now authorized to increase their production from 3.5 to 8.1 million tons between now and 1970. The Soviet Russians also agreed to assist the construction of a new Rumanian steel plant.

The weakening of the Soviet position in Eastern Europe has thus become obvious. It is possible that Rumania achieved more in 1963 with the methods of hard diplomacy than the Hungarian people with its heroic uprising of October, 1956. There are doubtless various degrees of East European resistance against Russian neo-colonialism. Herr Ulbricht will remain a pliable tool of Russian economic interests, since his survival depends on the political and military support of the Kremlin. Gomulka is in a dilemma. The more problematic his "Polish road to socialism" becomes, the more he needs the political backing of the Soviet Union. Czechoslovakia, as long as it remains frozen in its Stalinist rigidity, has less freedom to maneuver in foreign affairs than Albania. According to appearances, *the political cleavage of Europe is felt most strongly in the Danubian area: in Hungary, Rumania, and Bulgaria.* The successful rebellion by Rumania has in any case its deeper importance. It could become a turning point for Russia's European policy.

The Soviet Union, on the other hand, could retain its colonial possessions in Eastern Europe only if COMECON could be used to achieve a *full integration* of the economic potential of the satellite countries in the Soviet national economy. Through the resistance of Rumania and the unwillingness of other Communist-ruled countries, however, the Kremlin has been forced to retreat from its policy of total synchronization. It is true that resolutions of the COMECON still speak of new projects, such as the establishment of a common socialist bank, joint major planning projects, and coordinated investment policy. Measures that could not be accomplished in the heyday of Soviet centralism, however, will not be easier to achieve in a tug-of-war with the centrifugal forces released by the Moscow-Peking conflict. A group of German experts, the Research Council for Questions of Reunification, characterized the situation in clear-cut terms in July, 1963, as follows:

"The economy of the Eastern bloc is the victim of a profound chasm between ideological loyalty and the demands of practical economics."

What solutions to the problem are open to the Eastern bloc?

Up to the present time (September, 1963) the states of the COMECON have not even achieved multilateral clearance of payments, which has existed in the OEEC area since 1950 in the form of the European Payments Union. It appears, therefore, that the internal flexibility of COMECON continues to be severely limited. This is one of the reasons why its members would like to expand their East-West trade. When the American Secretary of Agriculture, Orville L. Freeman, recently took a trip through the countries of Eastern Europe, this desire was made known to him at every place he visited. It is reported that Eastern bloc governments are already putting forth feelers in Brussels, to see if they can make individual arrangements with the Common Market.

The July, 1963, meeting of the COMECON issued a call for the summoning of a *World Trade Conference* under the auspices of the United Nations, the purpose of which would be to oppose "trade discrimination" by the United States and its "NATO allies." The same line is reflected in Khrushchev's demand of May, 1962, for the creation of a "World Trade Organization," which in his opinion "must include all countries without any discriminaton."

Khrushchev's threat to press for a World Trade Conference should not irritate the West. Such a conference could easily prove a boomerang for him. The desire of the East European countries for closer trade relations with the West should, however, be given careful consideration. Bilateral talks on this subject are useful, but they only make sense if conducted with an eye on the over-all situation. All the satellite countries face the same problem: that of regaining their freedom of foreign trade. As long as these countries are obliged to conduct an average of 75 per cent of their foreign trade within the Eastern bloc, they are unable to develop any flexibility in trade with the West. Nor does the West enjoy much tactical leeway in this field. The favoring of individual states—such as Poland or Yugoslavia—has up to now led only to the strengthening of Communist governments.

This is an area in which fundamental decisions are needed. The West should not wait for Khrushchev's next *démarche,* but should develop of its own devices a coordinated policy with respect to Eastern Europe. The position taken by the E.E.C. Commission could well point the way for the governments of the NATO countries. In its sixth General Report, the Commission lays emphasis on its efforts to develop a "community-oriented total conception" for the solution of current and future problems of their relations with the countries of the Eastern bloc. The key phrase "community-oriented total conception" should remain central in our considerations and in all Western discussion of Eastern Europe. The Treaty of Rome extends in principle an invitation to *all* European countries to join the European Economic Community. The signatory governments declare in the Preamble:

"Determined to preserve and guarantee peace and freedom through this consolidation of our economic forces, *and extending an invitation to join our efforts to the other peoples of Europe who support these objectives . . ."*

It should be made clear that this standing invitation, insofar as it is directed toward the East, is addressed primarily to the peoples of the satellite countries, inasmuch as the Soviet Union itself constitutes a formidable economic empire. The West is in no way obligated to accept the dogmatic concept of an indivisible Eastern bloc. It would seem logical to begin by clarifying the relation between the E.E.C. and the East European satellite area, in isolation from other problems. Any step in this direction will, however, meet with the objection that for the next few years the architects of the E.E.C. should direct all their energies to organizing relationships with Great Britain, Scandinavia, and the other members of EFTA. To this it may be commented that British adherence to the E.E.C. has become an open political question in two respects: first through de Gaulle's veto, and secondly through uncertainty as to the attitude of the next British government. We know from Professor Hallstein's report to the European Parliament on February 5, 1963, that the fifteen months of negotiation in Brussels yielded a useful survey of the desires of Great Britain and the Commonwealth countries. Beyond the exchange of information, far-reaching agreement was achieved in a number of specialized areas. Should negotiations with Great Britain be resumed, the progress already made will not be wasted.

In contrast to the problem of Britain and the Commonwealth, the possibilities of including Eastern Europe in the E.E.C.—or of economic cooperation—need to be explored from the ground up. What is particularly needed is an expert analysis of changes in the economic structure and trade position of each of the countries in question. As a matter of fact, the organic economic circulation of Europe as a whole has been interrupted since 1914, most particularly by the economic nationalism of the successor states after the fragmentation of the Danubian region. The investigation must determine how much complementary need for the exchange of commodities between East and West has remained, and what possibilities exist for expanding the inter-European exchange of goods and services.

It will also be necessary to face the enormous obstacles in the way of a bridging of the economic cleavage of Europe. As matters now stand, a rapid increase in European internal East-West trade is not in the offing. What the East European countries particularly want is industrial equipment with extended terms of payment—that is to say, interest-free credits for building up the economic autarky of the Eastern bloc. They offer raw materials, certain foodstuffs, and special products in exchange. The Federal Republic could, for instance, obtain from Poland hard coal, veal, eggs, and the well-known "Polish geese" in large quantities. We cannot, however, injure our own coal-mining industry or the export opportunities of our E.E.C. partners in order to promote a greater volume of German-Polish trade. At the moment West Germany is in danger of becoming a battlefield among E.E.C. poultry, American chickens, and Polish geese.

A certain exchange of roles between West and East Europe has taken place since the last war. After World War I, and particularly during the great depression, the trade policies of East European countries were conducted under the pressure of large agricultural surpluses. In the present situation it is the "Western bloc" which is feeling the supply pressure of its tremendous stocks of agricultural products. The United States and Canada are particularly and continuously subject to temptation to feed the hungry stomachs in the Eastern bloc, either through gifts of foodstuffs or at preferential prices. In Canada, the annual wheat deal with Poland or China determines the electoral prospects of the parties in the prairie provinces, while the French government has been selling surplus wheat at a 50 per cent loss to both the Soviet Union and Spain. Canadian and American wheat sales to the Soviet Union and various satellites have assumed a prominent place in the news in recent months. The pressure of domestic political forces on the governments concerned is clearly evident in such transactions. It will therefore be no easy task to coordinate the East European policy of the West. Nobody can, however, expect better results if the Americans, the British, French, Italians, and finally the Germans of the Federal Republic each pursue their separate East European policies. Nor are individual conversations across the Iron Curtain an adequate solution to the problem. If we desire to exercise any influence on the course of events, then we must give the peoples of Eastern Europe a *Western answer* to the question of their future.

We cannot achieve our goal with economic arguments alone. The

West must also arrive at a political formula for Europe as a whole, which will be just as understandable to Rumanian shepherds as to the metal workers of Csepel and Pilsen and the miners of Upper Silesia. *If we believe in the unity of All Europe, then it is our historical task to help the peoples of Eastern Europe toward a share in the West European standard of living.* Any permanent solution of the problem of European peace must address itself to overcoming the socio-economic differential between West and East. We cannot afford to abandon these capable, gifted, and for the most part biologically advancing peoples behind the Iron Curtain to their fate. Their elementary drive to achieve a Western pattern of life is our silent ally in the contest of world politics. Tomorrow, however, the hatred of the rejected could be a dangerous neighbor.

What is to be done? President Kennedy, in his speech at the Free University in Berlin, mentioned the fact that aid under the Marshall Plan had been offered to the countries of Eastern Europe. He indicated that it was not too early to think of Europe as a whole. Such considerations lead logically to the concept of a new *Marshall Plan for Eastern Europe.*

When we approach this theme, we encounter a difficult question. How is it possible to help the peoples of Eastern Europe economically without hurting them politically? In purely economic terms, the East European countries are at present in a situation analogous to that of most West European countries before the European Recovery Program. The following are a few typical indicators of the economic situation in the satellite countries:

1. Their industrial power base is either too narrow or in need of further expansion. The recent breakdown of the electric power supply in Czechoslovakia is a case in point.
2. Their consumer goods industries and agriculture have been neglected.
3. Their sources of foreign exchange (tourist industry and export manufactures) can be made productive only through liberalization and through greater investment.
4. Backwardness in transportation hampers the productivity of the entire economy. Private automobiles are still considered a luxury.

5. The provision of housing has not kept pace with the rapidity
of internal migration or the requirements of the labor market.[7]

In all these fields, the countries of Eastern Europe could very well
stand an economic injection from outside. Communist governments,
however, are notorious for their lack of gratitude. They would accept
any Western aid deliveries which come their way without raising an
eyebrow (as they accepted UNRRA shipments at the end of the war),
and then use the goods to promote their Communist propaganda.

The only procedure which can be considered, therefore, is that of
rewarding measures of true evolution. A state which eliminates travel
restrictions behind the Iron Curtain, as Hungarians are now attempt-
ing to do, would, for instance, qualify for aid in the development of its
tourist industry. The test case would then be its willingness to permit
the construction of an American hotel in Budapest, or to permit the
self-administration of Western camping grounds on the Plattensee. In
exchange for trade concessions, the Eastern countries might undertake
to fulfill various Western wishes from a gamut which includes:

The joining of *emigrés* and expellees
Amnesty for political prisoners
Cessation of persecution of churches, freedom for religious activ-
   ity
De-collectivization of farms, allowance of a free internal market
   for agricultural products
Freedom of trade-union organization
Permission for opposition parties to operate.

[7] Motorization and housing are important elements for the productivity of a country.
Light on this subject is thrown by a comparison between two West European countries
and one state in East Europe, in round numbers:

MOBILIZATION OF MANPOWER IN
E.C.C. AND COMECON

	Population (millions)	Gainfully Employed (millions)	(as % of pop.)
France	47	19	40
German Federal Republic and West Berlin	57	22.5	39.6
Poland	30.4	8.2	27

The Polish figures are those for late 1962, based on official statistics (cited in *Narodowiec,*
Lens, June 11, 1963). What is surprising is the low degree of mobilization of Polish manpower, in spite of Poland's relatively young population compared to the aging in France
and in West Germany.

The *opening of an evolutionary avenue of escape through* a great common concept of the West cannot fail to make an impression on the technocrats, those who are Communists by compulsion, and particularly the intelligentsia of Eastern Europe. What is important is that we stop letting the Communists always dictate the themes for discussion, making sure instead that our themes become known in their domain.

There are good reasons for considering the E.E.C. the strongest trump card of the West, and Professor Hallstein Khrushchev's most successful adversary. Therefore the suggestion that the E.E.C. should articulate as a program its powerful magnetism toward Eastern Europe. Beyond this, a *working staff of the Atlantic Community for the problems of Eastern Europe* would be of the greatest importance. Participation of France in this joint undertaking is essential. The prestige of France will constitute an indispensable factor in leading the East European peoples toward Western Europe. France, in the eyes of these people, is the guarantor against the economic or political hegemony of Germany in an all-European community.

The West needs the concept of a constructive anti-Communism during the years to come. Europe must become the common objective of all European peoples: in friendship with America, in peace with Russia.

Part Two:

POLITICAL AND MILITARY
PROBLEMS OF EUROPEAN UNITY

CHAPTER VI

Soviet Russia's Foreign Policy: Ideology and Power Politics

BORIS MEISSNER

IN ACHIEVING THE STATUS of a great power as a result of World War II, Bolshevist Russia regained the world power position lost by Czarist Russia in the Crimean War of 1853-56 and the Russo-Japanese War of 1904-05.[1] The Soviet Union continues to exhibit revolutionary traits and does not regard itself as a saturated power. Containment of the revolutionary tide emanating from Moscow has brought into being that bipolar world, based upon a balance of atomic terror, to which we have become accustomed since the Second World War.

Since the future destiny of the world and of Europe in particular depends so greatly on how Soviet power is employed, knowledge of the nature and peculiarities of Soviet foreign policy assumes central importance. Only by clearly recognizing the various motivating forces which affect the Kremlin's foreign policy, and their interactions, will we be able to find the correct answer to the challenge from the East.

Soviet foreign policy could have been characterized, until recently, as an amalgam of world-revolutionary expansionism and national-imperial power politics. Alongside these two aspects, which remain as important as before, a new element has appeared since the end of the war: the need for a global balance-of-power policy to maintain the world power position gained under Stalin. A basic transformation in Soviet foreign policy has taken place under Khrushchev.[2] It has,

[1] See Stadtmüller, G.: *Die russische Weltmacht und ihr Rückzug (1783-1867)* (Munich, 1960); Rauch, G. von: *Russland im Zeitalter des Nationalismus und Imperialismus (1856-1917)* (Munich, 1961).

[2] See Mosely, Philip: *The Kremlin and World Politics* (New York, 1960), pp. 538 ff.; Meissner, B.: "Die Aussenpolitik Chruschtschows," *Osteuropa*, Vol. XI, 1961, pp. 601 ff.; Löwenthal, R.: "Chruschtshows Schritt in die Weltpolitik," *Ost-Probleme*, Vol. XIII, 1961, pp. 90 ff.

to an increasing degree, become a policy of world-wide scope. In addition to flexibility of style, it exhibits a trait of adventurousness that—except for the Berlin blockade and the Korean War—was missing in Stalin's policy.

The formation of Soviet foreign policy today is guided by an image of the world markedly different from the Communist view under Stalin. The United States and the developing countries of Asia, Africa, and Latin America occupy key positions in this new image. The new policy has had its undeniable successes, but it also involves dangerous risks. Its tendency to overstrain the resources of the Russian imperium violates one of the most important rules of foreign policy: the requirement of solvency.

The World-Revolutionary Aspect of Soviet Foreign Policy

Insofar as Soviet foreign policy expresses a territorially limited power policy determined primarily by specific Russian national interests, it has much in common with Czarist foreign policy. A decisive difference, however, lies in the fact that Soviet policy is dominated by an ideologically motivated basic drive to expand, which was unknown in Czarist Russia.[3] To this extent, Soviet foreign policy differs fundamentally from the foreign policy of traditional powers, not only in its goals and methods, but also in its dependence upon an internal totalitarian power structure.

During World War II, Western statesmen—who felt themselves linked to Moscow in a "Grand Alliance"—failed to appreciate the ideological determination of Soviet foreign policy. The path was thus cleared for that fateful chain of events which led from Teheran, via Yalta and Potsdam, to the splitting of Germany and Europe. In his study of American-Russian relations, George Kennan comments on the case of Franklin D. Roosevelt as follows:

"In his attitude toward the Soviet problem Roosevelt made a mistake to which members of the older Anglo-Saxon high society

[3] See Wittram, R.: "Das russische Imperium und sein Gestaltwandel," in: *Russland, Europa und der deutsche Osten* (Munich, 1960), pp. 83-84; Karpovich, M. M.: "Russian Imperialism or Communist Aggression?", *New Leader*, June, 1951. Concerning the influence of the internal power structure on Soviet foreign policy, see Hermens, F. A.: "Totalitarian Power Structure and Russian Foreign Policy," *The Journal of Politics*, Vol. XXI, pp. 434 ff.

are perhaps particularly prone: that is, he underestimated the ideological seriousness of the Russian Communists, he doubted the importance of principles in their psychology, and took the view that their involved, suspicious, irritable, and almost psychopathic political personality was merely a subjective reaction to the personal image of the opponent, not an ideologically determined fundamental attitude."[4]

The *leitmotiv* of Marxist-Leninist ideology is the revolutionary transformation of the world. This *leitmotiv* is expressed with particular clarity in the theory of foreign policy developed by Lenin, the central objective of which is fulfillment of the world revolution.[5] All Communists who claim adherence to the Marxist-Leninist ideology— and this is just as true of Tito and Gomulka as it is of Khrushchev and Mae Tse-tung—share a common belief in a perfect ultimate society as the final stage of history within this world. Since Marx, this utopia has been described as a "classless society," in which euphoric happiness, absolute justice, and eternal peace prevail. Institutions of political rule, social groups, and distinctive nationalities are no longer to exist in the "classless society." A single collective humanity is to replace the vital multiplicity of states and peoples, while a system of social norms, free of all compulsion, is to take the place of domestic and international law. Communists consider the realization of this ideal society to be the meaning of history, and therefore of all political action.

The aspect of "eternal peace," when coupled with the final revolutionary goal of the Communists, assumes particular importance in the

[4] Kennan, George F.: *Das amerikanisch-russische Verhältnis* (Stuttgart, 1954), p. 69.

[5] On the world-revolutionary aspect of Soviet foreign policy, see Goodman, E. R.: *The Soviet Design for a World State* (New York, 1960); Historicus (George A. Morgan): "Stalin on Revolution," *Foreign Affairs*, Vol. XXVII, 1949, pp. 175 ff.; Zinner, P. E.: "The Ideological Bases of Soviet Foreign Policy," *World Politics*, June, 1952; Diplomaticus: "Stalinist Theory and Soviet Foreign Policy," *Review of Politics*, Vol. XIV, 1952, pp. 468 ff.; Glaser, W. A.: "Theories of Soviet Foreign Policy," *World Affairs Quarterly*, July, 1956; Ulam, A.: "Soviet Ideology and Soviet Foreign Policy," *World Politics*, January, 1959; Mosely, *op. cit.*, pp. 523 ff.; Meissner, B.: "Aussenpolitische Theorie und Völkerrechtsdoktrin der Sowjetunion," *Internationales Recht und Diplomatie*, Vol. V, 1960, pp. 1 ff.; also the articles by R. N. Carew Hunt ("The Importance of Doctrine"), Barrington Moore, Jr. ("The Relations of Ideology and Foreign Policy"), and R. C. Tucker ("The Psychology of Soviet Foreign Policy"), in: Dallin, A., ed.: *Soviet Conduct in World Affairs* (New York, 1960).

Among earlier writers, Waldemar Gurian directed attention in a number of his writings to the important relationship of power-political and utopian-ideological elements in Soviet foreign policy.

area of foreign policy. This doctrine serves to clothe all Communist measures directed at the achievement of this utopian state of affairs, even if they constitute clear injustices or involve actual warlike operations, with the character of a "struggle for peace." It also provides a convenient rationale for denouncing as "dangers to the peace" any measures intended to maintain or restore peace, either currently or in the near future, if they tend to hamper the further advance of Communism in the world.

As Communists see things, the "liberating act" of the proletarian revolution occupies the central point in history. It thus serves as the starting point for a development that is to proceed, via the formation of a Communist world-state, to that utopian society in which no man is another's master. The road which leads by various stages to this final goal is that of world revolution.

Marx and Engels assumed that the proletarian revolution which they hoped to promote would break out almost simultaneously in the advanced Western industrial countries, including the United States. They attached little importance to the question as to how developments were to continue outside the Western industrial world. It was their opinion that the proletarian revolution, being of universal character, would also "totally change and tremendously accelerate" the development of the rest of the world. Accomplishment of the proletarian revolution, in the opinion of Marx and Engels, depended on three basic factors:

1. a highly developed capitalist system which is ripe for socialism
2. a revolutionary situation, in which a crisis involving the whole country coincides with a high degree of class consciousness and organizational preparedness on the part of the proletariat
3. the international character of the revolutionary process, which leaps across all national boundaries.

According to the original Marxian concept, the capitalist stage could not be skipped over without undesirable political and economic consequences. The bourgeois-democratic revolution therefore had to be completed before the proletarian-socialist revolution could start.

Lenin breached the "two revolutions" theory with his doctrine of "imperialism" developed in 1916. This doctrine, which still plays a central role in the foreign-policy theory of orthodox Marxism-Leninism, is based on the finding that capitalism, in its monopolistic and imperialistic stage of development, had developed as a world system after the end of the nineteenth century. Communists predicted that the unbalanced development and internal contradictions of capitalism would lead to worldwide crises and wars. The competition for hegemony among the leading industrial powers would lead to intensified competition on the world market and thus ultimately to wars of conquest. Such wars would be waged primarily to achieve a redistribution of capital investment areas, and of colonial possessions in particular.

Modern imperialism had found its primary expression in the building of great colonial empires and in the demarcation of spheres of influence by the great powers. Lenin, in a most unscientific manner, reduced the concept of imperialism to its economic factor alone. While he appreciated the importance of the national question, his ideological blinkers prevented him from recognizing nationalism as the decisive motivating force of modern imperialism.

Lenin's analysis led him to consider the entire system of bourgeois-capitalist states as a coherent body, ripe for overthrow as a whole. For this reason, a Communist seizure of power in a single backward country could set off the chain reaction of world revolution. It was no longer necessary to wait for ripeness for revolution, which according to Marx and Engels existed only in the most highly industrialized states. All that mattered now was a favorable opportunity for revolution, even in a semi-feudal country such as Russia. The important requirements were the existence of a revolutionary situation, such as that resulting from a war, and the ability of a disciplined party, such as that founded by Lenin and consisting mostly of intellectual professional revolutionaries, to mobilize the peasant masses as allies of the proletariat.

In a multi-national state such as Russia, the oppressed peoples were available as an additional revolutionary force. This is why the agrarian question, as well as the self-determination of peoples in connection with the national question, have assumed central importance in world-revolutionary strategy and tactics.[6] Within the same policy, the Communists undertook to support national liberation movements among the colonial and dependent peoples, so as to transform these "reserves of imperialism" into "reserves of the proletarian revolution." By allying itself with revolutionary nationalism in a united front, the social revolutionary movement could help to bring about a worldwide breakthrough of world revolution.

Lenin's doctrine of imperialism thus did not limit itself to justify-

[6] See Meissner, B.: *Sowjetunion und Selbstbestimmungsrecht* (Cologne, 1962).

ing the seizure of power by a Bolshevik minority in a backward country and the establishment of a minority dictatorship of a kind frowned upon by Marx and Engels. It led rather to a substantial modification of the previous concept of world revolution, with the developing countries assigned a new and important role.[7] The spread of world revolution, according to Lenin, should be based on the conscious conviction of the broad masses of the people, and not merely carried forward on the points of bayonets.

Soviet and Chinese Concepts of World Revolution

After hopes for an early victory of the world revolution had shattered, Stalin—in a manner quite consistent with Lenin's thinking—reworked the latter's ideas into a theory of "socialism in one country." This theory, which Stalin expanded in 1939 into a doctrine of "communism in one country," continues to serve as the ideological foundation of Khrushchev's domestic as well as foreign policy. In Stalin's day, it served to justify self-chosen isolation combined with concentration on building up the country internally and on strengthening the power potential of the Soviet Union. Under his aegis, the Bolshevik-governed state advanced to the "base of world revolution" and simultaneously to the "fatherland of all toilers." This development not only lent considerable momentum to the Russification of Marxism in its Leninist version, but also subjected the concept of world revolution to a new transformation.

Since Lenin, the term "world revolution" has had a dual meaning. It has signified the outward expansion of Communism on the one hand, while, on the other, it has been used to describe violent internal structural change. The Chinese Communists referred to these two aspects of the world revolution in their twenty-five point memorandum of June 14, 1963. We are accustomed to subsuming the incisive revolutionary changes that take place in the political, economic, and social structure of a country ruled by Communists—in Europe, usually as a result of Soviet intervention—under the term "Sovietization."

7 See Meissner, B.: "Die marxistisch-leninistische Lehre von der 'nationalen Befreiung' und dem 'Staat der nationalen Demokratie,'" *Moderne Welt*, Vol. IV, 1962-63, pp. 30 ff.; Löwenthal, R.: "Die Strategie der nachkolonialen Revolution in russischer und chinesischer Sicht," in: Boettcher, E., ed.: *Ostblock, EWG und Entwicklungsländer* (Stuttgart, 1963), pp. 115 ff.

With the consolidation of Stalin's rule, the external phase of the world revolution became for practical purposes identical with Soviet Russian efforts to achieve world rule. After the mid-1930's, however, there was little overt talk about the world revolution. Only recently has the growing importance of the developing countries aroused Khrushchev's hopes that the world revolution might be advanced by exploiting the revolutionary spontaneity of the masses, thus turning the Western front from behind. This hope has been realized so far only in Cuba. This is no mere coincidence: the intellectual tradition and difficult social problems of the Latin-American region make it particularly susceptible to revolutionary European ideas, even when a perverted variety of Marxism is involved.

The Soviet Russians do not share the Chinese opinion that the fate of the world revolution and therefore of world Communism is to be decided in the developing countries. It is, however, their belief that it is possible to draw this in-between world gradually into the Communist camp.

Recently, there has been a considerable resurgence in Western countries of the view that the world-revolutionary urge to expand has no great importance as a motivating force of Soviet foreign policy. This view does not correspond to the facts. The discrepancy is particularly sharp with regard to the internal phase of the world revolution, which under both Lenin and Stalin was pursued with unabated vigor. One need only recall how the internal structure of the Baltic states was forcibly assimilated to the Soviet model in 1940, a process repeated in the "Lands of People's Democracy" and in the Soviet Occupation Zone of Germany after World War II. The Berlin Wall cannot be overlooked as a monument to the already accomplished advance of the world revolution into the heart of Europe.

A drive for mastery of the world in the conventional sense, such as we encounter in history, would never have required such a thorough-going standardization of internal structures. It is obvious that in the case of Bolshevik Russia we have a very specific form of the urge to rule the world—one which has its roots in the foreign-policy theory of Marxism-Leninism. According to this theory, the world revolution is a step-by-step process, which leads to the final goal of the "classless society" via the Communist world-state, which has been introduced as an intermediate long-range goal.

Unlike the foreign policy of most powers, Soviet foreign policy involves long-range planning, which is oriented toward the intermediate goals associated with the various individual steps in the world revolution. The same long-range planning of foreign policy may be observed in the Chinese People's Republic, since it is the only Communist power which is already strong enough to challenge Soviet Russia's claim to leadership in the world Communist movement and to assert its own pretensions to world rule.

In contrast to Belgrade, the spokesman of reform Communism, Moscow and Peking are both firmly committed to the world revolution. They differ, however, concerning the individual steps to be taken on the way to the ultimate goal; as to the forces on which the world revolution should rely for support; and as to the most feasible methods for achieving the next intermediate goals.[8]

Peking appears to look with greater optimism on the opportunity to advance the world revolution in developing countries and in Southeast Asia in particular than does Moscow, which currently is more interested in maintaining and consolidating the status quo. The Chinese are also clearly prepared to take greater risks in order to cash in on their opportunities. In view of experience during the last few years, however, and in view of the basic military and economic weakness of China—which promises to persist for some time to come—it would be a misjudgment of the world political situation to base Western policy on the premise that the Chinese are more dangerous than the Soviet Russians.

It is, after all, Khrushchev and not Mao Tse-tung who provoked the Berlin crisis, and who went to the brink of atomic war in Cuba— where world revolutionary motives also played a certain role. Peking, which Moscow accuses quite falsely of wishing to advance the world revolution through atomic war, is quite correct in accusing Khrushchev of conducting an adventurous foreign policy not permissible to a Marxist-Leninist. The next set of goals, toward which Moscow is now aiming in its long-range foreign-policy planning, is much more dangerous for Europe, and therefore for the entire West, than is the Chinese activity in Southeast Asia.

8 Concerning the dispute between Moscow, Peking, and Belgrade, see Löwenthal, R.: *Chruschtschow und der Weltkommunismus* (Stuttgart, 1963); London, K., ed.: *Unity and Contradictions, Major Aspects of Sino-Soviet Relations* (New York, 1962); Meissner, B.: "Der ideologische Konflikt zwischen Moskau und Peking," supplement to the weekly *Das Parlament*, March 15, 1961; Meissner, B.: "Die Auseinandersetzung zwischen dem Sowjet- und Reform-kommunismus," in *Festschrift* for Hermann Gross (Munich, 1963), pp. 75 ff.; Meissner, B.: "Der Machkampf zwischen Peking und Moskau," *Osteuropa*, July, 1963.

The new party program of the CPSU, for which Khrushchev is largely responsible, sets the establishment of a "Communist world economy" within the framework of the "socialist world system" as a long-range goal to be accomplished before the creation of the Communist world-state.[9] Since the "Communist world economy" is to be based on a unitary production plan, it can only be brought into being within a state. In practice, this would require the federation and thus the incorporation of the People's Democracies, including Central and East Germany, into the Union of Socialist Soviet Republics, following the precedent of the Baltic states.

The "socialist world economy" also called for by the program—a short-range goal to be achieved within the framework of the Council for Mutual Economic Aid (COMECON)—is to be based initially only on an East European common market, but not a unitary production plan. In view of the peculiar structure of the People's Democracies, however, the creation of a common East European market would require at least a confederation. Whether these ambitious Soviet Russian goals can be achieved within the planned time limits appears highly questionable as things now stand,[10] since they are predicated on a further strengthening of Soviet hegemony—a development hardly desirable from the point of view of most other People's Democracies, Poland in particular. There can be no doubt whatever that Moscow would interpret a non-aggression pact between the NATO and the Warsaw Pact as a demarcation of spheres of influence, constituting a license for the Soviet Union to incorporate East Central Europe into the "base of world revolution."

The violent protests of Peking against Moscow's integration policy and the methods used to implement it, and its advocacy of a polycentric system within the Eastern bloc and the Communist camp—a subject on which Peking and Belgrade agree, however sharp their disputes about other things—are motivated by a series of reasons. First of all, the Chinese demand a voice in all matters involving the Eastern bloc and the world Communist movement. Secondly, they hold that the efforts of the Soviet Russians to expand their hegemonial leadership in the East European region into an empire constitutes a policy of great-power chauvinism. They feel that such a policy injures Chinese interests, the decline of Soviet economic aid being a case in

---

[9] Meissner, B.: *Das Parteiprogramm der KPdSU 1903 bis 1961* (Cologne, 1961), p. 48.

[10] Rhode, G.: "Politische und soziale Probleme einer Integration in den Ostblockländern Ostmitteleuropas," in Boettcher, *op. cit.*, pp. 22 ff.

point, and that it reduces the possibilities for promoting the world revolution in developing countries. Thirdly, they consider that the social transformation in world-revolutionary terms has not yet been completed in the individual Communist countries, the Soviet Union included.

Peking regards the accelerated integration of part of the Eastern bloc, on a basis of inequality and with China and its satellites excluded, as a violation of the principle of "proletarian-socialist internationalism," which Moscow interprets so as to justify its own exclusive position of domination.[11] In two places in its "Open Letter" of July 14, 1963, Moscow expresses the suspicion that "behind the rumpus about the world revolution" raised by Peking, other objectives are hidden "which have nothing to do with the revolution." However one may judge the ultimate motivations behind Peking's disagreement with Moscow, one conclusion may be drawn with certainty: that in the question of preventing both the accelerated integration of the European part of the Eastern bloc and the gradual incorporation of the countries of East Central Europe into the Soviet Union, there is a remarkable congruity of European and Chinese interests. In view of these parallel interests, the Chinese notion of coexistence—which resembles "cold war" more than "cold peace"—dwindles to insignificant importance.

The term "peaceful coexistence" was first coined by Stalin in 1927, although the idea contained in it had already been expressed by Lenin. For both the Soviet Russians and the Chinese, the phrase refers to a temporary armistice between the two antagonistic worlds.[12] Khrushchev views coexistence not only as competition in the economic field but also as a specific form of the class war. He is therefore just as unwilling as Mao Tse-tung to extend coexistence into the intellectual and ideological sphere. Nor is he inclined to comply with Belgrade's demand and make the coexistence principle the basis for relationships within the Eastern bloc.

The one genuine difference between the Soviet Russian and Chinese concepts of coexistence is the assumption of a longer period of coexistence by Khrushchev. The Soviet dictator regards coexistence

11 Meissner, B.: "Die interparteilichen Beziehungen im Ostblock und das Prinzip des 'proletarisch-sozialistischen Internationalismus,' " in: *Internationales Recht und Diplomatie,* Vol. VI, 1961, pp. 147 ff.

12 See Kordt, E.: "Koexistenz als politisches Phänomen," *Moderne Welt,* Vol. I, 1959-60, pp. 13 ff.; Meissner, "Aussenpolitische Theorie und Völkerrechtsdoktrin der Sowjetunion," *loc. cit.,* pp. 14 ff.

in its present form as the ideologial circumlocution for the condition of balance brought about by the atomic pact of the two world powers. He therefore shrinks from limited local wars, and prefers a Communist seizure of power on the order of the Prague putsch rather than a civil war. He accepts both "national wars of liberation" and civil wars, however, as permissible tactics of world revolution. Khrushchev clearly refuses to realize that these two categories of war which he approves can just as easily escalate into a world conflagration as can a limited local war—a type which Mao Tse-tung regards as a further legitimate form of "just" revolutionary war. As long as Soviet foreign policy retains its world-revolutionary goals and interprets the principle of "peaceful coexistence" in the manner indicated, any real relaxation of tensions is out of the question.

It is not only in determining the long-range goals of Kremlin policy, however, that the world-revolutionary aspect of Soviet foreign policy plays an important role. Even in those situations in which national problems or considerations of global balance-of-power policy predominate, Soviet foreign policy follows the strategic and tactical doctrines of world-revolutionary action laid down by Lenin and Stalin. These teachings emphasize fighting tactics of maximum flexibility and adaptability, including temporary retreats where appropriate. The necessary suppleness of mind is cultivated through training in dialectical thinking, which perceives the potentiality of contradiction in every situation.[13] One of the time-tested operating principles derived from Leninist-Stalinist strategy and tactics is that of defaming an opponent while at the same time lulling him to sleep with peace propaganda. Such propaganda also serves to cover up the essentially expansionist and aggressive character of the world-revolutionary motives underlying Soviet foreign policy.

Immediate measures of day-to-day foreign policy are thus integrated into the realization of long-range plans. The dogmatic principles underlying the ultimate objectives find compensation in an unbridled opportunism of method. There is no significant difference in this respect between Peking and Moscow. The Chinese are also pragmatists, and therefore not interested in dogmatic hair-splitting. They do, however, object to the reckless way in which Khrushchev has shaken the central beliefs of the Marxist-Leninist ideology in a number of cases.

[13] Grottian, W.: *Lenins Anleitung zum Handeln* (Cologne and Opladen, 1962); Meissner, *loc. cit.*, pp. 8 ff.

Although the ideological encounter between Peking and Moscow is unfolding against a background of concrete political differences, which are in no way limited to questions of world-revolutionary strategy and tactics, it does have its theoretical side. The latter is justified by the experience of the Chinese leaders, who were reared in the Confucian tradition that the stability of political rule depends essentially on the consistency of the dogma supporting its legitimacy.

The Nationalist Aspect of Soviet Foreign Policy

Beyond the world-revolutionary aspect of Soviet foreign policy, directed toward global rule by Moscow and the revolutionary structural transformation of the society of states, the nationalist aspect, the importance of which increased under Stalin, should not be overlooked. Its ideological justification is to be found in Soviet patriotism, behind which lurks integral all-Russian nationalism—one of the decisive motivating forces of Soviet foreign policy.[14]

Stalin did more than merely develop Lenin's world-revolutionary theory. He supplemented it with the imperial conception of a totalitarian national Communism, thereby building a bridge to ideas already present in the background of Czarist imperialism. Certain aspects of Soviet foreign policy under Stalin give the appearance of a continuation of Czarist Russia's traditional foreign policy, which was strongly characterized by the drive toward the open seas and by Pan-Slavic ambitions in East Central Europe. This continuity is particularly apparent in the policies of the Stalin era with respect to the Baltic Sea and the countries along its eastern shore, the Balkans, and the outlets of the Baltic and Black Seas.

The traditional expanionist goals of Russian Baltic policy were involved both in the Hitler-Stalin Pact of August, 1939—which resulted in the partition of Poland and in Soviet annexation of the Baltic republics of Estonia, Latvia, and Lithuania in the summer of 1940—and in the Hitler-Molotov negotiations of November, 1940.[15] At the direction of Stalin, Molotov demanded the inclusion of Finland in the immediate Soviet sphere of control, as well as Soviet participation

14 Barghoorn, F. C.: *Soviet Russian Nationalism* (New York, 1956); Sharp, S. L.: "National Interest: Key to Soviet Politics," in: Dallin, *op. cit.*, pp. 46 ff.; Meissner, "Sowjetunion und Selbstbestimmungsrecht," *loc. cit.*, pp. 109 ff.

15 See Meissner, B.: *Die Sowjetunion, die baltischen Staaten und das Völkerrecht* (Cologne, 1956).

in controlling the access routes to the Baltic (Great Belt, Little Belt, Sund, Kattegat, and Skagerrak). The Soviet expansion program is explained by Molotov was one of the factors inducing Hitler to make his disastrous decision to attack the Soviet Union. This turn of events completed the demolition of the *cordon sanitaire* which the Western powers had so painstakingly built up in East Central Europe, and opened the gates wide to a westward advance of Soviet power.

At Teheran in December, 1943, Stalin expanded the Soviet demands to include the northern half of East Prussia with its capital of Konigsberg. On that occasion, he also introduced the idea of the Oder-Neisse Line for the first time among high-level Allied statesmen, and made known Soviet interest in the control of the Kiel Canal.[16] According to the American and Russian minutes of the Teheran Conference, Stalin supported the Soviet demand for northern East Prussia by contending that it was "ancient Slavic territory," by claiming compensation for the portions of territory with mixed Polish and Ukrainian population, and by asserting the Soviet desire for an ice-free port.[17] The fact is, however, that Slavs have never inhabited the northern part of East Prussia. Nor did that province ever belong to the Russian Empire. The eastern border of East Prussia (including the Memel district) was for centuries one of the most stable boundaries in Europe.

The very fact that Stalin advanced a Pan-Slav argument of this kind is symptomatic in itself. The ploy about the ice-free ports of Konigsberg and Memel was not new; Stalin had used the same arguments in the negotiations with Ribbentrop to demand the Latvian ports of Liepaja (Libau) and Ventspil (Windau), and had been granted these ports by Hitler. Neither Roosevelt nor Churchill happened to remind Stalin of this fact, although both the United States and Great Britain had refrained from recognizing the annexation of the Baltic states by the Soviet Union.

In 1944, the Soviet Russians indicated their interest in occupying the island of Fehmarn, today crossed by the shortest transit route from Germany to Denmark and Sweden.[18] It was only with difficulty that the Western Allies managed to persuade the Soviet Union to with-

[16] See Meissner, B.: *Russland, die Westmächte und Deutschland, Die sowjetische Deutschlandpolitik 1943-53*, 1st ed. (Hamburg, 1953), pp. 27 ff.

[17] "Tegeranskaja konferencija rukovoditelej trech velikich derzhav" ("The Teheran Conference of the Leaders of the Three Great Powers"), *Mezhdunarednaya Zhizn (International Life)*, 1961, No. 8, p. 158.

[18] See Wagner, W.: *Die Teilung Europas* (Stuttgart, 1959), p. 83.

draw from the Danish island of Bornholm in the Baltic. Intervention by Churchill was necessary to assure that General Montgomery received the necessary reinforcements to reach Lübeck before the Red Army and thus head off a Soviet drive into Schleswig-Holstein.

The use of ideological formulations to cloak traditional Russian expansionist goals became quite apparent in the conversations of responsible Baltic statesmen with the Soviet leaders.[19] Professor Krėvė-Mickevičius, the Prime Minister and Foreign Minister of the Lithuanian transitional government after the occupation of that country by the Red Army in June, 1940, was told by the then Soviet Prime Minister and Foreign Minister Molotov:

"The efforts of the Russian Czars since Ivan the Terrible to reach the Baltic were not undertaken as a matter of personal pleasure, but because the development of the Russian state and the Russian nation made them necessary."

Stalin had already spoken in a similar vein to Estonian Foreign Minister Selter and his Latvian colleague, Munters, during the conclusion of "mutual aid" pacts in the fall of 1939. He emphasized in this connection that Peter the Great's efforts to gain access to the sea for Russia were not attributable to a personal drive for power.

But even in the case of the Baltic Republics, in which Bolshevist Russia's national-imperial power policy became so apparent, the world-revolutionary element was not to be overlooked. The Baltic states were subjected at a rapid pace to the same process of Sovietization which was later spread over a longer period in East Central Europe, following the principle known as "salami tactics." As "Union Republics," the Baltic countries were granted less autonomy than they had enjoyed under the Czars up to the Russification under Alexander III, and in some respects even afterwards. The "Lands of People's Democracy," on the other hand, did not entirely lose their sovereignty and were not subjected to as intense a degree of Russification.

The traditional goals of Czarist Russian expansionism are also clearly evident in Stalin's Balkan and Straits policies, as well as in his dealings with Turkey and Iran. During the negotiations with Hitler in November, 1940, Molotov demanded not only inclusion of Bul-

19 Cf. Meissner, B.: *Die Sowjetunion, die baltischen Staaten und das Völkerrecht*, pp. 62 and 82.

garia in the Soviet "safety zone" but also military bases on the shores of the Bosphorus and Dardanelles. Shortly afterward, he indicated Moscow's interest in placing Iran within the Soviet sphere of influence, and in obtaining access to the Persian Gulf.

Immediately after Yalta, Stalin demanded a control of the Turkish Straits limited to the Black Sea powers as riparian states, with joint Turkish-Soviet defense. This amounted to a repetition of the demand for Soviet bases along the Straits.[20] Turkey would be required at the same time to cede to the Soviet Union the Anatolian provinces of Kars and Ardahan (which the Czars had annexed during the nineteenth century but which Turkey had recovered after World War I), and to agree to border adjustments in the European part of the country. Simultaneously, in the Soviet-occupied northern region of Iran, an attempt was made to establish "People's Democracies"—the so-called "Azerbaijani Democratic Republic" and the "Kurdish People's Republic."[21] Only after invoking the United Nations did the Western powers secure the withdrawal of Soviet troops as provided by treaty.

As a response to persistent Soviet pressure against Turkey, as well as to the Greek civil war, the Truman Doctrine was proclaimed on March 12, 1947. This event marked the Western shift to a "policy of containment," which was to lead, via the Marshall Plan, to a rehabilitation of Western Europe.

After the establishment of the Cominform in September, 1947, Stalin shifted the main emphasis of his policy to the Sovietization of the East Central European countries, including the Soviet Zone of Germany.[22] Although the "Lands of People's Democracy" were at this time wholly dominated by Soviet power, Stalin did not go so far as to incorporate them into the Soviet Union. Pan-Slav forces were too weak to be exploited for this purpose, especially after the break with Tito's Yugoslavia.

The traditional expansionist goals of Czarist Russia had never extended so far to the west, nor was there any discernible Russian in-

---

[20] Meissner, B.: *Das Ostpakt-System* (Frankfurt/Main, 1955), p. 162.

[21] Geyer, D.: *Die Sowjetunion und Iran* (Tübingen, 1955), pp. 57 ff.

[22] Concerning the Sovietization of East Central Europe and the Soviet Zone of Germany, see Kertesz, E., ed.: *The Fate of East Central Europe* (Notre Dame, 1956); Birke, E. and Neumann, R., eds.: *Die Sowjetisierung Ost-Mitteleuropas* (Frankfurt/Main, Berlin, 1959); Schütze, H.: *Volksdemokratie in Mitteldeutschland*, 1960.

Concerning changes in Soviet methods of leadership and rule in the Eastern bloc, see Meissner, B.: "Das Verhältnis von Partei und Staat im Ostblock," in: *Die Sowjetunion in Europa* (Wiesbaden, 1962), pp. 63 ff.

terest in extending the borders of the Soviet Imperium to the Elbe and the Werra. National Russian interests would doubtless have been satisfied with a safety zone of friendly states in the East Central European region, and with a neutral attitude on the part of the other states, including Germany. Considered in purely nationalist terms, Russia's interest in perpetuating the partition of Germany may be eliminated by assurance that the East Central European countries will not fully escape from their relation of dependency, and by an arrangement with the United States which stabilizes a definite balance of power in Europe.

So far as national Russian interests are concerned, therefore, a re-unification of Germany seems entirely possible. As a precondition for such a development, however, it is first necessary that the Soviet Union be de-ideologized and Europeanized, and that the bipolar world be replaced by a multilateral power system giving greater weight to Europe. For the time being, the ideological forces motivating Soviet foreign policy are too strong to permit such a policy of self-limitation, even though it coincides with the clear interest of the Russian Empire, to become an immediate reality at the present time.

This situation reveals another remarkable parallelism between European and Chinese interests. Khrushchev's policy is directed at a gradual shifting of the existing balance of power within the framework of the "bipolar world." Peking, on the other hand, is not interested in a consolidation of blocs which would stabilize the status quo. It clearly prefers a loose concert of great powers, in which it would participate and which would afford it sufficient leeway to pursue successfully its own limited national-imperial power politics.

The collision between Russian and Chinese nationalism became predictable as soon as Soviet foreign policy, under Stalin, had turned anew to the traditional expansionist goals of Czarist Russia, in the Far East as elsewhere. This orientation is apparent not only in the Soviet annexation of Japanese territory, but also in efforts to expand Soviet influence beyond Tannu Tuva and Outer Mongolia into further border areas of the Chinese Empire.[23]

The "independent" People's Republic of Tannu Tuva was annexed by the Soviet Union in 1944. The following year, the Soviets also took over the Japanese patrimony in Manchuria, including the

23 See Mehnert, K.: *Peking und Moskau* (Stuttgart, 1962), pp. 314 ff.; Meissner, B.: *Das Ostpakt-System*, pp. 157 ff.

administration of the Chinese Eastern and South Manchurian railways, the naval base at Port Arthur, and the commercial harbor of Dalnij (Dairen). In 1946 Outer Mongolia, henceforth the "independent" People's Republic of Mongolia, was finally separated from the Chinese state. Mongolia's admission to COMECON in 1962 as the only Asian member of that body illustrated clearly its status as a Soviet protectorate.

The Soviet Union was less successful in its attempts to consolidate its position in Manchuria, and to secure footholds in Inner Mongolia and Sinkiang through the use of "mixed stock corporations." A Soviet-dominated "East Turkestan Republic" had actually existed in Sinkiang from 1944 to 1949. Through presistent negotiation, the Chinese succeeded in inducing the Russians to give up their privileges in Manchuria and to dissolve the "mixed stock corporations." Maps recently published by the Chinese indicate that they seek changes in their boundary with the Soviet Union, which include the Far Eastern Territory that China was forced to cede to Russia under the "Unequal Treaties" of Aigun (1858) and Peking (1860). These boundary disputes are certainly not the decisive issues in the conflict between Peking and Moscow. They do, however, illustrate the strength of Chinese nationalism, which had already become evident in the early development of a Chinese version of Marxism-Leninism.

The Chinese accuse Khrushchev of using the elimination of national, racial, and geographical barriers as a pretense covering up a policy of maintaining the rule of "master nations" over the oppressed peoples. They regard the Soviet Union as a European, not an Asian power, and consider themselves the spokesmen of the colored peoples. At the Third Solidarity Conference of Asian and African peoples in Moshi, the leader of the Chinese delegation informed the Soviet representatives that "whites have no business here." The Chinese likewise objected to the admission of Soviet newsmen to the Journalists' Conference in Djakarta, since "the Soviet Union is not an Asian country."

The Soviets, for their part, consider that the Chinese slogan, "the East Wind shall rule over the West Wind," reflects the ideology of racial warfare, not that of class warfare. The Soviet Russians are, however, just as guilty of national arrogance as are the Chinese.

There is significance in the language chosen by Stalin for informing his people of Soviet participation in the defeat of Japan. In his proclamation on this subject, he represented the war with Japan as Russia's *revanche* for the Japanese victory over the Czarist Empire in the war of 1904-05.[24]

"The defeat of Russian troops in 1904 left bitter memories in the heart of the Russian people. This defeat lay over our country like a blot of shame. Our people believed in and waited for the day on which Japan would be defeated and this shameful blot thus eradicated. We of the older generation have waited forty years for this day. And now the day has come."

The truth of the matter is that the defeat of the Czarist regime was greeted enthusiastically by all radical Russian parties, including even the Liberals, as a step on the road to freedom. Lenin himself had rejoiced in the Japanese victory as a prelude to the rising of the European proletariat.[25]

These examples confirm the historical experience, to which George Kennan has correctly pointed, that whoever currently wields the supreme power in a country is forced through his function of sovereignty into pre-existing patterns, which cast him in the role of a defender of traditional interests.[26] To remain permanently in power, he must identify himself—at least to a certain extent—with the national interest of the people over whom he rules. This phenomenon dilutes to a considerable degree the original ideological motivating forces. It does not, however, by any means indicate that they have lost their importance as political motivations. The latter is an erroneous conclusion suggested by observation of the specific Soviet foreign policy of the Stalin era.

It is easy to overlook the fact that the foreign policy of a state may be shaped by a multiplicity of motives. This is particularly true of a universal power such as the Soviet Union, with a sense of mission nourished from two different intellectual and ideological sources: Marxism-Leninism and all-Russian nationalism. Soviet imperialism, a synthesis resulting from the amalgamation of these two divergent elements, thus presents two faces. According to the shifting political

24 Stalin, J.: *Über den Grossen Vaterländischen Krieg der Sowjetunion* (Moscow, 1946), p. 232.

25 Rauch, G. von: *Geschichte des bolschewistischen Russland* (Wiesbaden, 1955), pp. 509-10.

26 See Kennan, G. F.: *Sowjetische Aussenpolitik unter Lenin und Stalin* (Stuttgart, 1961), p. 523.

situation, one or the other of these faces is brought to the fore. During the war, for instance, the Western powers were impressed by the national features of the Soviet system. Since the war, they have been frightened by its Communist traits.

Many observers of Soviet foreign policy have not yet realized that it is precisely the mixture of national-imperial and world-revolutionary factors, resulting both in a modification of Marxism-Leninism and in the simultaneous presence of nationalist and Communist motivations, which determines the essential nature and distinctive characteristics of Soviet foreign policy. Klaus Mehnert has suggested the simile of an airplane provided with two kinds of motors.[27] The pilot is free to use one motor, the other, or both, depending on the conditions encountered. The interaction of the two elements conditions the dynamics of Soviet foreign policy, but at the same time signifies a conflict of interests, which tends to become more acute as time passes.

The objectives of national Russian imperialism are more modest than those of the Soviet Communist variety. This does not mean, however, that Russian nationalists are in agreement as to whether the Soviet Imperium should be considered as saturated through its territorial gains in World War II. There are also differences in the way Soviet politicians evaluate various positions gained during the Second World War. The Beria-Malenkov group, which was not particularly nationalistic in its approach, was willing to release the Soviet Zone and agree to the reunification of Germany under certain conditions. Khrushchev, whose attitude is revolutionary and therefore more internationalist, as well as a number of leading Soviet military men more properly classifiable as nationalists, were opposed to such a policy. It is thus evident that the aforementioned ideological differences do not preclude agreement by adherents of different schools of thought on specific issues.

The fundamental contradictions between the national-imperial and world-revolutionary tendencies remain, however. They could very well provide the impetus for a conflict of interests, perhaps resulting in new approaches to problems for which the foreign-policy line now seems to be fixed. This statement applies—the Berlin Wall notwithstanding—to the Soviet policy on Germany and to the present *impasse* in German-Soviet relations.

27 Mehnert, K.: *Weltrevolution durch Weltgeschichte* (Kitzingen/Main, undated), p. 79.

The World Political Aspect of Soviet Foreign Policy[28]

The world, according to the foreign-policy theory of Marxism-Leninism, has been divided since the October Revolution into two camps: the capitalist and the socialist. The basic assumption of Communist foreign policy is therefore that of a bipolar world: the Communist world faces the capitalist world in a state of permanent struggle.

As early as 1927, Stalin visualized the two hostile systems as each grouped around a center; it was for him a foregone conclusion that the Soviet Union was the center of the socialist camp. He soon recognized that the United States would develop as the other center. This "two worlds" concept, which Khrushchev modified only slightly by directing more attention to the "in-between world" of the developing countries, was used by Stalin as the point of departure for his contribution to the foreign-policy theory originated by Lenin. The central feature of Stalin's teaching was his recognition that the world revolution was a long drawn-out process, which would pass through many phases, during which periods of revolutionary flood-tide and periods of revolutionary ebb-tide would alternate.

Opportunities for expansion were to be seized during revolutionary flood tides, without regard to agreements made with the enemy in the name of "peaceful coexistence" during the intermediate periods. The course of world politics since World War II has been shaped by two Soviet foreign-policy offensives which followed this theoretical directive.

The road for the first offensive, under Stalin, was paved by the Soviet military victories in Europe and in the Far East. The expansionist actions constituting this offensive were carried out without regard for the American nuclear monopoly. They included the division of Germany into three parts and the Berlin blockade, the Sovietization of East Central Europe, the Prague Putsch and the Cominform's conflict with Yugoslavia, the Greek civil war and the threats against Turkey and Iran, the Chinese civil war as well as the Korea and Indo-China wars.

Supported by Beria and Malenkov, Stalin shifted to a defensive

28 This section is based on two reports on foreign policy developments during the last few years, which the author presented at the annual conferences of the Göttingen Research Association in 1962 and 1963, and which are intended for later publication. In this connection, see also G. F. Kennan's Reith Lectures, publ. in German as *Russland, der Westen und die Atomwaffe* (Frankfurt/Main, 1958).

strategy in 1951 and 1952. The new policy was intended to secure existing positions and to consolidate the Eastern bloc, and was characterized by willingness to make limited territorial concessions, such as giving up the Soviet Zone of Austria in exchange for the neutralization of that country.

Khrushchev launched a second foreign-policy offensive after the Geneva summit conference of 1955. The Kremlin exploited the balance of atomic retaliatory power and the mutual promises by the two world powers not to make war on each other as a favorable opportunity to gain footholds in the developing countries of Asia, Africa, and Latin America. Using a cleverly compounded mixture of economic and military aid, cultural propaganda, and world-revolutionary infiltration and subversion, the Soviets were able to leap the dikes of the Western military alliances and to penetrate deeply into the Western sphere of influence.

Inspired by their lead in the fields of rocketry and space vehicles, the Soviets intensified their offensive in 1958 by issuing the Berlin ultimatum and reactivating the guerilla war in Southeast Asia. Starting from this position of strength, Khrushchev undertook to reach a global arrangement with the United States in the Camp David talks of 1959. These efforts have been intensified since President Kennedy's inauguration.

Khrushchev's first diplomatic efforts were directed at reaching a settlement based on the status quo *except* for the Western positions in Berlin and Southeast Asia, which the West would have to abandon. In 1961, however, he appeared ready to accept the status quo in its entirety.

Khrushchev had two reasons for reducing his demands. In the first place, the ratio of military and strategic power had shifted markedly in favor of the West since the spring of 1960. Secondly, the ideological conflict with Peking and Tirana had become increasingly aggravated. The erection of the barrier wall in Berlin and the Soviet guarantee of the neutrality of an independent Laos seem therefore to suggest a decision by Khrushchev, analogous to Stalin's decision of 1951, to shift to a defensive strategy. The building of the Berlin Wall could, of course, be interpreted as a demonstration of Soviet power, which did not fail to affect the morale of the Germans and the peoples of East Central Europe. Its basic intention was, however, defensive. When Khrushchev resumed the offensive by installing Soviet missile bases in Cuba in 1962, his move came as a surprise.

Faced with President Kennedy's decisive yet flexible response, and with an unfavorable diplomatic situation precipitated by Chinese Communist aggression against India, Khrushchev found himself obliged to dismantle a number of elaborate launching installations and to stage an ostentatious removal of the offending missiles. Why, therefore, did the Soviet leadership decide to accept the risks connected with the Cuba adventure?

One fact should be immediately obvious. There were no national Russian interests involved in Cuba, nor did that country constitute a traditional goal of national-imperial power politics. It is likewise hardly possible to interpret Cuba as a new case of Khrushchev's crisis diplomacy, since such a crisis—the purpose of which is to distract from internal difficulties or to lead to a new summit conference—could much more easily be provoked within the immediate sphere of Soviet power and influence, that is to say, in Berlin.

World-revolutionary motives, on the other hand, were clearly involved. These, however, were only of secondary importance. An expansion of the advanced position in Cuba would have made possible an intensification of Communist pressure in Latin America. After the setbacks which the Soviet Union had suffered in Africa and in Asia, it seems probable that the Kremlin was strongly interested in seizing the world-revolutionary opportunities offered by Latin America at little expense, as well as in outrunning Chinese competition.

Although these world-revolutionary considerations may have played a certain role, it nevertheless appears improbable that they were the decisive factor. Should the Cuban operation succeed, Castro's position would be strengthened. Should it fail, the result might easily be the end of Castro. For it is most unlikely that the Kremlin was ever prepared to risk a third world war to maintain Castro in power.

This leaves only one remaining explanation with a substantial basis. The motive which induced the Kremlin to essay the unequal duel in the Caribbean sun was worry lest the Soviet Union lose the world power position it had gained in World War II. The Cuban adventure was a desperate attempt to undermine the defense position of the United States, in order to head off a further shift of relative military power to the disadvantage of the Soviet Union. It was thus a compulsion to engage in world politics that induced the Kremlin to perpetrate an act of spectacular "brinkmanship" despite the unfavorable geopolitical situation.

In terms of domestic policy, Khrushchev is faced with a choice of rockets or butter. Insofar as they are dependent on their domestic resources, the Soviet Russians must tighten their belts considerably if they wish to keep the pace in the atomic armaments race, an enormously costly affair.

The fact should not be overlooked that the Soviet Union, with a Gross National Product which amounts to between forty and forty-five per cent of that of the United States, has undertaken to support a level of armaments production equal to the American output. The Soviet leadership does not enjoy unlimited freedom to dispose of available resources as it might judge desirable, since it must take into account the growing requirements of the Soviet population. The latter is no longer disposed to accept the same deprivations it was forced to suffer under Stalin.

It is true that a dictatorship is better able to allocate its resources and to emphasize the sectors of highest priority, even if its resources are lesser to start with. In the long run, however, as the fate of National Socialist Germany indicates, the superior weight of the opponent will carry the day. The United States, it should be noted, has in the countries of the E.E.C. and in Great Britain an economic potential on their side which is just as large as that of the Soviet Union and the other countries of the Eastern bloc combined. The only question is that of a better political and military organization, which will mobilize this potential to greater effectiveness in world politics.

Such a development could lead the Soviet Union to realize that the only way in which it can maintain its position as a world power is to limit itself to its more immediate area of power and to concentrate on internal development. Such a policy, which would approximate the line which Beria and Malenkov advocated for a considerable time, would require the Soviet Union to abandon world-revolutionary advance posts such as Cuba, to consent to the restoration of German national unity, to grant greater freedom to the countries of East Central Europe, and to recognize Europe as an autonomous political force.

Since the strategic and tactical doctrine of Lenin and Stalin anticipates such temporary retreats, such a change in course would not imply any final renunciation of the world revolution or of the dream of Soviet world rule. Historically, pretensions to world rule are never abandoned except through a long process of attrition. It will be more difficult to overcome the objections of certain nationalist circles, who fear that release of the Soviet Zone of Germany would lead to collapse of Soviet Russian hegemonial rule in East Central Europe. On this issue, the nationalists find themselves in agreement with the hard-bitten revolutionaries. Certainly, much time will pass before the Kremlin is convinced of the proposition that self-restraint such as suggested here would be desirable both in terms of Russian national interests and in terms of global balance-of-power policy.

By means of an offensive coexistence policy, which neither sacrifices rights of European peoples nor permits itself to be satisfied with superficial relaxations of tension, the West could contribute decisively to bringing about an accommodation of interests capable of serving as the basis for a durable order of peace in Europe. Former Secretary of State Acheson, in a widely noticed speech late in 1962, called for a common Atlantic policy in the question of the reunification of Germany and in matters involving the developing countries. The lack of such a common reunification policy has already become painfully apparent in connection with formulation of the pact suspending atomic tests. Such diplomatic initiatives would only be fruitful if coordinated with a common Atlantic policy toward Soviet Russia and toward the Eastern bloc.

The Interdependence of Soviet Domestic and Foreign Policy

However meager the prospects for a change of direction in Soviet foreign policy may seem today, there is nevertheless one important factor which suggests that the Kremlin may be ready for such a change in due time. The principle of the priority of domestic policy has since Lenin's time been an integral feature of Soviet foreign-policy theory, regardless whether the world-revolutionary or nationalist element is dominant in the particular case. This principle lays down the rule that maintenance of totalitarian one-party rule within the country takes priority in every case over the holding of particular territorial possessions.[29] The increasing interdependence between domestic and foreign policy since the rise of the Soviet Union to world power has not mitigated the operation of this principle. If forced to choose between internal concessions that might shake totalitarian one-party rule and concessions to foreign powers, the Kremlin, in line with the principle indicated, would always choose the latter.

It is in this connection that the struggle of the progressive sector of

[29] See Löwenthal, R.: "The Logic of One-Party Rule," in Dallin, *op. cit.*, pp. 58 ff.

the Soviet intelligentsia for greater freedom of opinion, for improved legal security, and for a higher standard of living in contemporary Russia assumes importance in the field of foreign policy.[30] The farther this struggle advances, the more thoroughly the progressive groups within the Soviet elite should become convinced that the internal regeneration which they desire cannot be achieved without a renunciation of imperialist foreign policy. Even though a rather long period of time may elapse before this insight gains general acceptance, it is still possible that internal pressure will persuade the Soviet leadership to make genuine concessions in the course of its foreign relations.

The world surrounding the Soviet Union is in a position to contribute appreciably to the acceleration of this process if it takes advantage of the opportunities offered by the trend toward a scattering of power in the Eastern bloc, if it cultivates contacts with the progressive forces within the Soviet world, and if it simultaneously makes the risks of atomic war—above all in Berlin—abundantly clear to the Soviet leadership.

[30] See Meissner, B.: "Bilanz der Entstalinisierung," *Die Politische Meinung*, Vol. VIII, 1963, pp. 29 ff.; by the same author, "Der Zweifrontenkampf der KPdSU," *Osteuropa*, July, 1963.

CHAPTER VII

The Ethos of Interdependence

STEFAN T. POSSONY

In the midst of an age of increasing interdependence, the North Atlantic Treaty Organization is falling into ever greater disarray. Because of continued nationalist isolationism, NATO is out of joint. American isolationism is technological and largely nuclear in nature; European isolationism manifests itself, above all, in the economic and manpower sphere. But there also exists a variety of European isolationism that is nurtured by nostalgia for the still unburied past. One branch of this isolationism is quite content to pass the major responsibilities across the ocean to the shores of the Potomac. The present trends must be halted and reversed; if not, the alliance will collapse, deterrence will evaporate, and Communism will take the risky plunge and attempt to complete the world revolution by means of nuclear war.

There is a widespread tendency to apply "gimmickry" to this troublesome situation and to endeavor to cure deep-seated moral and intellectual deficiencies by "re-organizations," new institutions, and additional headquarters. Institutional improvements, reorganizations and gimmickry have their place but, unfortunately, they will remain futile so long as the essential supra-national spirit is lacking within the governments and nations that form the NATO alliance.

Requirements

Beyond the currently existing outline treaty, the alliance could well use a sort of constitution in which ground rules for the management of the structure would be defined. We share with our English friends a certain suspicion of written constitutions. But it is useful to formulate, in clear language, the general ideas which should guide those nations that join together in a common purpose. It was Clemenceau who once offered a comment on a point that seemed perfectly obvious to his colleagues. One of his ministers reportedly objected: *"Mais, monsieur le Président, cela va sans dire."* Clemenceau replied: *"Monsieur le Ministre, cela va encore mieux en le disant."*

The following general principles of equity seem to be implicit in an alliance of interdependent democratic nations.[1]

1. Each member state enjoys equality of rights.
2. Each member state is obligated to contribute in proportion to its capabilities.
3. The NATO alliance commands the highest priority in the international undertakings of all members.
4. NATO can fulfill its purpose only if it dynamically develops to ever fuller cooperation and institutional interdependence.
5. All member states operate on the basis of trust toward one another.
6. All member states support each other in all difficulties.

On the basis of these self-evident principles, or premises—or, if you wish, platitudes—a common ethos may be elaborated and actions and procedures suggested, through which vitality can be infused into the tottering alliance.

1. Each member state, every one of which is under the firm obligation not to initiate aggression, has the absolute right of self-defense.[2]

In case of actual or clearly impending attack, this right, which includes the right to possess weapons of all types including retaliatory or "strategic"[3] systems, can be implemented instantaneously, both by defensive and pre-emptive action.[4] Implementation will be in accordance with previously formulated and periodically revised *explicit*

---

[1] See Preamble to North Alantic Treaty.

[2] See Article 51 of the U.N. Charter.

[3] See Article 3 of North Atlantic Treaty.

[4] See Article I, 10, 3 of the American Constitution; "No state shall . . . in time of peace . . . engage in war, unless actually invaded, or in such imminent danger as will not admit of delay."

rules of engagement. In the unlikely case that the precise form of enemy attack has not been anticipated in the previously formulated rules of engagement, the member state under attack will either take immediate action or will consult with the alliance in conformity with the exigencies of the situation.[5] The good faith of the member is assumed by all other members; all past treaties and provisions which curtail this right are rescinded. Those governments whose intentions and actions arouse the suspicion of other allies will be notified formally, should the majority be unable to act on the assumption of their continuing good faith.

2. Each member state must come to the immediate help of an ally who, because of attack, is invoking the *casus foederis*.

Instantaneous support will be provided, not dependent upon belated *ad hoc* decisions, but on the basis of pre-established rules of engagement. Such support need not come after the hostile attack has been initiated but can be of a pre-emptive nature, the rules governing the undertaking of pre-emptive action having been formulated beforehand. These rules could also include definitions of unilateral actions by member states which would be contrary to the spirit of the alliance and therefore would not be supported.

3. Support will be provided in the militarily most effective and efficient manner.

The utilization of key weapons will not be delayed through requirements for authorization for release. Weapons will be selected in accordance with pre-established rules of engagement and used in conformity with a pre-established and periodically revised scheme. For this purpose, all those NATO forces whose location and mission necessitates instantaneous action will be developed to the highest state of preparedness, including readiness to fire nuclear weapons instantly. Such a program, however, requires that the members affected agree to precautionary arrangements to preclude the abuse of such weapons for aggressive purposes.[6] The firing doctrine may also include all rea-

---

[5] See Article 5 of North Atlantic Treaty.

[6] Proponents of disarmament often propose stipulations which are predicated on enormous trust with respect to the Soviet Union. The alleged trustworthiness is justified by the argument that the Soviet Union and the United States have an identical interest in keeping the peace. This logic is hardly applicable to United States-Soviet relations but *is* applicable to NATO. Strangely enough, in debates on NATO questions this logic is usually forgotten and the opponents of "proliferation" implicitly agree that the logic does

sonable precautions against "escalation." Should a "pause" be instituted in the interest of avoiding full-fledged war, the alliance guarantees the attacked state that it will restore the *status quo ante* after the expiration of the pause.[7]

4. The NATO governments and their respective high commands communicate to each other their national intelligence estimates, including those on battle orders, anticipated technological trends, assessment of enemy intentions, information bearing on warning (including the timing and type of anticipated hostile action), and the strength and nature of operations in progress.

This provision does not imply a merging of intelligence systems, or a full exchange of information on intelligence methodology, or even an obligation to provide complete disclosure of findings. However, the alliance cannot operate effectively if there arises disagreement on the nature, the intentions, and the present and future strengths of the enemy. Hence the generalized intelligence needed for effective politico-military and technological planning and for command will be exchanged. The provision also implies the full sharing of data obtained, for example, from radar. Furthermore, there will be provided adequate reporting on current hostile actions and means of immediate verification. Institutionalized efforts to determine intelligence estimates for the entire alliance will be required, along with parallel procedures within each government for the utilization of these estimates in strategic decisions. Joint warning and surveillance systems (for example, through space satellites) will also be established. Those governments—and there are quite a few—which do not possess intelligence capabilities that allow them to reach meaningful conclusions will enter into liaison agreements with governments that have them, contribute to the cost of the intelligence services, if possible assume those minor functions which they are able to discharge, and otherwise delegate authority for the making of intelligence decisions to the "parent" member. (See also point 10.) They will also obligate themselves to use the intelligence findings in their own decision-making.

---

not apply to the allies of the United States. If it is impossible to achieve trust within NATO, we would be well advised to liquidate the alliance. Mutual allegations of "trigger-happiness" and "lack of maturity" cannot stand analysis. It is about time the presumption gains ground that each ally is innocent until proven guilty.

[7] Such guarantees must be applicable forthwith, and not in the dim future. The model of the British "guarantee" to Poland is not to be imitated.

5. The strategic decision-makers of each member government, the relevant military headquarters of all member nations, and all NATO command posts are linked by an effective and reliable communication system, as the technical prerequisite of instant NATO-wide decisions.

The concept of the "hot line" is of the utmost importance within the alliance. In particular, communication facilities within those areas which may be attacked first, or most devastatingly, must be immune to interference, spoofing, and surprise destruction. An adequate communication system also is required to enable the alliance to function during war.[8]

6. To ensure that NATO problems be given their full weight, each cabinet will include a minister for NATO affairs.

The U.S. Ambassador to the United Nations holds cabinet rank, while the Ambassador to NATO does not. The role of such a cabinet member for NATO would be to represent within each government the interest of the alliance as a whole and, in the case of absence or incapacitation of the chief of government, to replace him in NATO matters demanding immediate decision.

7. The authority of the Supreme Commander and the NATO council is increased.

Mere exhortation to recalcitrant members to fulfill their obligations has failed to produce substantial results. On the basis of suitable procedures, a legal capability must be developed that would obligate member states to fulfill their commitments. As a first step, there should be voting by a qualified or simple majority; the votes should be binding on all members, including those who cast a negative vote. At a later date, the possibility and usefulness of NATO-wide elections can be examined.

8. Each member has the right to declare, at any moment, a state of crisis.

Upon the declaration of a state of crisis, pre-established procedures will be instituted to initiate intensified consultation between member governments and high commands; moreover, various steps will be

---

[8] After the French government left Paris in 1940, lack of communications accelerated the defeat of the French forces.

taken to determine the precise nature of the threat. As a general rule, states of crisis should be declared whenever a member government (as in the case of the United States during the Cuban affair of 1962) is faced by the possibility of war.

9. Upon the demand of at least two member governments, the alliance declares a state of alert.

Such a declaration will be binding upon the member states, each of whom will be obligated to undertake certain precautionary measures, such as intensification of airborne alerts, missile count-downs, cancellation of leave, etc.

10. Each member government is entitled to delegate authority for strategic decisions to the government of another member state.

Smaller member states may delegate this authority to each other or to a larger state during a specific crisis or for a longer period. One specific member state may receive the authority to act for the entire alliance. Provision will be made to assure that the authority of a major state to decide upon the *casus foederis* is not paralysed by absence or incapacity of the chief of government. The necessary delegations of authority must be executed according to a previously formulated doctrine, which also would define the rules for partial delegations of authority, for methods of termination, etc. (See also point 4.)

11. The alliance is designed to prevent war, but if it fails in this objective, its purpose is to win. War will be conducted in such a manner that each belligerent aims to protect the population and resources of each ally as though they were his own.

Provisions are necessary for the management of the alliance after the *casus foederis* has come into play, including procedures to solve problems arising from captivity, incapacitation, or death of chiefs of governments and commanders-in-chief; re-arrangements of command structures after the conclusion of nuclear exchanges; coordination with forces outside the framework of NATO; the establishment of open cities and sanctuary areas; selection and exclusion of targets; rules of warfare; the appointment and control of operations of resistance leaders; commitments to occupied areas; precise doctrines for the reoccupation of lost territories; and formulas for truce and armistice agreements. The alliance is entitled to impose upon the technologically most advanced members an obligation to develop and use weapons without "overkill" characteristics.[9]

12. The alliance operates on the principle of sufficiency of defense.

All members of the alliance must be protected against each of the diverse military threats. More specifically, the entire alliance must have those modern defenses and counter-weapons which are technologically effective and such weapons must be available in requisite numbers. The entire alliance must have quantitative and qualitative superiority in all relevant weapon systems. Situations like the present, in which the Soviet Union possesses a medium-range ballistic missile force against which Europe, because it lacks retaliatory as well as counter-weapons, is defenseless, are intolerable and will be remedied as soon as they occur.[10]

13. Each member nation is entitled to effective, up-to-date weapons.

This requires, first, that each member nation be under the direct or indirect protection of systems used in modern warfare, or negatively, that no member be denied any system that other members deem indispensable for their own protection.[11] Second, each nation is entitled to design, procure, and operate modern weapons, and for such purposes to obtain support from its allies. Third, any notion that there will be two classes of nations—the nuclear "have's" and the nuclear "have not's"—must be rejected, especially if such a notion is based on mistrust or on hopes for accommodation with the opponent.

This does not imply that the most recent inventions and discoveries must be made available immediately or under all circumstances, or

[9] The unilateral U.S. decision not to press forward with clean nuclear weapons and not to develop neutron weapons is destructive of the spirit of the alliance; it is also nihilistic from the point of view of American national interests. The interests of the subjugated nations also are involved. However, the use of "discriminating" nuclear weapons presupposes larger forces and therefore is predicated on closer NATO-wide economic cooperation.

[10] "If we desire to avoid insult, we must be able to repel it; if we desire to secure peace, *one of the most powerful instruments of our rising prosperity*, it must be known that we are at all times ready for war." (George Washington's fifth annual address to Congress, December 3, 1793. Italics added.)

[11] The illogic of the Washington position, according to which Canada was forced to acquire nuclear warheads for the defensive missiles which guard the approaches to the U.S., while no such missiles are made available to Europe, and nuclear firepower for the defense of European cities is denied, is too obvious to require lengthy comment.

that technological leaders must make disclosures to members who are unwilling to contribute to technical progress or are incapable of using the new devices and who do not institute proper security systems. (See point 15.) But it must be the purpose of the alliance to improve the technological capabilities of all members, and to achieve an ever higher degree of cooperation so that the total capability of the alliance as a whole will be increased and its superiority over the opponent secured and enhanced.

Distribution of technological secrets will be accomplished according to a set of reasonable rules, including:

(a) No technological knowledge will be withheld from member nations if the enemy possesses weapons based on this knowledge or already has the prerequisite data. (b) No technological secrets will be withheld from member nations when such knowledge would decisively improve their defensive powers,[12] or when obtaining of the secret by the enemy would not necessarily increase his offensive potentialities.[13] (c) No secret or weapon will be withheld if it is indispensable to the solution of a critical defense problem in a member nation. If there exist imperative reasons against releasing information, the owner of the secret will supply the particular device or weapon system to the menaced country but will operate it with its own forces. (d) Secrets will not be withheld beyond a reasonable time (for example, five years) after initial incorporation into experimental models.

14. The entire alliance is armed according to a coordinated plan concerning types, numbers, and deployments of weapons and support systems.

This does not imply that individual nations cannot procure and deploy weapons not provided for in the coordinated plan. This plan should, essentially, define minimum requirements for the whole as well as for the parts, and it should facilitate technological division of labor, in order that the alliance as a whole can achieve a broader spectrum of technological and quantitative capabilities than can any individual nation. The plan also should facilitate the development, by several member nations acting jointly, of especially complex and costly systems.[14]

[12] E.g., small, clean nuclear weapons usable against an occupant.

[13] E.g., nuclear land mines blocking an invader's access.

[14] Nuclear weapons, radar, jet aircraft, and missiles have resulted from the scientific and industrial efforts of *several* nations; they are a result of the genius of the main nations which compose NATO today.

15. Each member state is obligated to adhere to the rules of a jointly managed system of security and counter-espionage.

In view of the fact that genuine sharing of technological secrets will never take place if disclosures to allies would assist Soviet intelligence collection, uniform rules for the classification of materials, the handling of classified materials and papers, the clearance of personnel, the handling of releases, and such, are obviously mandatory. In addition, counterintelligence should be considered a NATO-wide obligation. There is no reason why there should not be established a NATO-wide judicial system to handle all security cases that affect the security of the alliance as a whole. (See also points 3, 4, 5, 12, 13, 14, 16, and 18.)

16. The NATO area is declared a zone of military free trade in which each partner is entitled to buy military equipment from all other partners.

Nothing has poisoned relations within the alliance as much as the occasional refusal to sell military equipment to an ally, especially if such purchases would have strengthened the alliance as a whole and did not involve secret equipment. The merits of a common market for military goods are self-evident. A military common market would go a long way toward overcoming the specific industrial weaknesses of individual member states, and would have the added advantages (as a result of larger output) of lowering unit production costs for the entire alliance. It would also permit a more effective division of labor in areas of research and procurement. It should be noted that the marketing of fissile materials and many pieces of atomic equipment is presently prohibited by United States and British law. As a corollary to the common military market, the establishment of joint research and development facilities and of joint ownership (going beyond stock ownership) of industrial facilities and corporations should be encouraged.

17. The economic burdens of common defense must be distributed equitably.

It is recognized that specific formulas (e.g., each nation contributes x per cent of its Gross National Product) are unworkable. However, the impossibility of exact definition does not deprive the term "equity" of its meaning. The usefulness of an over-all NATO military budget and a NATO defense tax should be investigated. (Lack of space precludes further development of this complex subject.)

18. National legislation defining military obligations and bearing on other security matters must be equalized.

There is an urgent need, at least on the continent, to set up armed forces with compatible mobilization schemes, periods of service, reserve formations, officers' training, military pay, regulations, promotion and selection practices, and such. Regulation of defense industries and industrial manpower also seems advisable. Great differences in the military obligations of citizens of various countries should be equalized. There is need, furthermore, for uniform legislation on security matters. (See also point 15.) Whether or not it is necessary to harmonize the constitutional prerogatives of chiefs of government, cabinets, and military commanders, with respect to such matters as the initiation of war, procedures for succession, the right to abrogate the NATO treaty during battle, requires investigation. If there should be instituted new budget and taxation procedures, and additional types of election (see points 7 and 17), such legislation must be compatible throughout the alliance.

19. The member nations agree to establish close coordination between their respective legislative bodies and to ensure that bills affecting the security of the entire alliance will not be voted into law before consultation and mutual examination with representatives of allied nations.

The system of the American Congress through which bills are carefully investigated before enactment in public and executive hearings deserves to be adopted by all NATO legislatures. Such a system would make it possible for representatives of allied nations to testify on pending bills. In addition, the various parliaments should maintain liaison and correspondence committees attached to other parliaments, in order to provide mutual information on legislative activites. Reports and analyses should be published on a regular basis to facilitate legislative cross-fertilization and cross-checking.

20. Scientific procedures are used, to the fullest extent practical, to establish NATO operational plans as well as armament, production, enlistment, and civil defense schedules. These include adequate statistical documentation, technological forecasting, intelligence assessments, war games, legal, sociological, and operations analyses.

Most of the member governments are currently arriving at their decisions on the basis of studies prepared for them by national staff and research agencies. While this practice will continue, its short-comings—which include persistent misinformation concerning allied actions—are apparent. Henceforth, the decision-makers of the member states should be provided with documentation prepared by experts of many nations, who concentrate on determining the interests of the alliance as a whole.

The state of NATO's preparedness should be continuously evaluated in an objective and scientific manner by *at least* two supra-national operations-analysis groups. Critical reports on performance and on unsolved tasks should be rendered annually and used when formulating plans and budgets. Experts should be grouped together in formalized arrangements for continuous research on all perennial problems and in *ad hoc* groups for non-recurrent problems. These groups should have informational exchange with national operations-analysis groups and should be granted access to data and testimony on and from national echelons. The services rendered through operations-analysis techniques to the alliance as a whole should not be less but rather more elaborate than similar services now rendered to national governments and high commands.

21. The member nations agree to establish proper organs for the dissemination of relevant information and to provide improved facilities for more adequate public discussion, within allied nations, of NATO issues.

Public knowledge of NATO problems still is inadequate. Yet NATO will not flourish unless it has the full backing of public opinion. Until the present situation, wherein each country discusses NATO problems more or less from a national point of view, is overcome, no informed public opinion will develop.[15] It is necessary to make member nations realize that the alliance is not designed to supersede their national interests but, on the contrary, to uphold them in a period when they no longer can be protected by independent action.

22. The development of a NATO ethos and spirit, and the comprehension of interdependence, will not be left entirely to spontaneous intellectual progress but will be pursued by appropriate institutions and programs.

15 It should not go unnoticed that the press, as well as radio and TV, could do a far better job. American press reporting on NATO is deficient and not always objective. I presume a similar criticism applies to European media.

We are confronted with an enormous timelag in thought habits. Most of us still think instinctively within national frameworks and are able to address ourselves to the problems of "supra-nationality" only if we make a deliberate effort to do so. A rudimentary beginning in "NATO education" has been accomplished, but it has been only a beginning. It is necessary to provide suitable and large-scale training and research resources for politicians, bureaucrats, and soldiers,[16] as well as for the younger generation, and to support such efforts by establishing institutions of a new type (for example, an international academy of comparative administrative techniques or an international institute for the comparative study of military institutions). Care should be taken to appoint graduates of the NATO educational system to high positions within the NATO structure, and to expose a maximum number of the "national" personnel to "NATO education." The effort must be strengthened through additions to the curricula of existing universities.

Unity of Purpose

Most of the foregoing requirements for an alliance of interdependent nations are quite modest, staying within the limits of the cooperation that was achieved during World War II between the United States and Britain, but some have far-reaching, even constitutional, implications. Thus, the institution of "supra-nationality" does require a whole series of revolutionary steps. No purpose is served by pretending that supra-nationality has been attained or can be achieved if we only talk about it long enough. More is needed than speeches.

Most of our difficulties arise from the fact that modern technology has outrun, by a very long distance, the political institutions of all— I repeat all—member states. In particular, the necessity of activating the defense against nuclear aggression within seconds or minutes is in flagrant "contradiction" to procedures now used for the making of life-and-death decisions, which in all member states still are geared

---

16 One of the most impressive aspects of life in the U.S. is the willingness of many older people, including professors and high ranking officers and officials, to attend academic courses and seek degrees, usually at their own expense and as overtime work to their regular jobs. I have yet to encounter such a spirit among European career people, who usually are overimpressed by their rank and knowledge and hence consider it beneath their dignity to return to school. Few of these men realize the obsoleteness of their information.

to time tolerances of days and weeks. On the other hand, technology and rapidity of aggression are not the only relevant factors. The needed institutional changes should not lead to the curtailment of national and individual freedoms, but rather to their enhancement. If we intend to achieve supra-nationality we will have to institute it through a supra-national constituent assembly. This is a distant goal, but the scientific study of constitutional problems as they have been affected by nuclear firepower, nuclear submarines, missiles, and space and defense interdependence should commence forthwith. Let us do a bit more homework.

Many of the problems which are agitating our publics are of an illusory character and must be regarded as residual of earlier thought and action patterns. Residual "nationalism" explains, for example, the popular notion that the "proliferation" of nuclear weapons must be prevented,[17] and another notion that there should be two, three, or fifteen fingers on the trigger instead of one. Actually, the proliferation and trigger problems can be solved, quite simply, through defining doctrines and rules on engagement and firing—and such doctrines can even be given the highest "objectivity" through utilization of computers. Indeed, automatic response brought about through computers (two of which are needed to ensure against electronic malfunction) might add to deterrence, provided the attacker does not know the programmed doctrine and is unable to spoof the machine.

Can we still live with unilateral strategic decisions and, if so, to what extent? It is hard to see how we could live without unilateral decisions on the part of the United States. If the Soviet Union could expect that an aggressive move would be countered only after fifteen NATO members had decided upon a minimum risk course of action, strategic deterrence would no longer exist. China would not be deterred at all if the United States lost its freedom of action. And Cuba? Certainly, we must anticipate continuing shortcomings and failures in the NATO alliance. In addition, there is the paradox that if unilateral decisions on crucial matters remain permissible, the alliance

17 The U.S. government was so convinced that America alone had the "genius" to make a nuclear weapon that it almost failed to watch nuclear progress in the Soviet Union—why, those people just couldn't imitate what Professor Oppenheimer had accomplished. This same mentality presided over the drafting of the Atomic Energy Act. Today, this Act paralyzes the alliance, yet it is not rescinded, despite the fact that its original purpose, to prevent the Soviets from building the weapon, was not accomplished and the ineffectuality of the Act was demonstrated through its failure. In fact, because of its negative impact upon the alliance, the Act now has become an asset to the Soviet Union.

as a whole may act more effectively and rapidly. In this sense, continuing "nationalism" strengthens rather than weakens the alliance.

Great and self-reliant nations will not deprive themselves of the right to act according to their understanding of their best interests. This implies, negatively, that at a given moment *any* nation may lack the courage to face up to a nuclear threat and may desert from the alliance by giving in or surrendering to the enemy.

It is, therefore, a grave mistake to consider NATO as a panacea for all security problems and to deny that *national* defense remains a requirement of the greatest urgency and priority. But with the exception of the United States, no NATO nation has been satisfactorily maintaining its own defenses. The spectacle of France worrying *singlehandedly* about national security was so perplexing that it was bound to be misinterpreted. Many NATO nations indeed have been undermined because the *addormentatori*[18] they were picking as statesmen were congenitally unable to speak the truth about defense, or even to understand it themselves.

At any rate, nuclear weapons will tend to equalize the power differentials between big and small nations; hence "independence" will reassert itself more strongly in the future. But this will hardly lessen the *interdependence* of those nations whose goal it is to preserve both peace and freedom. Interdependence exists only for those nations who embrace both of these objectives. Those who are willing to discard freedom and those who want to embark upon aggression must seek independence, the former for a fleeting moment, the latter for as long as its endurance lasts. Otherwise, unilateral decisions, especially those decisions which affect other nations, tend to be self-defeating.

This is a lesson which was learned, to some extent at least, in the economic sphere: we are hopeful that the suicidal "independent" economic policies of the late 1920's and early 1930's will not be repeated. The lesson has still to be learned in the military sphere, where it is of far greater significance. Certain unilateral acts, like the ill-fated Skybolt cancellation and related ramifications, or the proposal to curtail the production of fissile materials—without asking first any of our allies whether perhaps they want to buy from our alleged surplus—are entirely destructive. So are occasional unilateral announcements from Washington that we will only fight in a second-strike configuration —how could we then come to the aid of Europe if the Soviets did not launch a simultaneous strike against both Europe and America? Uni-

[18] Soporificator or lullaby-ist. The expression is Metternich's.

lateral decisions to keep military budgets low—a game which Canada and some European allies have been playing with impunity—are equally inadmissible. If economic hardship were involved in a nation's preparedness, surely aid could be provided. But it is irresponsible for allies to obtain aid and then, in addition, to depend on the United States to provide the defenses.

The way to reduce the instances of unilateral actions is not to call big conferences every time a major decision has to be made. The need is for strengthening the understanding in all echelons of the facts of interdependence and of the supranational interest, as well as of the mutual obligations resulting from the passing of independence. Interdependent decision-making requires a new intellectual attitude and— at the risk of sounding professorial—a body of knowledge on supranational problems to supplement, and sometimes replace, the present body of knowledge which is permeated by awareness of national problems.

There is nothing magical or immutable about the current 15-nation membership arrangement. If the truth be told, we could rid ourselves of some members who do not really contribute to the common defense, and invite in their places other states who really should belong to the club.

There is a pressing need to simplify the structure in order to render it more effective. Consolidations of the military forces of several member states are in order. Certainly, to give just one example, it would not be sensible to consolidate the forces of Turkey with those of Portugal or Norway. But, to give another example, the consolidation of the continental defense forces of the United States and Canada could and should be advanced vigorously: the present arrangement is in the nature of a unified command, but due to an inadequate budget and a low degree of mobilization the Canadian contribution is disappointingly small.

Most urgently needed is the consolidation of several military forces in Europe. This urgency derives from the fact that Western Europe is a decisive front and, for a number of geographic reasons, is particularly difficult to defend. We can express this urgency in positive terms: if the military power of the free world is to make a quantum jump forward, such consolidation is imperative.

What should be consolidated? Some suggest a consolidation of the forces of France and Germany; others consider a federation of the Rhine, which would also include the Low Countries. The military consolidation of the entire Common Market (including Italy) also has its protagonists, and many argue that Britain, after attaining Common Market membership, should consolidate its forces with those of its continental partners.

From the viewpoint of surface battle logic, the military federation of the Rhine plus Denmark would seem a sensible first solution, provided this group entertains special—let us say confederative—arrangements with Britain, Spain and Italy.

Further analysis indicates, however, that consolidation for ground defense must follow a different technical-geographic logic than that for air and missile defense. The former suggests the Rhine federation, the latter, especially if at long last medium-range ballistic missile and antimissile forces will be deployed in Europe, a consolidation of all NATO members in Western, Northern, and Southern Europe. Again, manned strategic and space forces may require differing arrangements and, perhaps, no consolidation at all.

This subject could be discussed endlessly, yet it has been barely studied. It is therefore premature to venture proposals as to how consolidation can be effected. As an initial step, the French and Germans might undertake a scientific inquiry to investigate the advantages, disadvantages and modalities of bilateral consolidation. They would be well advised to pursue such a study together with experts from other NATO countries, if only to enlist the blessings of the entire alliance and to ensure against the suspicion that an attempt is afoot to resurrect and combine Napoleonism and Hitlerism.

But the ultimate question is this: can an effective alliance be maintained if there is no unity of purpose? The answer obviously is in the negative. Hence a second question arises, namely, whether the alliance lacks or does not lack unity, or, to put this differently: does the alliance have an agreed upon set of objectives?

If there had not been a rudimentary sort of unity with respect to our defensive purposes, the alliance never would have come into being. All member states are agreed upon the preservation of their freedom systems and upon the desirability of preventing war. This unity of purpose is weakened by doubts as to whether the preservation of peace is more important than the preservation of freedom, or vice versa, by arguments on whether there exists or does not exist a danger of war, and by grave uncertainties concerning the best implementation of the strategy of deterrence and the strategy to be adopted after deterrence has failed and the fire is upon us.

But let us assume that through all this confusion greater unity with respect to the defensive objectives of NATO will emerge.

Since the challenge of building a new type of alliance in the face of nuclear danger is most forbidding, some have thought it wise not to be concerned with objectives that transcend the minimum requirements for unity. But unity on defensive objectives is not enough. We may be performing astoundingly well in comparison with historic precedent. The important question, however, is whether we will be able to master the problems posed by the future.

There has been a great deal of debate on whether or not, since we are mainly interested in being left alone, the Western alliance should strive for "victory" or adopt any "offensive" or "positive" objectives at all. This sort of argument is essentially verbal or emotional exercise which prevents us from understanding the challenges as they really exist. It is quite true that most people in the United States and in Western Europe show no interest in how their fellow humans live behind the Iron Curtain. It is also true that very few volunteers would be found willing to launch a democratic crusade against the heretic Communist; or that if enough volunteers were to appear, a nuclear war would be the best means to further the cause of freedom.

But all this hardly matters. What matters is that we are living in the stream of history, and that (to paraphrase Engels) things will happen "behind our heads." For example, an uprising in a satellite state may occur at any moment, as indeed such uprisings have occurred in the past, to the surprise of those who had predicted the insuperable stability of dictatorial regimes. A cleavage between Communist governments may also occur and, while we cannot argue here whether or not the disputes between Yugoslav, Chinese, Russian, and Albanian Communists are genuine or really significant, these disputes have taken place. There is no reason to believe that the Communist empire henceforth will remain monolithic. Is the precedent of the splits in the Roman empire pertinent? Every dictatorship has exhibited the Faustian urge to halt time. The surprising thing is that the erosion of the Communist empire has begun so early.

The fact that one part of Germany is under a Communist regime, while the other part is under a successful system of freedom, lends a great deal of poignancy to the possibilities of uprisings and intra-bloc dissension. The national spirit, with its craving for unity, is not dead—it has proved to be one of history's least mortal forces. The quest for national unity in Germany will not abate on the part of those who live in *irredenta,* least of all if they also live under suppression while their more fortunate brothers are prospering. The notion that the split of Germany can be perpetrated is preposterous. The abnormal situation may be prolonged, to be sure, but some liberalization in East Germany will be the price the Communist dictatorship must pay to extend its miserable existence.

It is another fantastic error to assume that the Russian revolution, which has been going on for about 100 years or more, has come to a close. If there ever was unfinished business in history, the Russian revolution represents a prime example. We are so bemused by propaganda and counter-propaganda that we have completely failed to understand that the system in the Soviet Union is neither Socialist nor Communist—nor even in line with the "Marxist tradition"—and that Stalin carried out a counter-revolution. The Soviet state is a boa constrictor strangling society. Khrushchev simply eased the grip of the snake-state.[19] A comparison with Napoleon III, the first dictatorial phase of his regime, the subsequent liberal empire, and the terminal war, provides a useful parallel.

These ideological and historical comparisons are not introduced for the sake of erudition, but because a correct interpretation of the Soviet situation is necessary for proper forecasting. That the internal revolution has not advanced for years may be explained by the unending docility of the Russians; Oblomov lives on in the "new class." But according to Marx—and it appears he was fundamentally correct on this point—revolution is, above all, a social transformation *which takes place while the ancient regime is still in power.* Hence revolutions are not "made" by political means: political revolutions follow social transformations. There is little doubt that vast transformations are occurring within the Soviet Union, where, for that matter, the nationalism of the subjugated nations is surviving and kicking.

The question therefore is not whether citizens of California, East Anglia, the Provence, or the Rhineland are rearing to bestow the blessings of freedom on the helpless inhabitants of Gori or Kalinovka, but whether interdependence extends from the Atlantic into Eastern Europe, to the Urals, and perhaps (to go beyond President de Gaulle) into Siberia. The answer is that, indeed, interdependence does not stop at the Elbe River. It follows that the NATO alliance must consider itself as the *de facto* ally of those European nations, including

[19] The case of a state that may be compared to a boa constrictor was developed by Marx in his *The Eighteenth Brumaire of Napoleon Bonaparte.*

Russia, that are presently under the yoke of foreign dictatorship—and who are firmly convinced that they can count upon the help of NATO, regardless of whether our radio propogandists have been instructed to warn against "premature uprisings."

NATO is committed to such political principles as the right to self-determination, the principle of nationality, democracy, constitutional government, and freedom. True, our courage and resolution in upholding these principles often have been wanting. Nevertheless, the commitment is there and it is potent. Indeed, the persistent application of these principles has been the main cause of our successful *Knackwurst-und-Volkswagen-Demokratie*. History teaches that whenever a major crisis occurs, nations, by and large, will act in accordance with their ideas. Interdependence from Hawaii across America and Europe into Siberia exists, even today, in the fields of ideology and political morality.

In brief, multi-faced interdependence will demand NATO action as the old society gives birth to the new, to paraphrase Marx again. This hour will come—but will NATO be ready for it? Or will it continue to plan on the assumption of everlasting Soviet bloc "stability"?

Beyond the Cold War

The NATO alliance is not founded on the belief that the cold war will go on interminably. There has been much discussion on whether or not it would be feasible to liquidate the cold war by some sort of diplomatic agreement or by political accommodation. Any thorough sociological analysis shows that such hopes are foredoomed to failure. The cold war will not be halted unless and until the systems of freedom gain the ascendancy in Eastern Europe, the Common Market, and constitutional government are extended eastward, and the interdependence of East and West leads to an all-European open society. The Western world, including Eastern Europe, cannot continue "half-free and half-slave"—and this statement is not presented as a political sermon, but should be interpreted as a *constatation*. Unfortunately, the problem is not grasped by most of the political leaders in the West.

How are these objectives to be reached? Emulation of Bismarck's unification strategy of 1864-1870 would hardly be advisable or practical for the whole of Europe under present circumstances. If the NATO alliance can be vitalized so that it moves rapidly in the direction of cohesiveness and cumulative strength, then doctrines on world revolution and Communist intellectual commitments to advance the world revolution, if necessary by nuclear war, will become irrelevant: the Soviets will be blocked in their forward march and will be compelled to readjust to a new world situation.

As the Common Market and other integrative moves throughout NATO gain momentum, the balance of techno-economic power will tilt ever more decisively against the Communists. The futility of the so-called socialist economic system in transition to communism will become self-evident to everyone, perhaps even to the Central Committee studying the evidence. Once this happens, Soviet ideology is bound to undergo rather profound changes. Without exaggerating the importance of the indicators that exist today, there are some signs that "normalization"—this bland expression is deliberately chosen—in Eastern Europe is not impossible.

The key to all objectives, the negative and the positive ones, is therefore the proper construction of the NATO alliance and the achievement of clear-cut military superiority.

As a result of a substantial modification of the international power balance, the present cohesiveness of the Soviet empire will begin to decline. It surely will decline if we succeed in purveying pertinent information to the elites behind the curtain.[20] As NATO power grows, relatively and absolutely, individual East European states may reach out for greater independence, basing their policy on implicit or explicit assurances of NATO help. Should an event like the Hungarian uprising occur again, NATO's military power could be used as a deterrent against Soviet intervention; and if intervention were nevertheless risked by the Soviets the East European nation under attack could be supported effectively by means of limited war.

Limited war is a feasible strategy, i.e., one which does not pose the risk of escalation, provided it is waged under the umbrella of what Mahan termed "over-bearing power." Without such power, we must have patience.

The same arguments apply to the problems of German reunification. As late as July, 1963, Khrushchev still voiced the opinion that German re-unification will take place under a "socialist republic." But if NATO becomes a genuinely growing concern and enjoys power superiority, the chances are high that East Germany—perhaps its peo-

---

[20] Mere "communication" is not enough; the message must be reluctant, true, and persuasive.

ple, perhaps even its government—will move to end the foreign oppression. There is no point in speculating about the modalities of a
change in the German situation, or even to inquire whether it would
be useful in the next decades to re-establish Germany as a unified state.
Advisability of such a step would depend, among other things, upon
the status of "consolidation" in Western Europe.

To repeat, the point is to possess the military power which will
allow gradual and evolutionary reforms and readjustments through
deterrence of Communist counter-revolution or reconquest.

The fate of the Russian people depends upon NATO. In many
ways Europe bears the responsibility for the existence of communism
in Russia. Sooner or later the Russians themselves will want to establish a regime that is more compatible with the exigencies of the modern world and more in line with individual aspirations. If such a
moment arises, it would not be to anyone's interest if the replacement
of the Communist usurper would spark a civil war. The strength of
NATO should be available to persuade Russian leaders to carry out a
"revolution from above" and help Russia to accomplish a peaceful
transition toward a better life and toward interdependence with the
world of freedom.

There *is* a feasible strategy of peace and freedom. It consists in doing unto ourselves that which life is enjoining us to do; and to resist the
spirit of decadence and short-lived expediency.

"Blessed are they which do hunger and thirst after righteousness;
for they shall be filled."[21]

21 St. Matthew IV, 3.

CHAPTER VIII

France and the Defense of the West

F. O. MIKSCHE

THE FREQUENTLY HEARD ARGUMENT that expansion of the Atomic Club would encourage the political particularism of individual NATO countries is by no means unfounded. The current weakening of the Atlantic Pact is, on the other hand, largely a result of widespread mistrust, the actual source of which is the unsolved atomic problem. As the cracks in the structure widen, the greater the pressure of the non-atomic powers to achieve atomic status. By becoming atomic they hope to purchase not only political independence but also national security. Who can predict what will happen in ten years in such a turbulently changing world? An atomic arsenal cannot be created out of thin air from one day to the next. States that are unwilling to remain at the mercy of the unpredictable actions of today's "atomics" and that find it necessary to conduct an independent foreign policy for the defense of their vital interests also need to have autonomous military systems. The possession of a certain number of atomic warheads has become an essential feature of such a system.

It is therefore no wonder that France is pushing a crash program. No one can give her a guarantee that other states will not develop atomic weapons if she abandons hers. For technical and economic reasons alone, no modern industrial state will be able to manage without nuclear power a few years from now. In this field, as in many others, it is very difficult to draw a line between purely civilian and military use. The expansion of the Atomic Club cannot be stopped. It is therefore wiser to adjust to the consequences of this fact, rather than stubbornly opposing a fundamentally natural development. If the Americans were to assist France, they could still exercise a certain control over the production of atomic weapons. This they cannot do if they leave France to her own devices as up to now.

It is a predilection of American politics to make binding decisions without considering how they will apply to future situations. A case in point was the passage of the MacMahon Act (Atomic Energy Act), which forbids the divulging of atomic secrets or the furnishing of atomic weapons to other powers. Moscow is perfectly aware that the repeal of this law, even if the Administration in the United States should decide to seek it, would require a psychological preparation of public opinion lasting several years. This fact provides substantial leeway for Soviet policy. The threat to expand the Atomic Club is, however, exactly what could be a most powerful trump in Washington's hand. Moscow, on the other hand, is in a position to trade in atomic warheads just as in other weapons without violating international legal convention. Should it serve their interests, the Soviets would not hesitate to convert Indonesia, Egypt, or any other country that falls into conflict with the West into an atomic power on short notice, by furnishing a few "small" bombs together with "civil engineers." The Americans can do the same only after a complicated procedure in Congress, the outcome of which is uncertain.

The fact that the United States refuses to supply its own allies with research results long known to the Soviets, thereby forcing France to discover them anew at great financial sacrifice, is felt in Paris to represent an unfriendly policy. The American effort to reach an agreement with the Soviet intended to prevent the enlargement of the Atomic Club is likewise interpreted as unfriendly behavior toward friends. Washington's concern to prevent atomic war by means of this policy may doubtless seem justified. There is, on the other hand, no reason to assume that the new atomic powers would handle their nuclear weapons more recklessly than the United States. A factual basis does exist for Washington's fear that expansion of the Atomic Club would lead to a shifting of the present power relationships within the Western world with a resulting adjustment between the small and the large states.

If the atomic question is not satisfactorily solved in the near future, it may blow up the Atlantic Pact from within. That the Soviets, as some fear, might arm their satellites with nuclear weapons is an improbable contingency. Should they do so nevertheless, such a step would have only formal significance, since no satellite would dare to use its weapons without Kremlin approval. The proposal to establish

NATO as a multilateral or multinational atomic power likewise meets with little sympathy in Paris, primarily because it is totally unclear how such a plan would alter the present situation. It was principally French pressure for a greater voice in common defense matters that induced the Americans to attempt an "escape forward" in the hope that their project might still prevent an expansion of the Atomic Club. All these plans and ideas fall short in the face of the insoluble problem of authority to employ the weapons: By whom, how, and in what cases shall the order to fire be given? The fact is, that each NATO partner expects the other to take risks which he would hardly take himself, even in the extreme case.

Up to the present time, Europe has been furnished with atomic protection by the United States free of charge. From now on it is expected to pay for it—but without any substantial change in the situation, since any independent decision by the Europeans is blocked by the veto power which Washington reserves to itself under all circumstances. It is as though a number of people had jointly purchased an automobile; each receives a key to the door, but the ignition key is retained by the seller. It is therefore hard to understand why millions should be paid out, merely for the privilege of participating in the selection of targets and having a few sailors in the crews of submarines or surface ships.

A multilateral atomic force, for which Europe would have to pay heavily, would also eliminate any hope for the expansion of conventional forces. That is to say, it would foreclose precisely that program which the Americans have for years been urging us to undertake. With the heavy financial burdens which participation in such a plan would impose, it would be quite impossible for the Federal Republic to undertake defense measures essential for the safety of its population or to organize territorial defense forces. What is more probable is that after five years or so even the *Bundeswehr* would be forced to reduce the number of its divisions from twelve to eight.

Though the promotion of unrealistic proposals, such as that for a multilateral atomic force, as well as by lack of decisiveness in numerous international questions—even in cases involving their own interests such as that of Cuba—the United States has contributed decisively to a weakening of the NATO structure. The European members of NATO have gradually reached the conclusion that an atomic power would hardly be inclined to accept the risk of atomic retaliation in the defense of non-atomic states, for which reason it is the states with atomic forces in being which decide what shall be defended and what shall be surrendered. The non-atomic powers are worried, not without justification, that the atomic power might some day leave them in the lurch in a conflict involving the interests of the non-atomic powers alone. Since, last but not least, the atomic powers can be expected to defend only their own vital interests, the non-atomic powers suffer the additional fear of becoming involved in conflicts which do not involve their own interests. The atomic powers, on their part, fear that new possessors of atomic bombs may draw them into conflicts which are not their concern.

The saturation in destructive power achieved in recent years has rendered the concept of atomic superiority largely obsolete. Atomic weapons that are not intended as the central element of a particular strategy but which have the sole function of providing cover for the main element of a military system—that is, for the conventional forces—do not need to equal those of the enemy in either number or quality. A *force de frappe* of this kind does not require Sputniks, Vostoks, or intercontinental rockets. The geo-strategic situation is also a determining factor. An atomic arm with a range up to three thousand kilometers is sufficient for a European state. Even the ability to attack Moscow, Leningrad, or Kiev should have a sufficient deterrent effect on the Soviets.

No atomic power, regardless how strong, can be absolutely sure of completely eliminating every possibility of retaliation, even on the part of a small atomic power, through a single surprise attack. It is more probable that the effect of the remaining atomic weapons would suffice to inflict incalculable damage on the aggressor. For today no power is in a position to shield its territory reliably against every airborne attack. The annual maneuvers in the United States demonstrate that the Americans are not even able to destroy one-third of the approaching bombers in time—for long distance rockets, the disproportion is even greater. The Soviet situation is not much better. It may therefore be assumed that of one hundred atomic warheads fired by a *small* atomic power, one-third will reach their targets. This threat is enough to impress even an atomic great power.

There is an entirely ridiculous theory about the use of the "contra force" and "contra town" strategies for eliminating an enemy's aggressive power. The former endeavors to accomplish this by destroying the enemy's atomic military installations, while the latter concentrates the attack on large cities and industrial complexes. According to the theory in question, small atomic powers are particularly dangerous, since they are necessarily forced to aim their few atomic warheads at cities. The "contra force strategy," the targets of which are principally air fields and launching pads, requires the thousands of warheads available only to an atomic great power. The reality of the situation is that quite a few hundred of these countless warheads would destroy non-military targets, inflicting damage that the opponent could hardly accept as "contra force strategy" and would therefore answer with "contra town" retaliation. Since the Soviets, who are the aggressors according to all American calculations, do not possess thousands of warheads, it follows that they will presumably have no alternative to the "contra town strategy." As soon as this is admitted, the entire sophism about "contra town" and "contra force" strategies falls to the ground.

An effective strategy must take into account, not only the threats which may arise through political developments, but also those having their origins in the structure and weaponry of the enemy's armed forces, and in his strategy. No army can plan in entire independence of its enemy. There is a striking contrast, however, between the military thinking of the East and that of the West. The Eastern bloc endeavors to adapt its strategy to anticipated political and military developments. Technology is subordinated to political planning and not *vice versa*, as unfortunately seems to be the case in the West. In contrast to the Atlantic Pact, the Soviets use atomic weapons only to provide cover for their conventional forces, and not as the main element in their strategic planning. While the Western powers can play only the bass notes, the Soviets have the entire keyboard at their disposal. They are able to play bass and treble chords simultaneously in harmonic orchestration.

Why does the West—despite all its missiles, atomic submarines, and other wonder weapons—fear the conventional forces of the East? Why do the Soviets, tenaciously and at enormous expense, maintain one hundred fifty "old fashioned" divisions? Certainly, Moscow is not motivated by fear that the twenty-four NATO divisions will engage in aggression. The Soviet troops are essential for the support of subversive warfare; they may be deployed here and there according to the exigencies of the situation, assuring the offensive mobility of Soviet policy through subtly phased military pressure. For what Communism seeks is not open warfare, but rather the ruthless exploitation of all available opportunities. With such tactics, it endeavors to undermine Western positions throughout the world—in a war that does not seem to be a war, and yet is a war.

There is no doubt that the foreign policy of a state gains credibility when that state is in a position to employ its own atomic deterrent. It may therefore be assumed that the expansion of the Atomic Club would lead to a reliable balance of power, since it would involve a distribution of risks with consequent reciprocal neutralization. It is in no way suggested that Europe should emerge as a third force between the United States and the Soviet Union. All that is proposed is to give Europe the ability to act in those cases where it would be difficult to expect an American President to take risks on account of Europe.

NATO atomic strategy today is based one-sidedly on the United States, with the result that both continents are excessively dependent on each other. Were this strategy to be replaced by a more balanced one, then Western policy would acquire a badly needed element of flexibility. Such a distribution of risks would considerably narrow the Soviet range of political operation. A European atomic power could, of course, find itself facing problems like those with which the United States must cope today, as in the Cuban case. Should Algeria go Communist tomorrow or the day after tomorrow, would France risk the destruction of Paris?

In considering these problems, one always returns inevitably to the same conclusion: that it has become impossible to conduct an independent policy today without one's own atomic cover—just as it has become impossible to act flexibly in foreign policy if one depends entirely on atomic strategy. And it is here that the French *force de frappe* assumes questionable proportions. It is merely a political instrument to wring concessions from the Americans? Or is its possession intended to permit the French to exercise a certain hegemony over the other European states? Or shall it some day become the nucleus of an all-European atomic force? Only General de Gaulle himself can answer these questions. Is the *force de frappe* intended only to provide cover for conventional forces, or is it the main element of a French strategy? *Voilà la grande question!* Should the latter be the case, then France would be running a danger similar to that faced by Great Britain or the United States. For these two powers find themselves today in the position of a chess player who has undertaken to play without pawns. The more powerful pieces may then be used to checkmate the enemy only when one's own king is in danger.

The *force de frappe* alone offers no reliable guarantee, either for the defense of French interests or for the security of Western Europe. The fact remains incontrovertible that in the future as at present it will be impossible to do without sufficiently large strong conventional troops. In order to regain political flexibility, the West must therefore make itself more independent of atomic weapons. However one turns the problem about, the answer remains: a substantial expansion of conventional forces has become an absolute necessity. It is of course to be admitted that Western Europe can be defended just as badly with the twenty-four divisions existing today as it could be with the thirty called for by NATO plans. For to cover the thirteen hundred kilometer front between the Alps and the Baltic without having to take recourse to atomic weapons, at least sixty to seventy divisions are necessary. To make these available, it is neither necessary to appropriate more funds for national defense nor to withdraw additional manpower from the economy. What is needed is the establishment of a new system which uses our available human resources under economically acceptable conditions. In a study which the Inspector of the Swiss infantry, Supreme Corps Commander Max Weibel, published in the NATO journal, *The Fifteen Nations*, in July, 1960, it is stated that: "Switzerland can mobilize fifteen divisions, that is three per million inhabitants, whereas the peoples of Western Europe exploit only five per cent of their defense capability compared to Switzerland." Weibel then points out that NATO could have five hundred divisions if it used the Swiss system. The examples of Switzerland and Sweden show that it is possible to achieve an incomparably more reliable defense with the funds currently expended, if correct military policies are consistently followed. It would, of course, be a mistake to base the NATO organization exclusively on the Swiss model. Western Europe needs both highly mobile regular troops and skeleton divisions with a peacetime strength of thirty-five hundred men per division, the latter being expansible in militia fashion in case of need.

A military policy such as indicated here could only be carried out by an integrated Europe. Without such integration there can never be real Western European defense, for financial reasons if for no other. De Gaulle is correct, to be sure, when he says that a state that no longer has an autonomous strategy ceases to be a sovereign state. If this is the case, however, then it is necessary to press for the foundation of that state which is capable of conducting an integrated military policy and arming itself with both atomic and conventional weapons, to whatever extent is required for achieving a capacity for political action.

CHAPTER IX

Berlin and the Western Cause

FRANK L. HOWLEY

I̱f you are interested in yourself and in Western civilization, then pay heed to the City of Berlin. For Berlin is a mirror, a mirror in which we see ourselves, our strength and weakness, courage, timidity, despair, and hope. Here we see our Western civilization with all of its ramifications. Here we see the Eastern civilization which has dedicated itself to the destruction of our way of existence.

Berlin is a city with a long and exciting history, to which I am proud to have made a modest contribution. Among those concerned with Berlin's recent history, its present situation, and its future prospects, I am identified as a commander, an executive, a "doer" rather than a philosopher. I hope, however, that my readers will not apply the title "Beast of Berlin" given me during the Blockade days of 1948 by the Communists, who hoped to identify me as a contemporary of *Pithecanthropus erectus,* or at best of Neanderthal man.

I have been too closely and personally concerned with Berlin to view its problems solely in terms of cold analysis. Four and one-half difficult years at the end of the war and happy memories of student days thirty years ago remind me of the popular Berlin song, "I have left some of my luggage on Kurfürstendamm so I must come back again." In my case I have left a bit of my heart in Berlin, so I cannot be unfeeling about the City or its magnificent people.

The present brief survey of the Berlin situation is based less on library research than on my general background and years of practical experience administering and negotiating the city's problems. For this reason, there will be a minimum of quotations and few references to sources.

Berlin's Past

Berlin is more than a wall, more than a city, more than a conflict of declarations and actions by France, Great Britain, America, and Western Germany on one side, the Soviet Union and its satellites on the other side.

A few reminders of Berlin's ancient past will suffice. According to the State Department book, *Berlin: City Between Two Worlds:*

"Prior to its destruction in World War II, Berlin had for many decades been a center of commerce and industry, not only for Germany but for Central Europe as well. Back in the Middle Ages it was one of the free towns that formed the Hanseatic League in the pursuit of international trade. Beginning in 1871, Berlin was capital, in turn, of the German Empire, the Weimar Republic, and Nazidom, with the business of government employing a substantial portion of the population. Since Frederick the Great's time Berlin has been a cultural center, drawing to it scientists, musicians, writers, and artists from many countries. . . ."

Charles B. Robson remarks in *Berlin: Pivot of German Destiny:*

"For our purposes, however, the period when Berlin was a member of the Hanseatic League and temporarily occupied a leading position among the cities of the frontier is not so interesting as the period succeeding it, which began with the subjugation of Berlin-Cölln by the Hohenzollerns, who became Electors of Brandenburg and established their residence in Berlin-Cölln about 1450. . . . Medieval Berlin, which grew up at the ford of the Spree about 1200, had—like its neighbor across the river, Cölln—important functions as a center of communication. . . . In 1709 a few years after his accession, Frederick I consolidated the administration of the "Royal Prussian Court," uniting Berlin and Cölln with the neighboring towns that had in the meantime sprung up on the western side of the river . . . Berlin's function as a center of traffic had already been improved by the construction of a system of canals. . . . For Germany as a whole, Berlin was located quite far to the East. . . . Berlin, had by the eighteenth century become a refuge for religious emigrants from half of Europe. . . ."[1]

[1] Charles B. Robson, *Berlin: Pivot of German Destiny* (Chapel Hill, University of North Carolina Press, 1960).

Berlin has been for centuries on the frontier of Europe's and Asia's conflicts of religion, commerce, and ideology.

Here in Berlin are two great civilizations face to face as they have been for more than one thousand years. Both meet the accepted definition of civilization. Both represent advance in man's society over savagery. In considering the present problems we have to bear in mind that for more than one million years man made very little progress from savagery. It was only five thousand years ago that in Egypt, Mesopotamia, Indochina, and elsewhere man at last raised his eyes from the mud and saw a star. The birth of our Western civilization can be dated from about five hundred years before Christ when there was almost an explosion in the advancement of our understanding of religion, government, and art. Greece teamed with man's interest in himself, his fellow man and his gods. This was the beginning of our Western civilization.

Although we all recognize the dangers and possible inaccuracies of broad generalization, we may, for comparative purposes, consider that the Eastern civilization in modern dress again confronts Western civilization in the City of Berlin. The East is analogous to that of the Persians of the seventh century before Christ. The Persians with their vast hordes assembled before the mountain pass of Thermopylae were as different in civilization from the Greeks confronting them as are the Eastern Communist-directed forces today from the West.

Members of the Eastern and Western civilizations have sometimes changed sides. An Eastern chieftain, Clovis, after conquering what is present day France, accepted Western Christianity at Rheims along with three thousand of his followers in the year 496 A.D. In more recent days we have had the examples of Hitler and Castro who were reared and trained in Western philosophy but rejected their backgrounds and accepted the leadership principles of the East. What are the great differences between East and West? Why are men willing to die for these differences?

Edward Gibbon wrote in his *Decline and Fall of the Roman Empire:*

"Under a democratic government the citizens exercise the powers of sovereignty. . . . they acknowledged that the true principles of social life, laws, agriculture and science which had been first invented by the wisdom of Athens were now firmly established by the power of Rome under whose auspicious influence the fiercest

barbarians were united by equal government and common lan-
gauge. . . . Homer as well as Virgil was transcribed and studied
on the banks of the Rhine and Danube. . . ."

As Wenzel Jaksch wrote in his contribution to the recent volume,
Berlin and the Future of Eastern Europe:

"We owe to Christendom the introduction of two basic concepts:
the moral equality of men and the solidarity of peoples. . . . Europe is not only an incubator of ideas but also a battleground of
ideologies. The seeds of the contemporary East-West conflict were
probably sown when the fateful schism between the Roman and
the Greek Christian churches took place. . . . Europe's unsettled
eastern frontiers were for centuries a major problem for the survival of Western civilization. I need only to mention the successive waves of Avarian, Magyar, and Turkish invasions up the Danube River into the heart of Europe, the last of which was repelled
at the gates of Vienna in 1683. . . ."[2]

According to the Western beliefs which have come to us from
Greece to Rome to the Rhine Valley, we as individuals have the right
to determine which beliefs are best for us, have the right to decide
our relationship with our fellow men and have the right to determine
our relationship to our God or gods. This basic philosophy grows out
of our definition of civilization which originated in the Latin word
"civis" (citizen). The citizen determines his fate. Opposed to us is
the notion that a self-appointed god, a dictator or a selected group of
individuals known as an oligarchy can determine what is best for all
of us. This is the concept of the Hitlers, the Stalins, the Khru-
shchevs, and it was that of the Persians twenty-seven centuries ago.
They too had no use for the freedom enjoyed by individual citizens—
they placed their trust in despotism.

Today, the East with its modern propaganda can make their system
seem extremely efficient. The Soviets can maintain order, work out
inventions, put a man into space but so can we of the West and we can
do it better and, at the same time, create greater individuals and
greater governments despite our diversification. If any proof were

2 Wenzel Jaksch, "European Unity in the Age of Atomic Weaponry," in David S.
Collier and Kurt Glaser, eds., *Berlin and the Future of Eastern Europe* (Chicago, Henry
Regnery Company, 1963), pp. 2-4.

necessary, one might compare the democratic government of West Berlin with the "stooge" government in East Berlin and compare great leaders of the past such as Professor Reuter and Frau Schroeder and today's Willy Brandt with the political chameleon, Walter Ulbricht.

Those of the East have always shown a tendency to underestimate the will and the strength of Western civilization. The Persian king, Darius, with his vast army and a background of victories, could not believe that a handful of Greeks would even fight against his forces. He was incapable of understanding that the five hundred Greek Spartans, preparing themselves to fight Thermopylae against Darius' thousands, could laugh when they were told that the Persians were so numerous that their arrows would blot out the sun and answer, "Then we will fight in the shade created by their arrows." So it is in Berlin today. Khrushchev cannot believe that to the people of the West, Berlin is worth a war. It is contrary to his philosophy to understand that a handful of Western troops supported by two million unarmed civilians are willing to continue to block his efforts to take over control of the West. Nonetheless, he will fail to destroy our concepts of mankind just as Darius failed to destroy the Greek civilization which gave us the basis of Western greatness.

Berlin, 1945

To understand the progress made in Berlin, we must look back to the first week in May, 1945, when the War was over and Berlin was completely crushed. My personal introduction to present day Berlin took place on June 17, 1945, when I led the American preliminary reconnaissance party from the Dessau area to Berlin. Conditions in the dying city of Berlin cannot be adequately described. The Four Horsemen of the Apocalypse had been there and were still there. Although the War was officially terminated, the dead were everywhere. More than 200,000 bodies were buried in the rubble of destroyed homes and offices. The nauseating sweet smell of the battlefield polluted the air. Hunger was universal, the average ration being less than nine hundred calories. Famine was just around the corner. The average Berliner was underweight at least thirty pounds. A loose collar was the sign of starvation. Pestilence was rampant. Dysentery was killing the old and young. Typhus, typhoid fever, tuberculosis, venereal diseases all were having their way. During the month of July, 1945, in one sector of Berlin, records showed that 92.4 per cent of all babies born alive died within ten days.

War's destruction had been almost complete. What the fire bombs didn't accomplish, the last ditch fury of a mad Hitler did. Before our arrival, the Soviet Army had had two months during which its soldiers, infuriated by past wrongs and drunk with conquest, murdered, looted, and raped at will. Even today the cry *"Hure, Hure"* or *"Komm, Frau"* sends a shudder through the memories of those who were there. Systematically, though unscientifically, the Soviets dismantled and took all which had not already been destroyed. From power plants to abattoirs, from machine tool plants to cows, from clothing to bathtubs, everything which they deemed of value and which could be ripped out, dismantled, or hauled away was taken. This high Soviet policy was deliberately planned to enrich Russia and to cripple Berlin.

From the very beginning two great problems confronted the West. First, how to revive Berlin so it could serve as a future capital of a democratic Germany. Second, how to prevent the Soviets from imposing their will on the people of Berlin and the rest of Germany. These were two problems which went hand in hand then and continue even today. On departing from the post of U.S. Commandant in Berlin during the autumn of 1949, I wrote in my official report: "Since our arrival in Berlin, the impact of Western Military Government policies upon the Germans has been tremendous. We have succeeded in reviving the social and political life of the City. We have guided Berlin Germans to a concept of democracy similar to our own. We have not succeeded in reaching agreements in those fundamental conflicts between Russian Communism and Western democracy. In Berlin, as elsewhere in the world, the aims of the Communist Party, called there the Sozialistische Einheitspartei Deutschlands,[3] have been to get complete control of the economic and political life of the City.

---

[3] The Sozialistische Einheitspartei Deutschlands (Socialist Unity Party of Germany, abbrv. SED) resulted from the merger of the Communist and Social Democratic parties on April 21, 1946. The merger, forced by the Soviet Military Administration over the objections of rank-and-file Social Democrats, was limited to the Soviet Zone and Soviet Sector of Berlin. A referendum of Social Democrats in the Western Sectors of Berlin rejected the merger overwhelmingly. Through a compromise reached in the Kommandatura, both the SED and the SPD (Sozialdemokratische Partei Deutschlands) were licensed in all sectors of the city. (Eds.)

The German Communist Party in this struggle has been aided, advised, directed, and supported by the Russian military administration. It is impractical to separate the missions of the Soviet military administration and the Communist Party."

Upon our arrival in the City of Berlin in 1945, we found a Soviet appointed government, completely under control of Communist leaders. Admittedly there were front men for camouflage. Old Dr. Werner, with the title of mayor, was no Communist, but his deputy, Maron, was Moscow trained and cracked the whip. All key functions of the appointed government were Communist controlled, including education, welfare, food distribution, trade unions, and police. The struggle of the Soviets to maintain this complete control is the story of our struggle which continues even today.

At the beginning, the Berlin Allied Kommandatura, composed of British, French, American, and Russian committees and executives, played the leading role in reviving the City. Much was accomplished, though frequently accomplished despite Soviet interference. There were, for instance, no law courts at first except those established by Military Government. Finally, despite Soviet interference, which at times took the form of kidnapping judges, the present judiciary system was created in Berlin and control gradually transferred to the German people.

It was the Western demand from the very beginning that the people of Berlin be allowed to vote and determine what sort of a government they wanted. This election took place on October 20, 1946, when the Sozialistische Einheitspartei, although it had enjoyed every unfair advantage, polled only 19.8% of the votes city-wide. The SPD won 48.7%, the CDU 22.2%, and the LDP 9.3%.[4] This crushing blow to the Communist SED was followed by new attempts on the part of the Soviets to regain control of the government by direct and indirect methods. Since all city legislation had to be approved unanimously by the British, French, American, and Russian Commandants at the Berlin Allied Kommandatura, the Soviets used their veto so as to give de facto veto power to the SED minority in the City government. Even so, the duly elected government of Berlin would not capitulate or be intimidated. Mobs hauled in Soviet trucks to the City Hall, which happened by chance to be in the Soviet Sector, beat elected officials, in-

4 CDU is the abbreviation for Christlich-Demokratische Union, and LDP stands for Liberaldemokratische Partei. (Eds.)

terfered with their governing, and made it necessary for the Magistrate of the City of Berlin to finally move to the Western Sectors for protection from Soviet brutality.

During these developments the Western Powers were learning. They were discovering the intent of the Soviets. They were losing their illusion of the wartime alliance. They were developing a mutual respect for the people of Berlin. The Soviet attempts to maintain their complete control of the City despite Four-Power agreements need no repeating at this time. The hunger blockade of Berlin, imposed upon two and one-half million civilians, as well as upon the troops and families of the Western Allies, was a desperate attempt to drive out Western troops and enable the Soviets to take over control of all of Berlin by force. Its failure is now history, as is the record of courage shown by the men, women, and children of West Berlin, supported loyally by the French, British, and Americans and fraternally by the German people of what is now the Federal Republic of Germany.

We can best appreciate the miraculous progress of present-day Berlin by recalling economic conditions at the end of World War II. Transport facilities, for example, were virtually non-existent during the summer of 1945. Railroad centers had been targets for repeated aerial attacks. All forms of surface transport had suffered enormously during the final suicidal struggle for the German capital. The subways had in most areas been subjected to artillery fire and flooding. Rivers and canals were blocked by blown-up bridges, sunken barges, and a mass of debris. Sewer pipes which had hung under bridges had spewed their poisonous contents into the rivers and canals of Berlin.

The building and housing situation in the City would have made a suitable picture for Dante's Inferno. In some boroughs, such as Kreuzberg, the destruction amounted to eighty per cent of all property. There were those who recommended that Berlin be abandoned, that a new city be established elsewhere. One city planning group estimated that in the center of Berlin, the shattered buildings, if levelled, would form a basis for new building on an over-all elevation of more than eight feet over previous streets.

For that first winter, there was little or no fuel. Work gangs using American Army trucks, saws, and other equipment, cut from the Grunewald approximately 250,000 round meters of wood. This helped, but was of little significance in a city the size of Berlin, and provided no heating for homes. At the same time, public health was handicapped by a lack of hospital beds. Of the 38,000 existing in 1943, only 9,300 remained available on July 1, 1945. Few hospitals had anaesthetics. There was a great scarcity of narcotics, sulfa drugs, and bandaging material. Vaccines were almost nonexistent. The police and fire departments, such as they were, had been hastily recruited by the Soviet almost from nothing. Within their ranks the Russians had placed a hard core of Communists in most of the strategic positions. Modern forms of communication—newspapers, magazines, radio— were not available to the people. It was a common sight to see trees and buildings plastered with handscribbled notes, frequently containing pathetic messages from members of a family to other members of the same family, telling each other where they could be found.

As late as February, 1946, there were more than sixteen thousand non-German displaced persons in the U.S. sector alone. Added to the general public welfare problem was a great influx of Germans forced from their homes in Czechoslovakia and Poland. More than two million such unfortunates passed by railroad through Berlin during the first two years. Soon, also, the city's welfare funds, food, and facilities were further burdened by returning members of the German Army who had been released from Russian prisoner-of-war camps because they were too sick or too feeble to be of use for the Soviet forced labor gangs. The educational system of Berlin was operating only on a most limited scale, though it had been well organized by the Soviet, who had placed in charge a trio of Moscow-trained Germans—Wandel, Winzer, and Wildangel.

Manpower was mostly womanpower. Ragged, weary, ravaged, German women could be seen on all streets removing the debris by hand, brick by brick, stone by stone.

The West Berlin Miracle

Now let us consider a few facts concerning the miraculous advances made by Berlin industry. From a beginning of nothing in 1945, industry had increased in 1950 to a value of one billion, 790 million Deutsche Marks and in 1960 to nine billion, 600 million Deutsche Marks. At the present time, despite the Soviet-erected wall and despite increased Soviet interference, West Berlin's industrial production has risen to 12.3 billion Deutsche Marks in 1962, not counting 1.55 billion DM worth of building construction. This production is,

furthermore, diversified among a number of industries, with investment goods accounting for approximately half the total. The largest
single industry is that of electrical products, accounting for about
twenty-eight per cent of Berlin's total output. (See Table One at end
of article.)

The geographical distribution of deliveries by Berlin industry was
as follows in 1961:

To German Federal Republic	7,630 million DM
To Soviet Zone and Soviet sector of Berlin	60 // //
To foreign countries	1,400 // //
Total (including deliveries within West Berlin)	9,590 million DM

It is significant that even before erection of the Berlin Wall, shipments from West Berlin to the Soviet Zone and Soviet sector of Berlin accounted for only .63 per cent of West Berlin's total output.

Before World War II, half of Berlin's employment was accounted
for by its function as the capital of the German Reich and as a center
of commerce for Central Europe as a whole. Today, West Berlin's
employment is built almost entirely around a core of industrial production, and servicing the needs of what is today the largest industrial city between Paris and Moscow. Despite this drastic readjustment, the unemployment rate in West Berlin was less than one per
cent in 1963. The distribution of employment among fields of activity is shown in Table Two.

Despite West Berlin's great economic progress, it has not yet been
able to achieve complete self-sufficiency. It is still partially dependent
on financial aid from the West. The budget for the first half of 1962,
which is summarized in Table Three, indicates aid from the Federal
Republic amounting to 751.2 million Deutsche Marks. Between 1945
and 1960, West Berlin received aid from the United States totaling
4.57 billion Deutsche Marks or $1,143,000,000. Over the past ten
years, aid to Berlin from the Federal Republic (which has increased
as American aid has tapered off) has averaged approximately 830
million Deutsche Marks per year. Any fears that United States or
West German aid might benefit Communist-controlled East Berlin
or Sovzone Germany should be quieted by the fact that West Berlin
exported only 64 million DM worth of goods to these areas in 1962,
out of a total export trade of 7,987 million DM. In the same year,

West Berlin imports from the Soviet Zone and West Berlin amounted to 165 million DM, among total imports of 8,810 million DM.

West Berlin's economic recovery has been characterized by a strong emphasis on personal initiative and private enterprise, as well as a full and varied supply of consumer goods. Economic activities in East Berlin and the Soviet Zone have, by contrast, featured collectivization of farms and almost complete socialization of state ownership of industry. Consumer goods have been deliberately neglected to advance industrial capacity, with indifferent results since the workers lack incentives to work more efficiently. Mismanagement and collectivization of farms in the Soviet Zone made necessary the purchase of 20.2 million DM worth of badly needed food from West Germany in 1962, despite the fact that the Soviet occupied zone formerly exported foodstuffs.

The great contrast between East and West Berlin and between Sovzone and West Germany is not, however, to be found in economic statistics alone. It is to be found in political matters, in social conditions, in the things that make life worth living. In West Berlin it is the students and their parents who determine the course of study to be taken, whereas in East Berlin the state decides which students will study what subjects, its own needs being controlling.

Joachim Tiburtius, the West Berlin Senator in charge of education, has written: ". . . in our school system in West Germany, on the other hand, every effort is made to give each child, regardless of the social group to which he may belong, the educational opportunities best suited to his intelligence, his particular aptitudes, and his sustained interest. . . . We hold our education of every kind should have as its objective the development of personality through learning. On the other side of the Brandenburg Gate, the purpose of education is . . . determined by the needs of the State rather than by the needs of the students or the wishes of their parents. . . ." In the West there are democratically elected governments; in the East there is a one-party government by appointment—in the West is freedom—in the East is slavery. What the German people in East Berlin and East Germany think of the so-called German Democratic Republic is dramatized by the Soviet-built wall across Berlin, a wall built to forcefully the people of the East in what the Soviets had maintained was a workman's paradise.

The Berlin Wall is an admission on the part of the Soviets of the complete defeat of the Soviet system when confronted by Western civilization. The Berlin Wall dramatizes for all the world to see that

the German Democratic Republic, as a "dictatorship of the proletariat," as a government for the people, is a myth; that it is truly not
German, certainly not democratic, and only on paper a Republic.

Future Possibilities for Berlin

The past is instructive, but what about Berlin's future? How can
the West help West Berlin to progress and stay free? The problem
is complicated by a wall across the City of Berlin, separating its free
from its enslaved boroughs—separating the principles by which we
live in our Western civilization from those which guide the Eastern
concept of life.

In London, Paris, Bonn, and Washington, there are units called
task forces, which study the situation day and night and plan for all
contingencies. They face the problems of helping West Berlin stay
free and of developing steps designed to extend freedom to East
Berlin.

How do these task forces work? At what do they aim? Expressed in
military terms, they are endeavoring to determine whether Western
policy should attack, hold, or retreat. Expressed diplomatically, it
comes out as follows: Should we exercise positive initiative, maintain the status quo, or negotiate a disengagement? These three alternatives are sometimes called the policies of liberation, coexistence,
and appeasement. To arrive at decisions, most of the task forces, regardless of nationality or language, go through a process known as an
estimate of the situation. In studying the situation, consideration is
given to every factor involved in the reasoning processes which will
help to arrive at a decision—a broad decision to attack, to hold, or to
retreat. Once that decision is made, the wheels of government, military pentagons and various state departments work out every detail
to implement the decision that has been made. Therefore, it is rather
important to us that we consider how this estimate of the situation
is arrived at.

M-O-E-O-D

The American military achieve this estimate by a series of guiding
principles—M-O-E-O-D. Each letter represents a part of the study
process. "M" stands for mission—what is our mission in Berlin? "O"

stands for opposing forces—what are the factors confronting us and what assets do we have in order to accomplish our mission? "E" stands for the enemy's possible actions to prevent the accomplishment of our mission. "O" stands for our opportunities for accomplishing our mission. After this study is completed we arrive at a decision—"D"— and that decision determines the plan to be followed, the actions to be implemented, the risk to be run.

The first step is to consider the mission. What is the mission of the United States of America in Berlin? Despite the diversity of opinion on the subject, the minority views, and irresponsible debates, as well as the serious discussions, it can be fairly stated that American policy and hence the U.S. mission in Berlin is determined primarily by an idealistic concept—so idealistic that at times it may seem unrealistic. Its essence is that most of the American people want the rights of Western civilization for the German people. Frequently this is called self-determination. In applied terms the United States wishes a united Germany with Berlin as its capital. This union is to be accomplished by free nation-wide elections. In order to accomplish this mission, the United States, according to the policies developed during the Kennedy Administration, will negotiate and discuss almost any idea except in three areas where we will not negotiate or compromise. The first is the matter of Western troops remaining in Berlin until the mission has been accomplished. The second is that the United States will not stand or tolerate interference with rights of exit and entrance to and from Berlin and West Germany. The third is that we will maintain, by whatever force necessary, a viable existence for the people of West Berlin.

To describe the British mission in Berlin is not as simple. There are many indications that Great Britain would, to use a popular term, like "out"—in a word, be rid of the whole vexing problem of Berlin. They would like gracefully to withdraw as they have done or are in the process of doing, from India, Kenya, Ghana, Tanganyika, and British Guiana. Yet, Great Britain will stick to its agreements with the United States and NATO. They will stay in Berlin until a satisfactory solution is reached. It is very important for all of us to bear in mind, when we consider Great Britain, that they are the greatest negotiators of modern times. They will negotiate and debate up until the last moment. But make no mistake—when and if a use of force is demanded they will fight and there are no greater fighters in the world today.

In evaluating the French mission, it is difficult to gauge General de Gaulle's total thoughts on Berlin. He has on many occasions shown scorn for meaningless negotiations with or concessions to the Soviets. But it also seems likely that General de Gaulle and a fair percentage of the population of France are not unhappy over a divided Germany and a divided Berlin. For despite the praiseworthy rapprochement between General de Gaulle and Chancellor Adenauer, there is still fear of German militarism. Not so much of German militarism against France, as a fear that a strong, united Germany may create a world war into which France will be drawn. Despite this, France will stick to its commitments and, under the inspired leadership of Charles de Gaulle, France is completely dependable.

West Germany's Mission

The country with the greatest stake in Berlin, of course, is West Germany, The German Federal Republic. West Germany and West Berlin want a united, free, Western-oriented, Germany with a united, free Berlin as its capital. Also, as a negotiable subject—West Germany wants back the lands taken by the Poles and the Russians. But this can wait.

The *bête noire* of the entire German situation is of course the U.S.S.R. What the Kremlin wants has been crystal clear since the end of World War II and was undoubtedly planned before the end of the war. Soviet Russia wants a united Communist-controlled Berlin as a stepping stone to a united Communist-controlled Germany. The Communists have changed their techniques and shifted their tactics, but their basic mission has never altered.

Opposing Forces

So much for missions, now what about opposing forces? The U.S.S.R. has, in Germany, twenty-two divisions plus the armed forces of the Soviet Zone regime, as opposed to the Western strength of only eleven thousand in surrounded West Berlin. In the event of an all-out nuclear war, the Soviet Union would not stand a chance against the forces of the West because overwhelming numbers of surface troops would not be decisive. That the Soviets know this was indicated by the speed with which Khrushchev withdrew his missiles from Cuba when confronted with the blunt ultimatum that they be removed or that the Soviet Union would be held responsible for their activities.

The various Eastern Task Forces are constantly measuring and planning for various types of military action against the West. The West faces questions such as: Should the defense be at the Rhine River, or should we attack towards the Oder? Should tactical atomic weapons be used immediately or should a policy of escalating be followed? Should control of atomic weapons be integrated under NATO or co-ordinated with the United States playing the leading role?

Economics are also a factor in the juxtaposition of opposing forces. The Soviet economy is state-controlled. Production is based upon the needs of the state with little regard for consumer goods. The work force, compared with that of the West, is primitive except in certain special areas. While the planned economy of the East had produced certain spectacular accomplishments, statistics show that economic growth in the Soviet Zone is slowing down and that it never was comparable with the tremendous expansion in West Germany and West Berlin.

Like West Germany, West Berlin has chosen its own government through legitimate elections, and enjoys all the freedoms of a democracy. The so-called "German Democratic Republic" is a government of Soviet stooges hated by the people. It is a police state with only one operational political party, the so-called "minor parties" being tools and puppets. The people of East Berlin and the Soviet Zone are resentful, depressed, resigned, and at the moment somewhat hopeless. There is no force like the power of the people and, in West Berlin as in West Germany, the people are free, determined, and hopeful. Even the song, "Das ist die Berliner Luft-Luft-Luft," reflects truly the optimism of the free people of West Berlin.

Possible Enemy Actions

We now turn to possible actions which the enemy might take against us. Aside from acts of nuisance, such as banning transit of members of the Bundestag when they desired to meet in Berlin, the wall is the greatest psychological weapon against the West. The Soviets can maintain the wall and increase their control over contacts between East and West Berlin. They seized control over political life in East Berlin during the blockade in 1948, and have never relinquished it. Unfortunately, the Jessup-Malik agreement under which the Soviets lifted the blockade in May, 1949, did not require the Communists to relinquish their dictatorship in East Berlin, nor did the ensuing Foreign Ministers' Conference restore unified government to the city.

This seizure of a third of the City of Berlin by the Soviets was contrary to all allied agreements and contrary to all international principles of integrity. Nonetheless, the wall built across Berlin is simply a physical proof of a condition which has existed since the blockade.

The Soviets can also interfere with West Berlin by means of clearance papers (Warenbegleitschein). Since the blockade, all civilian shipments by barge, by rail, and by road have had to have clearance papers approved in the Soviet occupied sector of Berlin. At first, a Russian stood in back of the East German representative who stamped approval on the papers. That pose of using the East German representatives as agents of the Soviets has long since disappeared. By means of clearance papers, the East German Government can hold up and interfere with shipments, can accomplish almost a complete blockade with a minimum risk of war. By holding up clearance papers, orders from West Germany and foreign countries can be discouraged. This action by the Soviets against us is quite likely.

The Soviets might also consider a complete blockade of land, water, and even air; accomplished directly or indirectly as was done the last time in the blockade in 1948. Such a drastic step is not likely, for the Soviets do not want war with the West and this would be almost a sure way to bring such a catastrophe about.

Similarly, the Soviets might, under one pretext or another, occupy West Berlin, either with Soviet troops or Zonal German police and army units. This might be an especially tempting possibility, if the Soviets and their communist stooges were successful in causing uncontrollable rioting in West Berlin. This action by the Soviets, so long as Western troops are in Berlin and willing to fight, would seem too risky for the Soviets unless they desire war.

Opportunities to Accomplish Our Mission

Let us now consider our opportunities for the present and future. Shall we attack, hold, or retreat? Expressed another way, shall we exercise positive initiative, defend actively the status quo, or negotiate a disentanglement?

Before considering alternative courses of action, it is well to recapitulate the rights enjoyed by the Western powers in Berlin. What are the legal bases for being there? In the first place, the Western powers are in Berlin by right of conquest. The Soviet claim that the U.S.S.R. alone captured Berlin was placed in its proper perspective some years ago by General, later Ambassador, James Gavin at the Allied Kommandatura. The Soviet General, Kotikov, repeated, as he had already said ad nauseam, "We Russians, alone, captured Berlin." General Gavin's quiet answer was: "When I look in back of me, I see a long line of white crosses over Germany, through France, down through Italy, and across North Africa. Don't you, General Kotikov, ever again tell me that you Russians alone captured Berlin." If the Western Powers have no rights in Berlin by right of conquest because they did not physically capture Berlin, then by the same reasoning, the Soviets have no right in Saxony and Thuringia which were captured by the Western armies.

A second right which the Western Powers have in Berlin is the right obtained by Allied agreements. At the end of the war, the American troops withdrew from Saxony and Thuringia, back from all the Czechoslovak border, and turned over to the Soviets for military occupation this vast area as part of an international agreement whereby Berlin would be occupied by the Western Powers jointly with the Soviet Union. A third justification for our being in Berlin lies in the Allied high-level agreements which planned postwar Germany at various conferences of the European Advisory Commission, the meeting of heads of government at Yalta and Potsdam, and the blockade lifting conference at Paris in May, 1949. These inter-governmental arrangements were based upon a postwar, united Germany with Berlin as its capital.

We might consider a fourth right, and that is the right of the German people who, though conquered, cannot be deprived, consistent with international law, of their right of sovereignty. The German people are entitled to enjoy Western civilization with its self-determination. If the Soviets prefer to ignore these rights, they had better recognize that the Western Powers are in Berlin by the desire of all true Germans and by the right of power. We're there; we intend to stay there. We have the strength to assert, maintain, and continue our rights in Berlin with or without Soviet approval.

Let us continue, even though sketchily, what might be done by the Western Powers in Berlin. If our decision were to attack we might smash the wall and if necessary, occupy East Berlin as well as West

Berlin and force decision on a city-wide basis, following decisions arrived at by the Berlin Allied Kommandatura and the elected government of West Berlin. Short of that, we might permit the people of West Berlin and West Germany to harass the wall and the Soviet stooges instead of employing the police of West Berlin and the military to hold back the wrath of the people of West Berlin. We might cut off all contact, employ a complete boycott of East Berlin and the Soviet Zone, it being borne in mind that East Germany particularly needs trade with West Berlin and West Germany. We might, in an all-out "short of war" program, use against the Soviets and their East German stooges the tactics which are used by the Communist-directed revolutionary forces all over the world. These Soviet tactics employ the principle of sanctuary. North Viet Nam is a sanctuary against South Viet Nam. Tunisia was a sanctuary against Algeria. The Congo Republic is a sanctuary for guerrilla operations against Portuguese Angola. West Berlin and West Germany could be used as sanctuaries for guerrilla operations, for sabotage, industrial slowdown, passive resistance, and revolt against the Communist government of East Berlin and East Germany. The German Federal Republic might establish at Bonn Soviet Zone Land governments in exile; might establish West Berlin as a land with full participation in the German government at Bonn. West German troops might be stationed in West Berlin just as Soviet Zone troops are stationed in East Berlin. The Western Powers might apply pressures of direct and indirect forces against Soviet operations not just in Germany but in other parts of the world.

The Soviets have succeeded in Africa, Asia, and other parts of the world in implementing such actions. There is no justification for the assumption that such tactics would not succeed against them in Germany without producing an all-out war. Nonetheless, it is generally reasoned that these positive operations would not be supported by the German population of the East or the West. Life is not that desperate. A new generation has grown up in the ten years since the uprising on June 17, 1953. In the capitals of the West there is great fear of actions of this sort escalating into an all-out war. Against the chance of successful uprisings is the Soviet record of cruel suppression exercised after the 1953 uprising when more than fifty thousand workers were imprisoned, at least two hundred executed, and fifteen hundred shipped off to Soviet slave camps.

Probably the most powerful reasons of all against positive attack, direct and indirect, are the announced peaceful aims of the American, British, and French governments. President J. F. Kennedy in the summer of 1963 at Bonn and Berlin reaffirmed U.S. determination, but at the same time stressed conciliation and peaceful negotiation as means of settling East-West differences. President Kennedy, in a speech at the American University in Washington, emphasized a "Strategy of Peace" to attain, by negotiations, "Just and peaceful settlements . . . at least we can help make the world safe for diversity." There is a dominant spirit in the West of "Pacem in Terris" and of what amounts to our endeavoring to attain the objectives of our Western mission by peaceful methods. So, for the accomplishment of our Western missions, attack would seem unlikely.

The next opportunity would be that of our maintaining the status quo in Berlin. The status quo policy includes a willingness to discuss and negotiate with the Soviets almost any subject except the three which have already been mentioned. No negotiation is possible concerning our troops remaining in Berlin, our communication being maintained, and a livable life for West Berliners being sustained.

In favor of the status quo is the Western belief that time is on our side. The West believes that while we maintain our rights, and while West Berlin continues to expand industrially and improve socially, people in the Zone and in East Berlin are becoming increasingly disillusioned with the Soviet system. The hope is that some time in the future a united Berlin and a united Germany can be obtained short of using force. Such a policy of status quo encourages an intensification of recognition by East and West on technical levels while the West adamantly refuses to consider any recognition of so-called "elected" East Berlin officials. Justification for such technical contacts is made on the basis that it is mainly the hypocrisy of one-party elections which deprives the people of East Berlin and East Germany of their right of self-determination. It is, furthermore, logical that most technical men in areas from power to sewage disposal, from telephones to the S-Bahn, from mail to trade and industry are men selected or appointed primarily for their skills rather than wholly for their political convictions.

During the blockade of Berlin, there were extensive exchanges in these technical areas and today in 1963, such contacts are continuing as indicated by the following report:

Contacts between East and West Berlin, 1963

1. *Mail*

   Mail is exchanged several times during the day at checkpoint Zimmerstrasse Ecke Friedrichstrasse.

2. *Interzonal Trade*

   Authorities are permitted to cross the border in two cars without being controlled by Border Police.

3. *S-Bahn*

   stopped running between East and West except for one line ending at East Berlin's Friedrichstrasse Station. S-Bahn trains in West Berlin run on power from the East. Station platforms are illuminated by West Berlin power.

4. *Subway*

   Two West Berlin subway lines still pass through East Berlin but only one makes a stop—at Friedrichstrasse. Persons authorized to enter East Berlin may leave the train there.

5. *Water and Gas*

   Each half of the city has its own water and gas supply but 90% of West Berlin's sewage flows under East Berlin. A small amount of gas comes to West Berlin from the East to illuminate certain border stations.

6. *Power*

   A small part of West Berlin's power consumption is supplied from the East and is paid for under a general trade agreement.

7. *Telephone*

   In 1952, the East Berlin postal authorities cut telephone communications with West Berlin. West Berlin telephone officials have one service line into East Berlin but it is not for public use. The three Western Allies have a telephone line to the Soviet Embassy and the Russians have lines to the Berlin Air-Safety-Center and Spandau Prison.

8. *Police*

   The West Berlin Police has a teletype line to the Headquarters of the People's Police. Before August 13, 1961, files on wanted criminals were exchanged and search actions discussed.

9. *Fire Department*

   The West Berlin Fire Department maintains radio communications with the East Berlin Fire Department for cases of fire near the sector border.

10. *Burials*

For the transfer of the dead from and to West Berlin a special permit is required by the East Berlin authorities. Applications are usually answered within three days and may be initiated through any West Berlin funeral parlor.

Last and least attractive as an opportunity for the Western Powers in Berlin is that action bearing the unpleasant name "retreat." This could be done as skillfully as it was done in Laos. Those who were in a position to know must have realized that acceptance of a troika government made up of conservatives, communists, and neutralists could only result in a communist take-over. In Berlin, the West might accept, under the principle of retreat, the withdrawal of British, French, and American troops, leaving only a symbolic force—sort of a military attaché's guard. This tactic would satisfy the timid as a skillful disengagement from Western obligations. The same thing would result if Western rights in Berlin were turned over to the United Nations. Of course, turning any part of Berlin over to the United Nations would solve nothing. It would simply cause additional confusion and facilitate Soviet control.

Another retreat would be that of the creation of a "free" city. As this has been suggested by the Soviets, the result would be that West Berlin would lose its freedom and simply fall under the control of East Berlin and the Soviet Zone government. Any Soviet sponsored elections could only result in mockery of democracy. A "free" City of Berlin, as understood by the Soviets, would be a City of Berlin cut loose from its ties with the West and with the German Federal Republic. Another form of surrender would be to accept a common Soviet-controlled currency for all of Berlin. This has been proposed by the Soviets on many occasions. Only the naive think that complete political control would not follow financial control.

We can rule out any thought of retreat from Berlin. Such an action would be impossible after the pledges which have been given by the government of the United States as expressed in 1963 by President Kennedy and in 1961 by the then Vice-President Lyndon B. Johnson, who promised Berliners, "We mutually pledge to each other our lives, our fortunes, and our sacred honor."

Decision

A review of the statements of Western leaders and the actions of Western governments over the past decade or so leads inescapably to the conclusion that as of this date the decision of the Western powers concerning Berlin is a decision actively to maintain the status quo and to react vigorously and forcefully against any attempts on the part of the Soviets or their Sovzone German puppet government to impose their will upon West Berlin, to interfere with the continued growth of West Berlin, or to deprive the people of West Berlin of their freedom. Those familiar with me and my writings will recognize that a policy of the status quo is not to my personal liking. My studies and observations in various parts of the world have convinced me that communist governments get into power by force, stay in power by force, and can be deprived of power only by force.

Berlin deserves our understanding, sympathy, and active support. Berlin, as the Greeks at Thermopylae, is blocking the pressure of an outdated Eastern civilization and is exposing for all to see the brutality and unproductiveness of Soviet slavery. Berlin is preserving for the Western world the right of free men to decide for themselves what is best for them—the right to decide their relationships to their fellow men and the right to decide their relationship to the eternal.

TABLE ONE

WEST BERLIN INDUSTRIAL PRODUCTION

Industrial output: 1950	1,790 million DM
1960	9,600 million DM

Breakdown of 1960 output by branches of industry:

Electrical industry	28.4%
Food	11.9%
Clothing industry	11.0%
Machinery	10.2%
Tobacco industry	6.8%
Chemical industry	6.5%
Printing	4.7%
Non-ferrous metal industry	3.6%
Steel construction	3.4%
Miscellaneous	13.5%

TABLE TWO

Distribution of Employment Among Fields of Activity, 1960

Industry and crafts	40.2%
Public services	20.4%
Trade	13.0%
Construction	8.4%
Private services	8.0%
Transportation	6.0%
Banks and insurance companies	2.2%
Utilities	1.2%
Agriculture	0.6%

TABLE THREE

West Berlin Budget—First Half 1962

	Revenues in million DM	Expenditures in million DM
General administration	29.1	82.4
Restitution	232.2	289.9
Police and judiciary	15.4	220.7
Schools	2.1	151.4
Cultural affairs and arts	10.0	105.1
Labor and social welfare	62.5	400.5
Youth and sports	8.9	65.0
Health	51.7	163.6
Construction and housing	14.6	114.5
Commerce, transportation, utilities	2.6	38.0
Public institutions—commercial enterprises	8.9	68.2
Financial administration	90.4	186.0
Aid from the Federal Republic	751.2	——
State and community taxes	704.6	——
Total	1.984.2	1.885.3

Part Three:

TOWARDS EUROPEAN-AMERICAN PARTNERSHIP

CHAPTER X

The Challenge of Our Time

EUGENE DAVIDSON

Tʜᴇ ᴄʜᴀʟʟᴇɴɢᴇ has often been defined: it is essentially the problem of mastering the technological revolution that produces each year newer and more formidable weapons with which to subdue man's natural environment and also to destroy it, by means of inherited responses—both social and psychological—that were barely adequate to cope with the relative simplicities of preceding centuries. The hand that drew the bow is the same human hand that can press the red button; the heads that made the decisions that in the Thirty Years War reduced the population of much of Central Europe by two-thirds have not grown in size or cerebral capacities under the hats and caps of Washington, Bonn, Paris, London, Moscow, or Peiping. What changes in political thinking that have occurred in the twentieth century have come out of this technological revolution and out of the reactions to the history that was, in part, a consequence of that revolution. The grandiose and sinister illusions of National Socialism were but one example of a marriage of a falsely construed history and an all too well understood order of the machines. And the Nazi state itself emerged because the statesmen of Europe and the United States had no sensible solutions for the problems of Europe after World War I. They too were unable to adjust their thinking and their decisions to the demands of a technology that helped to produce a world-wide depression or to the submerged longing of the peoples of Europe for an order with a deeper significance than the one that had brought on meaningless and devastating wars followed by vast unemployment. The deaths of millions of young men were not requited by the spurious world order of a League of Nations that was unable to restore the

155

balances of the nineteenth century or to create the viable concepts and organizations that would make them unessential.

When President Kennedy came to Germany in the summer of 1963 and told his German and European audience that an attack on any part of their territory would be considered an attack on the United States he made a pronouncement that had a very mixed history. For this, of course, was a continuation of the doctrine of Woodrow Wilson and Henry Stimson, of Franklin Roosevelt and Wendell Willkie—to mention only a few of those in the United States who thought the One World had come much sooner than turned out to be the fact. These men lived and made their speeches in an era of lofty principles where self-determination was to be a cornerstone of a world made safe for democracy. It was, however, a selective brand of self-determination. It was a principle to be applied to Poles, to Czechs, to Slovaks, to Serbs, and Croats, but not to the Sudeten Germans, or to the Austrians, or to the people who lived in Danzig, or Vilna, or Memel, for in these cases it clashed with the power goals of those who had won the war. Words like "disarmament," "respect for obligations solemnly undertaken," "collective security," "open covenants openly arrived at," were used in a high rhetoric that covered the brute realities of a continent dominated as a result of American intervention by a weak France and its alliance of succession states. Words about democracy were conspicuous in the speeches and in declarations of the leaders of these newly created countries too, but the ancient oppressions of which they had so bitterly complained were as virulent as ever in the lives of their mixed peoples. Thus the Sudetenländer, presumably an integral part of the multinational state of Czechs, Slovaks, Ukrainians, and Hungarians, were discriminated against economically, politically, and socially by the ruling Czech hierarchy; when the depression came, the Sudetenland was the most distressed area in Czechoslovakia. But no account of this catastrophe or of the vindictive political decisions that had helped to bring it about could eradicate the sedulously cultivated myth of a flaming Czechoslovakian center of democracy that had succeeded the feudal empire of the Austro-Hungarians. The legend remained fixed in the minds of the American statesmen who had helped to found the country and then to perpetuate its mythology. The Polish Corridor too, although called by many leaders among the Allies themselves the likely origin of the next European war, became part of the system of legality. Henry Stimson, who had a compact solution for everything he regarded as a breach of

international decorum, wanted the heads of countries that misbe-
haved or committed aggressions against this unstable order to be
ignored in the councils of the powers as one might ignore a person
dropped from the Social Register for unseemly conduct if he turned
up at a social gathering. Stimson would have preferred sterner sanctions than this social ostracism, but at the least he wanted to summon
the moral forces of the twentieth century to maintain what he regarded as a world order. While the *Realpolitiker* moved deftly behind
the slogans of international solidarity, the problems themselves remained.

Out of the non-order that followed World War I, three major world
views competed for establishing the conditions their proponents declared essential to the welfare of the race or to a preferred section of
it. The first was that of the neo-Wilsonians, who wanted to outlaw
war, to adjust differences between nations by way of reason and juridical argumentation. The second was that of Soviet Russia, who with
the appearance of Hitler quickly adopted the concept of the world
alliance of peace-loving nations. These could, on suitable occasions,
include friendly capitalist powers, for the just war in the Communist
lexicon was defined as any war in which the Soviet Union took part
and the peace-loving nations were either its allies or countries that
would condone what actions, military or otherwise, she felt necessary
to undertake on behalf of her security. The Russian state was based
on a series of interpretations of the nature of the industrial revolution:
an international order would be achieved when these dogmas were
universally accepted. Nazi Germany, too, could easily identify the
just war: it was the war on behalf of the race, against Communism,
against the international conspiracy dominating both the Soviet Union
and the nations of the capitalist world—that of the Asiatic Jew who
had been conspiring for centuries against the culture-bearers of the
West.

Thus three imaginary worlds came into conflict, each of them exclusive—although for the brief interlude of the Hitler-Stalin pact it
seemed as though the anti-democratic systems might range themselves
against the Western powers in a powerful alliance of coerced populations, millions of whom accepted their bondage with enthusiasm,
turning the vast technological resources of their countries into anything that served the state, whether they were ordered to manufacture
tanks or automobiles or gas chambers. Before them were placed the
perverted slogans of the machine age that were as appropriate to Soviet

Russia as to Nazi Germany—"the common use before individual use," and over the concentration camps "Work brings freedom." When this short-lived alliance was disrupted by Hitler's attack of June, 1941, the tattered banner of collective security was raised again, and on its behalf Roosevelt was ready to accept the sacrifice of entire populations, Poles, Germans, Czechs, and as it turned out the whole of Eastern Europe to the fantasy of the four policemen and the post-war collaboration of the great powers, one of which was to be the China of Chiang, that would have an identical interest in seeing to it that the peace of the world was kept. Neither Roosevelt nor Churchill would negotiate with the high-minded and courageous men of the German resistance, for part of the Anglo-American stereotype was the long-lived menace of Prussian militarism and the Junker caste which it was believed they represented. The American and British leaders had only contempt for the idea that the army generals and the civilians who were risking their lives and those of their families against the Third Reich without any support whatever from the outside world could found a state that would be a long-range improvement over that of the Nazis. It was the German general staff, the prosecution kept telling the court at Nuremberg, that was the eternal enemy of the peace-loving nations, making and unmaking governments at will. The idea of dealing with its representatives to shorten the war and get rid of Hitler was waved aside as merely another crafty device whereby the Germans sought to escape the consequences of their defeat.

But with the collapse of Germany and Japan the hollowness of the post-war design immediately became clear. Russia had no idea whatever that Hitler had been defeated in order to produce a "bourgeois" version of the four freedoms which she would join with the West to protect. Nothing in Marx or Lenin or Stalin, excepting the latter's virtuous protestations to his Western colleagues on such occasions as those at Yalta or Teheran, could have given rise to such illusions. When Roosevelt at Yalta spoke of the need for free elections and a free press for Poland, Stalin told him briskly that those principles were well-known, and went on to talk about something else. The notion that Stalin's post-war plans were the same as theirs was part of the interpretation of history placed upon his remarks by such men as Harry Hopkins and Joe Davies and the other busy emissaries who plied between Washington, London, and Moscow.

The image of the four policemen, however, faded slowly. The war in Greece, the Berlin blockade, the Korean War, the uprisings in East Germany, in Poland and Hungary, the building of the wall have played havoc with the myth that Prussian militarism was the chief danger to the peace of the world. They have brought an American president—who may not always have had the friendliest feelings for the Berliners of whom he unexpectedly proclaimed himself one—to declare himself the stoutest of champions for the maintenance of Allied strength in that city and to this date at least have prevented him from giving away the Oder-Neisse territories, a gesture believed desirable by so many of his advisors as well as by so many Germans. Treaty-breakers, the anathematized if somewhat sketchy outlaws of Cordell Hull, have been replaced by the unmistakable threat of the enemy coalition from Cuba to Laos. The brush fires that appear at intervals in Africa, or the Far East or the Mediterranean or near our own shores are met in one form or another by an *ad hoc* coalition opeating under the uneasy direction of the United Nations—surely a curious description of a body representing one of the great cleavages of history.

But the Western alliance is an inescapable necessity. In it both European and American policy at long last deal with realities from which much hypocrisy and many illusions have been burned away. We do not have One World, but we have working alliances of half a world that, in their power and well-being, remain a magnet for the oppressed millions of Europe and Asia. We have a nascent European and American order that has emerged not only from Hitler's diabolism but from its own failures. It is an order that corresponds to the material demands of mass production and mass consumption, an order in which each historical entity may take its place in a wider culture. It is an order in being and prospect, but it is far from complete. The challenges remain and they appear in many forms and places: unemployment in the United States and England, the farm problem wherever there are farms, the drive for equality among the colored races, the unreconciled differences in NATO and the Common Market, the continuing inflation, to mention a few of them. The European Economic Community has accomplished everything Speer had boasted the Nazis had done for Europe, without threats or violence, with no need to erect a wall to keep its workers from fleeing to the other side.

This collaboration of the West has nothing in common with the flimsy alliances and pretensions of post-Versailles Europe. The statements of its leaders about their common purposes and goals correspond to the realities of the need for defense both of territory and a culture. It is only a start: the alliance is threatened at many points from without and within, by the enemy at the perimeter and also by passivity and irresolution inside the fortress. But no matter how strong the French drive for a third force under the hegemony of Paris might be, what could this possibly come to in a time of genuine crisis? France has more than once called upon her friends for help when civilization —which her leaders always held to be coequivalent with the boundaries of France—was threatened. De Gaulle may sulk within his tents, but who can doubt where in the moment of crisis he or any successor must stand? But de Gaulle's moves toward more independence should be easily understandable to an American who believes the United States should have dealt resolutely and immediately with Castro's rocket pads because they represented an intolerable threat and calculated affront about which we could not debate either with our enemies or with our friends. And on this matter, it should be remembered, de Gaulle understood the need for taking action better than some of President Kennedy's own advisors.

While every country must be the final judge of its vital interests, the over-arching alliance of the West is an essential part of the vital interests of each of its members. France alone against Russia would be a lost cause; the United States without Western Europe, or Western Europe without the United States, would be fighting a last desperate struggle.

The loose confederations that have united the Western world since the war may not survive in their present forms; they need remodeling, to be adjusted to the growing strength of Europe, to the tactics demanded by the new weapons and to what we learn as we develop the common front. But the forces that brought these confederations into being remain the same; no one can secede from this history or stand alone in its stream.

Nevertheless we are not the creatures of a dialectic. Although the forces making for union are powerful they can be misdirected. A resourceful adversary will do his best to promote any differences that may be exploited in the alliance that keeps him from the mastery of the continent and of the world. But the Polaris submarines that disappear from the surface of the sea for two months at a time sail for us all, for de Gaulle as well as for Kennedy, and the German divisions on the front line are the divisions of the West. This is more than a military alliance, for the boundaries between the two world forces are far more ideological than geographical. . . . Reality has, in a sense, been simplified for us. Perhaps we can say that our capacity for coming to grips with it has improved since the earlier part of the century. For we confront the naked question of survival—not only of physical survival but of that of the culture we have inherited and to which we have contributed. Is the nature of man with all its limitations and dead spaces such that he can learn to live, when he has the choice, in a disciplined freedom, to forego shortrange advantages, to make sacrifices for the common cause—or is he rather in the age of technocracy the creature that needs to be handed the blueprints, to learn to recite in each generation a different version of a distorted history as one big brother succeeds the other and denies his works?

At least these basic changes have become manifest in the climate of the postwar years: the boundaries between states are losing their significance; the welfare of the people of Western Europe, even including the population of the Tyrol, is not felt to be at the mercy of the mapmakers as was the case after 1919. The causes of both World Wars are wholly lacking among the countries of the Western alliance: their cooperation is based both on necessity and on a consensus of purpose that is as widely shared as the spontaneous demonstrations in Germany for de Gaulle and for Kennedy would indicate. In the case of de Gaulle they stood for reconciliation, the end of centuries of hostility and of war that is now unthinkable between the two countries. In the case of President Kennedy they had many significances, the chief of which was manifest in the shadow of the wall. The West needs to know its massed strength and to rely on it, to have the will to increase the flow not only of goods across its borders but of ideas as well, and to be as ready to sacrifice for this free community as are the zealots of the enemy cadres, to think beyond the local gain and privilege to the general purpose and to be ready to take risks on its behalf. For this is the first and last line of civilization. Either we will maintain it or the whole world will perish or—what is worse—be delivered to the men who have themselves become machines.

CHAPTER XI

Franco-German Reconciliation and European Unity

LOUIS-HENRI PARIAS

THE CURRENT Franco-German reconciliation is a link in a growing chain of European and world unity. This can be said without indulging in illusions that minimize the number or complexity of the political, social, economic, and religious problems which block the realization of such unity. Nor need we fail to keep in mind that Franco-German reconciliation is only one of many phenomena competing for the attention of Europe and of the world.

But the uniqueness and interest of this reconciliation—after the Franco-German conflicts which preceded it and paved the way for it, and in view of the repercussions which it promises to have on the European Community, the Soviet Union, the African countries, and the United States—are to be found in the lesson in political philosophy that this reconciliation offers. We are, in fact, witnessing a phenomenon in which human destiny is finally finding the road of liberty and justice, after having groped for it for centuries under the successive domination of European powers, the German Empire, and France in particular. Franco-German reconciliation thus appears in a perspective linking it to the history and the future of Europe, and to the ancient dream of European unity.

This lesson in political philosophy emerged during an examination of the various methods available for dealing with Franco-German reconciliation. Two such methods were apparent from the start. Each opens up different horizons, but neither exhausts the subject. Either of the two ways of handling the theme circumscribes us, so to speak, within limits which prove (if such proof is required) that the total environment of Franco-German reconciliation is far more extensive than the political era in which it originated or the historic-geographic space which contains it.

To speak of Franco-German reconciliation within the immediate frame of reference of the recent treaty formalizing it would mean to limit ourselves to present considerations, thereby eliciting an approach determined by the nature of short-range phenomena. Such a treatment would be limited to a factual chronological account of the conversations and agreements which culminated in the rapprochement of the two peoples. To speak of reconciliation within the framework of the French and German past would mean to limit our consideration to the historical reasons for unity—reasons which one or the other of the two powers sought to exploit in the interest of its own hegemony throughout a century of struggle.

These two methods of dealing with the subject lack perspective, even when combined. They involve the student with the details of a historical phenomenon and the events leading up to it, without penetrating its deeper meaning. The only way in which the historical problem of Franco-German reconciliation may be grasped in its total magnitude is to consider it as a whole, taking a bird's-eye view of it and at the same time opening our eyes to its unsuspected dimensions.

This approach requires us to treat Franco-German reconciliation as a stage in an evolutionary phenomenon which is itself a crucial aspect of a greater evolution. The immediate evolutionary happening is itself a step toward higher and more complex evolutionary processes. The formation and unification of economic and political Europe helps to make possible the more remote unity of the world. Such an approach to Franco-German reconciliation surmounts the limitations of the immediate history leading up to it and of the geographical space in which it is occurring. This reconciliation thus appears as one of the links in the chain of what Teilhard de Chardin has called the "phenomenon of planetarization."

The importance of this link in the evolutionary chain can, of course, be understood only if studied in its historical evolution. This evolution continued throughout the thousand-year struggle between the German Empire and France, to the day on which the exhausted people of Europe saw that their unity was possible in the face of the menace to their security posed by an outside power—a power which had drawn much of its vital dynamism, its ideology, and its technology from European genius. The forces of history had thus worked in the interests of liberty, justice, and unity for the peoples of Europe. The

European community thus emerging is itself destined to become one of many "links in the chain" of the liberty, justice, and unity of future humanity.

The Dialectic of Tradition and Utopianism

Everything said so far leads up to an interpretation of history, to a guiding idea. This idea, which will remain basic throughout our considerations, may be stated thus: *History is what prepares nature to submit to liberty.* This truth is made apparent by the study of those phenomena which, considered in terms of European unity, divided our peoples for so many centuries and bring them together today. These phenomena outline clearly the lines of force of an irreversible evolution, which continues inexorably despite historical reverses. Toynbee has with great perception examined its forward march through the twenty civilizations that constitute humanity's historical experience. But the political thinking of the greatest German philosopher, Immanuel Kant, offers a higher discipline for our intuition and judgment. This rigorous thought finds in Franco-German reconciliation experimental confirmation of an entire political philosophy formulated a century and a half ago—a confirmation which justifies our belief in human progress.

Following the order of our research and observations, and relying on Kant's political philosophy, we shall show how the thousand-year struggle of the German and French peoples—in the traditional and utopian forces which nourished it, and in the reconciliation which followed it—presents a case of intimately linked political finalism and naturalism, culminating in the triumph of liberty, justice, and unity for these two nations today and for Europe tomorrow, under the pressure of historical necessity.

We shall therefore study successively:

1. The roles played by tradition and utopianism in this thousand-year struggle of our two countries, the changes which the encounter of traditional and utopian ideologies produced in political reality, and the appropriate criticism of these phenomena; and

2. The way in which exhaustion of the European peoples removed any tendency toward hegemony, particularly in France and Germany, thus permitting Franco-German reconciliation

in the face of the Eastern menace to the security of these two peoples and the peoples of Europe.

The Franco-German struggle had its origin in the breakup of the Carolingian Empire. By dividing the ancient realm into three kingdoms, and by leaving Lotharingia to the appetites of the "sister" powers east and west of it, the Treaty of Verdun (843) ushered in this thousand-year conflict from which we are just emerging.

The problem is simple. The Western world was at that time under the mystical influence of three politico-religious myths:

> the power of Caesar,
> the era of Constantine,
> Carolingian unity.

These three myths were to nourish the Western tradition and to be alternately exploited and combatted by princes of the middle ages and modern times. On the one side, the Holy Roman Empire of the German nation sought to reunite Caesar, Constantine, and Charlemagne in a single elected leader: the "demi-god" emperor. On the other side, the feeble hereditary monarchy of the Capets set forth to assault this "demi-god" on feet of clay. The myth belonged to the Germans. The French were moved by utopianism. But both the elected emperor and the hereditary king remained unaware that they were prisoners: the one of a static historical era, the other of unforeseeable evolutionary changes.

Ernest Lavisse, the author of a monumental history of France, has emphasized the way in which hereditary monarchy gave rise to the national idea. In the tenth century, Germany seemed the closest to unity among the states which had formed Charlemagne's patrimony. But this almost achieved unity slipped away. A little later it was definitely lost, and opportunities to realize it were not to reappear until modern times. What is at the root of this German destiny? What caused the failure? Germany, in the era of its decline, had not found "that continuity of monarchical action by which the other countries were constituted states which then became nations." France, on the contrary, was to achieve at a very early date that continuity which it was to employ in order to frustrate the centralization and unification of the Holy German Empire, by fighting against a hereditary imperial crown.

But the hereditary Capetian monarchy, by constituting the French state, permitted the French nation to become aware of itself and to awake the peoples of Europe and the world to the national idea. While it is true that the hereditary principle is legitimized by the myth of monarchy by divine right, and is thus rooted in traditional ideology, the continuity engendered by this principle also operates to create a strong state, a centralized nation, and a nationally conscious people—thus opening the door to utopian ideology. An "enlightened despot" such as Frederick II is the typical incarnation of this idea in the eighteenth century. Monarchical continuity could not in fact exist without territorial and administrative centralization, without national consciousness. Through the effects of discoveries and the flow of ideas, especially the idea of liberty which Christianity brought to the world, the state forged by Philip the Fair, Richelieu, and Louis XIV was to become conscious of itself through the subjects who administered it and the people that feared it. National continuity was to take the place of monarchical continuity.

National awareness emerges as a result of monarchical continuity during the centuries from the Renaissance to the present. European unity can no longer be achieved except through the unity of nations. For Europe to become a political reality, it is first necessary that each people marked by historical destiny discover its national being and its national unity.

The hegemony which the great ruling families exercised successively over the peoples of Europe tended to inhibit the development of national awareness by these peoples. By conducting a diplomatic and military struggle against German unity, the French monarchy alone, unknowingly and with no desire to do so, prepared the road for the national awareness of the French people and other peoples as well.

While the Germans remained fixed in a static historical era—that of the Holy Roman Empire of the German nation—France discovered the modern state and national awareness. Throughout this millenium of history, the Holy German Empire appeared as an admirable and outworn myth, which French foreign policy jealously kept in the state of anarchy into which it had fallen. (Consider, for instance, the treaties of Westphalia which stabilized this anarchy in 1648 and those of Vienna which attempted to renew it in 1815, despite the tempest of national liberation emanating from the French Revolution and Napoleonic hegemony.) This is how the internal policy of the French monarchy—unknowingly and paradoxically—paved the way for the

revolution of 1789 in France and the revolutions of national liberation of 1848 throughout Europe, while its traditional foreign policy
was devoted to preventing national unity or destroying it through
diplomacy and wars.

The Holy Alliance of the kings was the last resurgence of the
monarchical principle against national awareness in nineteenth-century Europe. To become convinced of this, one should read the journal in which Baron vom Stein set down his impressions at the Congress of Vienna. Stein records the disillusionment and bitterness of
the Prussian patriots and reformers who, in taking the leadership in
the war of independence and the German nationalist movement
against the Napoleonic occupation, had believed that their country
would then undertake to accomplish the unity of Germany. Stein
wrote that the treaties of Vienna ended the German national movement with a "farce." And in 1832 the great historian Ranke declared:
"Never has our country been divided into so many pieces and frag-
ments foreign to one another. Never have the principalities enjoyed
such a degree of independence, and never have princes and subjects
been more jealous of it.

After the defeat of Napoleon, the German Confederation established by the treaties of 1815 simplified the Gothic fragmentation of
the German Empire, but the spirit of division championed by Talley-
rand at the Congress of Vienna survived the revolution that had
sought to destroy it. This spirit is summed up in a remark which a
French minister (Marillac) made to his king (Henri II). The minister defined the traditional foreign policy of the French monarchy
with regard to the German princes in these words: "Under cover, to
keep the affairs of Germany in the greatest possible state of confusion."
Ranke exclaimed in desperation: "Is it not necessary to renounce
completely, without deceiving ourselves any longer, any hope of
achieving German unity?"

The Impact of Revolutionary Nationalism

In France as elsewhere, the Holy Alliance of kings was so unpopular
that it provoked "the malady of 1815" amid the keenly felt but divergent aspirations that agitated the nations. Protesting against it, the
French song-writer Béranger proposed a "holy alliance of the peoples." The nationalist movement is irreversible. Can it be that the

terrible collisions that were to take place in the twentieth century, under the pressure of German nationalism, were the result of having suppressed it too long? One might think so in reading certain German eighteenth- and nineteenth-century texts, which suggest a reserved attitude toward the charge that the revolution and Napoleon III brought about frightful wars by facilitating German and Italian unity.

The ideas of 1789, carried across the various parts of Germany by French soldiers, aroused a feeling of nationality in that country. "This dear Holy Empire, how can it stay on its feet?" sing the companions of the wine cellar in Goethe's *Faust*. "German patriotism proceeds from human rights," Albert Sorel observes. The rights of man, as we know, are the legacy of Rousseau. And "Jean-Jacques Rousseau was welcomed in Germany like a Christopher Columbus," in the curious wording of Dubois-Reymond—a Prussian like all the descendants of refugees from the revocation of the Edict of Nantes.

The principle of popular sovereignty bequeathed to us by the author of the *Social Contract* was to give rise to the nationality principle. This is why the nationalist and ultra-royalist Jacques Bainville was able to write in a book about our two peoples, which caused a considerable stir in the 1920's: "Having abandoned the cosmopolitanism of the eighteenth century—a time when a German intellectual such as Lessing claimed to have no idea of love of fatherland, a time when the superiority of French civilization was unchallenged and, receiving general consent, was realizing the unity of the European world—thinking Germany turned to the most violent nationalism through the transition introduced by Rousseau and adapted to German conditions by Herder. . . . Herder, nourished by Rousseau, proposes a cosmopolitanism in which the great conflicts of nationalities and races are in gestation. This cosmopolitanism admits that every people has something precious and sacred, which no one has the right to destroy: namely, national character, the soul of the race. Language, through which this soul expresses itself, also serves to define national character. It is therefore the absolute duty of each people to cultivate and develop its own personality to the fullest extent. . . ."

This affirmation of German nationalism can be observed in the last years of the eighteenth century and the early part of the nineteenth. "Will not the Germans finally defend their own rights?" wrote the Nuremberg journalist Erhard in 1794. "I am no aristocrat at all, but I can no longer admit the pretension of French reason to establish guardianship over my German reason." Many similar texts could be cited. They would simply show us that the hegemony of the great ruling families was to be replaced (alas!) by the hegemony of the nationalisms. In 1807 and 1808, while the streets of Berlin were echoing from the steps of French nationalists, Fichte gave his famous "Lectures to the German Nation." They were to become the classical theoretical work of German nationalism. A century and a quarter later, the Third Reich was to pursue this political aberration to the point of delirium.

The pendulum of history, the motor of human psychological and moral progress, often swings so strongly as to cause incalculable suffering. But even though it may be necessary to fight the evil emanating from an idea so intepreted by certain men as to render it insane, the idea itself is not always responsible, but often rather the ignorance, selfishness, or mendacity of those who have appropriated the idea for their private property, preventing it from making history. As soon as an idea begins to fertilize reality, its explosive force—intensified by the struggle among men and by the suppression of the idea over the centuries—is able to produce abnormal and catastrophic historical situations. Even if we sympathize with Toynbee's declaration: "Everything opposed to nationalism is for me a victory of the human race," the nation nevertheless remains an essential *organic stage* in the evolution of humanity. We cannot, in the twentieth century, conceive of European and world unity except in the form of a supra-national and supra-continental unity based on the reality of nations and continents. *Political Europe is founded from the beginning on the national awareness of the peoples constituting it, and on their irrepressible desire for harmony and unity.*

The Judgment of Kantian Liberalism

The process of history has appeared to us so far as the interaction of ideas and reality. It is when reality, the nature of things, is penetrated by ideas that true history is born. Kant, in his political philosophy, defines history as one of the meeting places of the intelligible and the sensible. We have, as we have indicated, made a conception of this sort the guiding idea of our considerations: "History," wrote Kant, "is what prepares nature to submit to liberty."

But the encounter of ideas and reality does not necessarily result in the progress of liberty in the world. The great European ideologies have not always changed reality so as to advance the cause of liberty. The most sacred and true ideas have sometimes given birth to frightful worlds; how much worse the offspring of false and mendacious ideas! Ideas need therefore to be subjected to a criterion of their worth, to a human ethic, to a conception of the world, to a metaphysic.

For Kant, the criterion of historical progress is liberty. This liberty must involve a modification of reality. Liberty is the penetration of rational order into the order of perceptible or empirical data. The meaning of history will therefore be found in the progress of liberty among men. And politics itself as well as economics will find their ultimate realization in this progress. This progress of liberty, which we shall call Kantian liberalism (and which should not be confused with the liberalism of the physiocrats or of industrial capitalism) leads humanity to the republican state. The *republican state,* which is compatible with many types of government including monarchies, is the opposite of the *paternal state.* The latter seeks to impose upon its citizens its own conception of life and happiness—that which is appropriate to domination and despotism. "The essence of all government," Kant wrote, "consists of this: that each person concerns himself with his own happiness, and that each has the right to engage in commerce with every other person with this intention. The function of government is not to take this concern out of the hands of private persons, but solely to assure their harmony in accordance with the law of liberty."

These, according to the philosopher of Konigsberg, are the rules for true peaceful coexistence. The latter will lead freely to a federation of free states and to perpetual peace, the final ideal of humanity. Very different states will be able to take part in this federation, provided that they are moving toward common goals of liberty and justice. In the distance looms the idea of an ecumenical state, which can only be achieved through an elite of "enlightened" men and by taking advantage of established governmental structures.

Finally, as Kant sees it, the liberty which is the end of history should also be its means. "Kantian liberalism," writes Mr. Jean Lacroix, "is *a reformism based on a dual criticism of traditionalism and utopianism.* Kant's political philosophy is dialectic in that it proceeds from an antinomic conception of historical experience, which is the simultaneous result of moral experience and national finality."[1]

[1] *Le Monde,* August 11, 1963. M. Jean Lacroix is the philosophic critic of this paper. He is a professor at Lyon. The article in question is a review of Georges Vlachus, *Kant's Political Youth,* and E. Weil, *Kant's Political Philosophy,* both published by the Presse Universitaire de France in 1962.

This judgment of Kant's political philosophy proved a valuable guide to us in developing the present discussion. As soon as it has been determined to classify Franco-German reconciliation as one of the great events of the twentieth century, the need to understand the liberty that our two peoples may gain from this event suggests the next logical step: an analysis of the spirit of Franco-German relations during the last ten centuries. This analysis, extending over the entire historic struggle of our two countries, makes evident the phenomenon of "Kantian reformism," based on a dual criticism of the traditionalism and the utopianism which have oriented German and French politics.

Under the pretext of defending the idea of Empire, of protecting "German liberties," of freeing oppressed minorities, of proclaiming the principle of popular sovereignty, of affirming the natural right of peoples to self-determination, or the pretext of asserting the priority of the nation or the race, etc., the politicians of France and Germany sought to exploit traditionalism or utopianism to secure the triumph of their common instinct of domination—an instinct which led *ipso facto* to the subjugation of one of the two peoples and of the powers allied to it at the time.

But behind this hegemonial instinct there always remained the *ancient dream of unity* which haunts humanity. For this dream to be realized, it must first come to fruition here or there—in each province, in each country, within each continent—while waiting for this ancient dream to "precipitate" in the manner of chemical reactions, producing a unique substance in which each constituent element is perfectly complemented by its union with the other elements. Now this perfect complementation which, to "precipitate" European unity, must come into existence between our two peoples, requires that France and Germany acknowledge a common spirit, the *spirit of Europe*. This is a spirit which transcends the level of their particular interests, does not injure them, but quite to the contrary promotes their economic, social, cultural, and religious accomplishment, being guided by the principle of subordination which already governs the constitution of Federal Germany, and which should govern each province with regard to its nationality, each nation with regard to its continentality, each continent in relation to the world, and—so far as we are concerned—each European nation in relation to Europe. This principle of subordination is the constituent factor of a unity broader and deeper than merely the simple juxtaposition of the political and geographic structures of nations among themselves—a juxtaposition which gives free rein to the spirit of domination.

Paul Hazard has spoken to us of "the crisis of European conscience" in a book that has become classic, analysing the revolution of ideas which, beginning with the Renaissance and even in the midst of the century of Louis XIV, started the chain of events leading to the political and social upheavals familiar to us. But even though a European awareness existed at a very early date in the field of culture (the cultural cosmopolitanism of the seventeenth century based upon French civilization), the same cannot be said for the fields of economics, social welfare, politics, geography, and so forth. Modern times, by reducing distances, by enlarging economic systems, by concentrating specialized activities and by bringing about the appearance east of Europe of a common immediate menace to the liberty and security of its peoples, have fostered the broadening of this awareness in areas in which it had not yet surmounted the geographic level of the province, of the nation, of treaties or of alliances. This is how the economic life, the societal life, and the political life of the European nations have in our contemporary period become penetrated by the European conscience, the European spirit.

But such an awareness and such a spirit remove the mortgage of the goals of domination pursued successively by the great European powers. These hegemonial goals were, as we have indicated, gratified under the cover of traditionalism (such as the hegemony of Charles V, that of Louis XIV, or the imperialism of Queen Victoria) or that of utopianism (as in the case of the French Revolution, the Napoleonic Empire, or Hitler's Reich). While traditionalism served the protection of Europe's historical liberties, utopianism fostered the progress of human self-knowledge and of individual and national liberty. In order for such a common awareness to arise in Europe—an awareness sanctioned today by "technical Europe" and which will be sanctioned tomorrow by "political Europe"—it has been necessary in this twentieth century for the hegemonial instinct of the great nations, justified by the convenient pretext of spreading traditional or utopian ideologies, to emigrate beyond the Oder, to that great empire of the steppes, the reservoir of all the great invasions that, over the course of the centuries, overflowed the extreme western peninsula of Asia. It so happens that the emigration of this hegemonial instinct was made possible by contagion of Europe's most recent "utopian" virus, cultivated for the last 46 years on its easternmost marches. It is at this price—a disturbing price, since it may lead to a paralysis of history in Europe—that the European community has acquired the faculty of knowing itself.

The experience summarized shows how strikingly Kant's philosophical dialectic concerning the political evolution of the world is justified by the empirical situation. This philosophy illustrates a coherent plan of nature, a "kind of natural necessity of final effectiveness," a deception which obtains from men what reason could not have obtained. The liberty and the unity of the European peoples, those of Germany and France in particular, are initially a liberty and a unity forced by necessity, before becoming a liberty and a unity determined by higher objectives. Nature paves the road for liberty by permitting the birth of a "free" European community, determined by the necessity in which the nations of Europe find themselves—the necessity of awaking to their unity in the face of the immediate threat to their security from the East.

European awareness is also in the process of realizing an objective which neither Charles V, nor Louis XIV, nor Napoleon, nor Queen Victoria, nor Hitler were able to achieve, and which the Concert of Europe disdained, because of the instinct of domination that falsified their great designs of unity or equilibrium. European awareness is achieving this objective through the economic community which is now developing and the political community which is being prepared. There is no doubt that Franco-German reconciliation will be the cornerstone of the future European community.

Toward a European Polity

Our argument may be summed up as follows: the national idea permitted the peoples of Europe to become aware of themselves, but nationalism also limited this self-awareness and gave rise to the same political ills as did monarchism. It was necessary for Russia to expand to a world power in order that Europe might surmount the nationality principle as a final political objective, becoming aware of itself as a federal entity *endowed with* power." The two national states capable of fostering the constitution of this federal entity are, of course, the two complementary powers of Western Europe: Germany and France.

Until very recently, monarchical and national powers have "parodied Europe" because of the hegemonial spirit which was dominant in Paris, Vienna, and Berlin. Behind the Europe of the monarchies or of the nations, there was always skulking the hegemony of one monarchy or one nation. Hegemony is Europe's "Trojan horse," its malady, the "virus" which forbids its existence as a political reality. Only a complementary Franco-German policy will permit the birth of a political Europe. The history of the last European millenium has been a game of hide-and-go-seek between the Germanies and France —a deception constantly renewed, which under the pretext of European equilibrium or unity has nourished the spirit of hegemony, and therefore that of division between the two constituent powers of Europe: Germany and France.

Today, Germany and France need to look at each other face to face so as to get to know each other, to understand the ways in which they complement each other, and the extent to which such complementation is a constituent factor for the Europe of tomorrow. The existence of a world power to the east of Europe may serve to stimulate such an awakening as well as the crystallization of Europe in its natural dimensions. What is to be avoided is that other nations or other continents, such as the United States or the Soviet Union, practice with regard to Franco-German reconciliation or that of Europe in general the same politics of anarchy which France practiced for centuries with regard to the Holy German Empire, which was condemned to picture-puzzle fragmentation by the treaties of Westphalia.

CHAPTER XII

America's Changing View of Europe

FRITZ T. EPSTEIN

THE ASSUMPTION THAT AMERICA has ever entertained a single image of Europe, or that a "standard" American picture of Europe exists at the present time—an assumption which the title assigned for this contribution might seem to suggest—is in no way supported by factual study of what Americans have said and written about Europe during the various phases of recent history. In a country with the freedom of speech and publication traditional in the United States, it is never possible—except at those moments when emotional mass thinking paralyzes and overwhelms rational individual thought —to discover or specify a standard image of Europe typical of and suggestively effective on broad strata of the population. There are impressions and conceptions, as well as preconceived judgments of European countries, that change from time to time. But there is no single American picture of Europe, the metamorphosis of which could be recorded.

The German Chargé d'Affaires in Washington, Dr. Hans Thomsen, submitted on March 27, 1939, a report to Berlin concerning the objectives and limitations of American foreign policy. In this report, which takes up five large pages in Volume VI of the *Documents on German Foreign Policy* of the Hitler era, Dr. Thomsen passes the following flattering judgment on American thinking:

"In general, the average American understands nothing of European history and European politics; he has an opinion on everything, however, if it is only suggested to him often enough. In addition, there is the proneness to wild enthusiasm and the emotionalism for which the American is well known; instruments upon which every agitator and every world reformer can play."[1]

The reference to "agitators and world reformers" was obviously directed at the President of the United States, Franklin Delano Roosevelt. Six years later, Colonel-General Jodl declared in a statement recorded in the War Diary of the German Supreme Command on May 13, 1945:

"The Allied delegation has no comprehension whatsoever of our German problems or those of Europe. This is especially true of the American college professor."[2]

It goes without saying that such blanket judgments of the intellectual attitude and political maturity of a people not subjected to a totalitarian propaganda machine must always be treated with appropriate skepticism and reserve.

Attempts to piece together into a unified image the tiny mosaic stones on which attitudes toward other peoples are registered, constitute one of the criteria by which historical writers and journalists attempt to gauge relations among nations. Gustav Stolper has said that it is simple to see a country from outside, but difficult to see it *correctly* from outside.[3] It is difficult when the problem is not only to judge the partner correctly in a specific situation—an accomplishment prerequisite for any successful foreign policy—but also to know the process by which the partner has arrived at *his opinion* which, consciously or unconsciously, determines his actions. With these thoughts in mind, the *Deutsche Rundschau* is currently sponsoring analyses of the image of Germany in various countries and regions of the world. The editors have correctly pointed out that the studies of the notions entertained in one country about another are *more* than mere analyses of nations; they are also analyses of cultures.[4]

The picture which Europe presents, with its societal and social, its

[1] *Documents on German Foreign Policy, 1918-1945*, Series D, Vol. VI (London, H. M. Stationery Office, 1956), p. 131.

[2] *Kriegstagebuch des Oberkommandos der Wehrmacht*, Vol. IV, Part 2 (Frankfurt/Main, Bernard & Graefe, 1961), p. 1500.

[3] Gustav Stolper, *German Realities* (New York, Reynal and Hitchcock, 1948).

[4] Series of articles: "Deutschland von draussen gesehen," introductory remarks. *Deutsche Rundschau*, Vol. 89, No. 7 (Stuttgart, July, 1963), p. 30.

economic and scientific, and its military and political aspects, is of such a dazzling and self-contradictory multiplicity, that an attempt to abstract out of it an American image of Europe would be a futile undertaking.

Considerations of time and space limit this paper to a highly eclectic treatment of certain American statements which bear on the political picture of postwar Europe: the picture of Europe as seen and characterized by Americans, and the *Wunschbild* of Europe as Americans would like to have it. There is, as we have noted, no *single* American picture of Europe. Instead, brief attention will be given to a procession of images of Europe—a variety of alternating and shifting impressions and distortions of Europe heard in American public statements since the end of the war. These citations will serve to characterize briefly the ideas and beliefs on which the European policies of Presidents Truman, Eisenhower, and Kennedy have been based; to delineate the contrast between George Kennan and John Foster Dulles; and to clarify the inseparable connection of the Berlin question, the German question, and the East European question within the framework of postwar American-Soviet relations.

American historical and political-science treatment of Europe is currently subordinated to and coordinated with the over-all problem of worldwide American-Soviet rivalry, which has determined and overshadowed the destiny of the world since the end of World War II. The political contest between the United States and the Soviet Union has extended not only to Europe, but to Asia, Africa, and South America as well. It is, however, Europe, always Europe, to which the two world powers direct their concentrated energies as champions of opposite ideologies and social orders. The so-called Old World continues to represent an inexhaustible reservoir of material and intellectual values that neither the free world nor Communism cares to abandon. A basis exists, therefore, for the contention that since the war American thinking about Europe has been very strongly influenced, consciously or unconsciously, by the Soviet image of Europe and Soviet European policy—so strongly, in fact, that the term dependence is not entirely out of place. A survey limited to the European aspects of post-World War II American-Soviet relations would still include the most urgent and vital questions of contemporary world politics: the problem of security, including atomic policy, defense, deterrence, and disarmament; and the problem of reunification, or the questions of Germany and Berlin. The observations to follow should, therefore, always be understood against the background of the question, whether or not explicitly stated: How does the Kremlin look at the matter, what does the Kremlin say? European problems—as seen from America—must in the present situation be understood in terms of the contrast between the United States and the Soviet Union and the efforts to reach a settlement.

As early as 1952, Carlo Schmid saw looming on the horizon the danger that the relationship of the United States to Germany was, or could become, a function of the fluctuating American relationship with the Soviet Union.[5] Schmid's perception turned out to be correct. A decade later, the historian Kurt Borries was able to describe the German question as the historically conditioned and sanctioned mutual orientation of East and West in German destiny.[6]

National Socialism, which claimed that it was entitled to be regarded as the final liquidator of the philosophy of the French Revolution, has always been regarded in America as standing in absolute opposition to all the values which are anchored in American national and political consciousness. Except for a few outsiders, Americans have always rejected it emphatically and fought it with determination. The same applies to other European authoritarian ideologies.

The American historical judgment of Hitler and of National Socialism is firmly established. William Shirer's book, *The Rise and Fall of the Third Reich,* has darkened further the shadows in the sombre picture. Shirer failed to take advantage of the opportunity to show the lights as well as the shadows, that is, to do justice to the German resistance movement against Hitler. Within the last few months an American, David L. Hoggan, has appeared upon the scene as an apologist for Hitler with a book entitled *Der erzwungene Krieg* [The Unwanted War],[7] initially published in Germany, which in this author's opinion contains many grave errors in selection and interpretation of historical data. Hoggan has been presented to the German public as the champion of a movement in American historiography comparable to the

    5 Carlo Schmid, "Die Aussenpolitik des Machtlosen," *Aussenpolitik*, Vol. III, No. 1 (January, 1952), p. 18.

    6 Kurt Borries, *Deutschland im Kreis der europäischen Mächte* (Stuttgart, Bernhard Tauchnitz Verlag, 1963), p. 208.

    7 David L. Hoggan, *Der erzwungene Krieg: Die Ursachen und Urheber des 2. Weltkriegs* (Veröffentlichungen des Instituts für deutsche Nachkriegsgeschichte, Vol. I). (Tübingen, Verlag der Deutschen Hochschullehrerzeitung, 1962.) See also: Hermann Graml, "David L. Hoggan und die Dokumente," in *Geschichte in Wissenschaft und Unterricht,* Vol. 14 (1963), pp. 492-514, and William L. Langer's letters to the editors of this journal, *ibid.*, pp. 556f, and of the American Historical Review (October, 1963), pp. 304f.

historical revisionism which followed World War I, and certain circles
in Germany have greeted him with unrestrained enthusiasm. Actually,
Hoggan is practically alone in his views. It would, however, be a mistake not to pay careful attention to the effects of this misleading book
—even though it provides a miserable historic foundation for neo-
Nazism—since its promoters have made secondary schools their special
target of distribution.

A publication of the United States Department of State issued in
1950 under the title *Postwar Foreign Policy Preparation, 1939-1945,*
brings out the fact that American peace planning during World War
II did not anticipate any far-reaching difference of opinion with the
Soviet Union. Even less did the possibility of a subsequent cold war
enter into American calculations. Almost all evaluations were based
on the assumption that after the war the Soviet Union would work
closely and honestly with the Western powers. Only very occasionally
were doubts expressed in official documents. One of the few exceptions
may be found in a memorandum of the Departmental Committee on
Germany dated September 23, 1943, in which the statement appears
(p. 559: "The Political Reorganization of Germany") that it was "a
marked disadvantage, both from the viewpoint of political warfare
against National Socialism and from the viewpoint of preparing the
democratic forces of Germany for action," that the United States and
British Governments had never announced their support of a future
German democracy. Instead, a democratic program for Germany had
made its appearance under tacit Russian patronage. This could lead
to a situation in which Communists would secure control of the German democratic movement, resulting in the establishment of Russian
hegemony in Germany. Such a development could only be prevented
by Anglo-American support of moderate elements, encouraging them
to participate and to transform the movement into a genuinely democratic one.

In evaluating the phraseology of this memorandum, it must be
kept in mind that the ideas expressed implied criticism of an ally by
an agency of the United States Government at a time when differences
were being belittled and criticism of the Soviet Union was more or
less taboo. The memorandum, nevertheless, contains not only a prophetic warning of the coming struggle of East and West after the war
with Germany as the prize, but also an explanation (among others)
for the passive and negative attitude of the Western powers and America in particular toward the German resistance movement. This atti-

tude, which is deeply to be regretted, refused to take into account the German and European aims of the anti-Nazi resistance. Those who today still regard this movement as reactionary disregard fifteen years of historical research. There is tragedy in the fact that for a long time the democratic West shared the judgment of Hitler and his spokesmen regarding the resistance movement and the attempt to assassinate Hitler on July 20, 1944. In the latter case, the Western propaganda agencies permitted themselves to be completely taken in by Goebbels' propaganda about the conspiracy of an officers' clique. We are justified in asking the question: How would Europe look today if the Allies had been willing to encourage the German resistance and to make concessions in case of a successful overthrow of the National Socialist regime, instead of committing themselves to the politics of Unconditional Surrender and the Morgenthau Plan?

In a conversation with Roosevelt's envoy Sumner Welles on March 1, 1940, Ribbentrop explained the "German Monroe Doctrine" of National Socialism:

"The German Monroe Doctrine signified that there existed a German sphere of interest in Eastern Europe which was no concern to England, France, and other Western countries; this was a matter that Germany had to discuss with only one power, Soviet Russia, with whom an understanding had already been reached."[8]

While American wartime diplomacy viewed in retrospect evinces inconceivable blindness regarding the postwar politics of the Soviet Union, the National Socialist-Communist accommodation which Ribbentrop so highly praised represented an even greater historical blunder from the German point of view. It led, at the end of the war, to the carrying into practice of a "Soviet Monroe Doctrine" for Eastern Europe and East Central Europe, penetrating deeply into Central Germany ("Mitteldeutschland"—currently the "German Democratic Republic," in fact, the Soviet Occupation Zone).

Gustav Stolper, one of Germany's leading economic writers during the Weimar Republic and a refugee in the United States since 1933, published a book entitled *German Realities* in 1948[9]—a book that Theodor Heuss called "a matter not of human sentimentality but of

[8] *Documents on German Foreign Policy, 1918-1945,* Series D, Vol. VIII (Washington, Government Printing Office, 1954), p. 823.

[9] See note 3, *supra.*

intellectual passion."[10] It portrays the shocking balance of two years of American occupation policy in Germany, drawn with the acute perception of a scholar intimately familiar with both the American and the European economy. Stolper observed conditions in Germany as an economic adviser to former President Herbert Hoover during the latter's mission to Europe in February, 1947. There was no other book then, and there is still no other book, that describes so persuasively the biological, moral, and material destruction of Germany at the end of the war and the interdependence of German and European economic life, and which analyses and criticizes so competently the questions that seemed most urgent in 1947—the issues of reparations, of the German war potential, and the consequent demand for an internationalization of the Ruhr, and the questions of socialization, decartelization, and the future constitution. Stolper concluded his book with these words: "The future of Germany is the future of European liberty. In Germany it will triumph or die."[11]

One must look far—or more accurately, one will look in vain—to find an analysis which judges the role of the Soviet Union in what were then the present and the future more realistically than Stolper does in the final chapter of his book. No deceit could hide from him the fact that the Russian Occupation Zone of Germany was already almost totally Sovietized in 1947. That this development was inevitable, Stolper observes, was clear from the outset to anyone with the most rudimentary knowledge of the nature and functioning of the Russian system. At no stage in its history had Soviet Russia ever indicated that it possessed the faculty for cooperation on a basis of equality with any partner whatsoever. One of the mysteries which future historians will have to unravel is how the responsible leaders of America, after their experiences during the war, could have erred so badly on this point. At the moment of decision to establish a West German state, Stolper predicted, a Soviet Germany would "in fact if not in name, be ready to be integrated into the system of Eastern European states under the thumb of Soviet rule."[12] Stolper summarized the Soviet policy of those days in the formula that the Kremlin sought a bolshevized Eastern Germany as a springboard for the bolshevization of all Germany, and a Communist Germany as the last stage preparatory to a conquest of

[10] Gustav Stolper, *German Realities;* postscript by Theodor Heuss to the German edition: *Die deutsche Wirklichkeit, ein Beitrag zum zukünftigen Frieden Europas* (Hamburg, Claassen & Goverts, 1949), p. 369.

[11] Stolper, *op. cit.,* English ed., p. 256.

[12] *Ibid.,* p. 240.

Western Europe by the Communist parties. Should the siren song of Communism fail to captivate the German people, it was still possible to fall back on a Soviet appeal to traditional German-Russian anti-Western friendship, that is, a revival of the politics of Rapallo.

Stolper underestimated the regenerative potential of Western Europe. He believed that the best that a generous Marshall Plan could accomplish—and the basic ideas of the Marshall Plan are in part attributable to Stolper[13]—was to maintain Europe in a state of semi-viability. He also believed that Germany's military history had come to a definite and final end. Germany, he thought, would remain "an uncanny mystery to the world"[14] until it recovered its power of speech. Germany *has* recovered its power of speech, but has remained a riddle for many—particularly in recent months.

The events of the Korean War intensified European fears that the Soviet army could easily overrun the armies of the West. An American evaluation of West European armed forces in 1951 led to the conclusion that twenty more divisions were needed to guarantee a minimum defense of Western Europe. To make up this deficit of forces, the Americans demanded West German rearmament—thereby upsetting the Allied German policy of the immediate postwar years and raising anew the question of Germany's position in Europe. Walter Lippmann believed at that time that the Americans would have to remain in Germany until that nation—through its own sovereign decision and action—should become integrated into a European system.[15] By this he meant, first of all, a reconciliation between a reunited Germany and France, sealed by a Franco-German alliance through which the two states should commit themselves to a common foreign policy. These are the ideas of an American in 1952, and not those of de Gaulle in 1962! Until Germany and France had fully made peace with each other, the armed forces of the Atlantic Community would have to keep up the "Watch on the Rhine." Starting with the principle that German unity and European unity were inseparable, Lippmann concluded that a European system could only come into being when a German-French partnership existed.

Lippmann pointed out that recognition of the German eastern

13 Toni Stolper, *Ein Leben in Brennpunkten unserer Zeit—Wien, Berlin, New York—Gustav Stolper, 1888-1947* (Tübingen, Wunderlich, 1960), pp. 462 and 468.

14 Gustav Stolper, *op. cit.*, English ed., p. 256.

15 Walter Lippmann, "Amerikanische Gedanken zur deutschen Einheit," *Aussenpolitik*, Vol. III, No. 12 (December, 1952), p. 782.

boundaries of Potsdam by a reunited Germany would mean renunciation by the United States of all right to participate in the reorganization of Europe east of the Elbe, and actually east of the Rhine. A reunited Germany would have to cultivate good-neighborly relations with Poland. Only when German-French-Polish understanding had been achieved would it be possible to speak with any certainty of a unified Europe and of a European system.

The official policy of the Truman Administration vis-à-vis the Soviet Union was the *policy of containment* championed by George F. Kennan. This policy left no doubt that America was determined to call a halt to Soviet and Communist expansion. It led to the Korean War, in which the Soviet Union scrupulously refrained from direct intervention, leaving the active role to Communist China.

Not the least of the factors contributing to Eisenhower's electoral victory of 1952 was his promise to bring the Korean War to an early end. The Republican platform of that year denounced the Truman Administration's policy of containment or dike-building as "negative, futile, and immoral."[16] The prospect of a policy of liberation for the Soviet-enslaved peoples, to be conducted by a Republican President, was held out as bait for the voters of Polish, Czech, and Hungarian descent. Eisenhower's supporters promised the discontinuance of an anti-Communist war, while at the same time they demanded or announced a policy which did not seem to shrink before the risk of a new war. It soon became apparent, however, that the Eisenhower Administration was just as loath to incur the risk of a war with the Soviet Union as the Democratic Administration had been. On two occasions, that of the uprising in the Soviet Zone on June 17, 1953, and that of the 1956 October Revolution in Hungary, the Eisenhower government found itself facing the inescapable question of how seriously the liberation policy proclaimed by John Foster Dulles was really meant. And on both occasions it turned out that Eisenhower's policy of liberation was in no way different from the Truman policy of containment.

The so-called policy of liberation revealed itself as "a policy of inactivity plus empty words," which aroused unrealistic and vain hopes.

Neither Eisenhower nor John Foster Dulles took any pains to hide the fact that the policy of linking Germany to the West through military integration was based to a certain degree on distrust for the Ger-

[16] Republican Party, 25th Republican National Convention held in Chicago, Ill., July, 1952, *Proceedings* (Washington, 1952), p. 313.

man people. Germany was considered to be continually tempted to play off the West and the East against each other.[17] In the Senate Committee on Foreign Relations, Senator George D. Aiken (Republican, Vermont) asked Secretary Dulles on June 6, 1958, whether a reunited Germany might not be a threat to the peace of Europe and possibly the whole world. The Secretary answered in pertinent part:

"I think it is very important, Senator, that a reunited Germany should be integrated into the West through its association with NATO, through its participation in the Brussels Treaty of the Western European Union, through participation in the Coal and Steel Community, Euratom, the common market, and things of that sort.

"I believe that a Germany which was left in a position of neutrality, or some people call it disengagement in the center of Europe, would be under an almost irresistible temptation to play one side or the other, and that that would be a very dangerous situation, dangerous for the West, dangerous for the Soviet Union, and dangerous for the Germans, themselves. . . .

"So the answer to your question is this: I would not think it was wise or prudent to try to buy reunification of Germany at the price of having Germany an independent country unrelated to the West. . . ."[18]

American discussions of the European future are marked by a basic difference of opinion concerning policies on Berlin and Germany, depending on whether the question of reunification is regarded as an acute and urgent issue of *Realpolitik,* or as purely theoretical, imaginary, and utopian at the present time. A growing current in American public opinion leans toward the latter view. Walter Lippmann, previously an advocate of reunification, caused a sensation during the spring of 1959 by shifting over to the camp supporting the theory of the inevitable and unlimited coexistence of two Germanies. His reasoning was that honesty required admitting the fact that, for the foreseeable future, German reunification had ceased to be practical politics. As long as Germany remained divided, special protective meas-

---

17 Herbert von Borch, "Amerika und Russland," *Aussenpolitik,* Vol. X, No. 2 (February, 1959), p. 72.

18 United States Senate (85th Congress, 2d Session), Committee on Foreign Relations, hearings, *Review of Foreign Policy, 1958* (Washington, Government Printing Office, 1958), pp. 804-05.

ures would be necessary for Berlin. Lippmann's proposal was to transfer Berlin to United Nations trusteeship, and to write a statute for Germany which would regulate the right of free access to Berlin, relationships between West and East Berlin and between the two Germanies, as well as the symbolic presence of Allied and United Nations troops in Berlin.[19] More than once, Lippmann has criticized harshly the West German attitude toward negotiations about the future of Germany. He predicted not long ago in the New York *Herald Tribune* that there will soon be Germans who are more interested in reunification than in petty bickering about degrees of diplomatic recognition.

On the occasion of Lippmann's change of opinion, a liberal weekly, *The New Republic,* circulated a questionnaire that became the basis for a symposium on the German problem. Louis C. Halle, a former member of the Planning Staff of the Department of State, pointed out in his reply that the world was becoming increasingly accustomed to regard the existence of two Germanies as normal, just as after the foundation of the Reich in 1871 it had been considered normal to have two Germanies, one of which was called Austria.[20] After the end of World War II, opinion had been widespread in the United States that the Soviet Zone would become for West Germany what Alsace-Lorraine had been for the French after 1871. This had not turned out to be the case, and the world outside Germany had come to accept the division. Halle believed that widespread support for the partition existed even inside Germany; for a new generation was emerging, to which the two Germanies would appear normal. Less and less was being said about a liberation of the inhabitants of Central Germany and the only hope—if any hope existed at all—lay in a step-by-step easement of the situation, a liberation through evolution.

In a speech on U.S. policy toward Germany, Senator Wayne Morse (Democrat, Oregon) remarked on August 19, 1963:

"We share, and sympathize with, the ultimate objective of the reunification of Germany. . . . The partition of Germany became a fact. The government set up by the Communists became just as real as if we recognized it. . . . The separation and dismemberment of the country became a German legacy from the Third Reich.

[19] "Solution for Berlin," *The New Republic,* Vol. 140, No. 19 (May 11, 1959), p. 9; and Walter Lippmann, "The Problem of Berlin," *ibid.,* Vol. 140, No. 22 (June 1, 1959), pp. 9-10.

[20] Louis J. Halle, "Back to 'Normalcy,'" in "Solution for Berlin," *loc. cit.,* pp. 9-11.

"So I think, it is fair for Americans to ask the Bonn Government if the Communist Government is not just as real as it can
ever get. And does not rejection of any and all dealings with the
East German Government really confirm and harden the Division
of Germany, and make impossible any change in the status quo?
Is Bonn satisfied to keep reunification as a hypothetical objective
instead of a practical one? And how long does it think the rest of
the world—the rest of the Western World—will respect and share
its policy of non-recognition when that policy has no apparent
objective, no apparent end, and no apparent relationship to
reality?"[21]

The Administration in Washington was, as could be expected, prompt
and emphatic in disclaiming Senator Morse's views.

But there are not a few Americans who argue in the following way:
The Germans, in 1933, entrusted their fate to Hitler, a *hasardeur*.
He lost the game, and now they wince and wriggle and writhe, rather
than reconciling themselves to their fate. Within twelve years, Hitler
ruined Germany, a great power even after her defeat in 1918. Through
the dizzying events between 1933 and 1945, the Germans completely
lost historical perspective—the awareness that long periods of preparation are needed for changes which are to last. The Reich, entirely deprived of its moral credit within twelve years, might need, perhaps, 120
years for becoming once more *one* Reich of the Germans in the West
and the East.

In the present situation characterized by a frozen status quo, some
consolation may be derived from Lincoln's Springfield speech of June
16, 1858, in which he spoke of the house divided against itself that
could not stand, and expressed his conviction that a state could not
remain permanently half slave and half free.[22]

The boundaries of 1937 are frequently invoked in Germany today.
It is true that the division of Germany into occupation zones was undertaken on the basis of the borders of December 31, 1937 (with the

21 *Congressional Record* (88th Congress, 1st Session), Vol. 109, No. 128, August 19, 1963
(Senate), p. 14474. Morse's ideas bear great similarity to those of Senator Claiborne Pell
(Dem., R. I.); see Pell's article: "Berlin: A New Approach," reprinted from *The Nation*,
June 22, 1963, in *Congressional Record, loc. cit.*, June 19, 1963, appendix, pp. 3913-14,
and Pell's remarks in the Senate, August 28, 1963, p. 15257.

22 Abraham Lincoln, *The Collected Works* (Roy P. Basler, ed.), Vol. II (New Bruns-
wick, Rutgers Univ. Press, 1953), p. 461. Quoted by Willy Brandt in speech of Feb. 12,
1959; see *Aussenpolitik*, Vol. X, No. 4 (April, 1959), p. 209.

exception of East Prussia, which Stalin had demanded).[23] The question, however, whether the Allies, in choosing this date, intended to set a precedent for the territorial provisions of a future peace has not to my knowledge been considered or clarified anywhere in the whole voluminous literature on Allied war aims. Golo Mann has characterized the borders of 1937 as a state of affairs belonging to the past, something which has become imaginary and which only an ivory-tower conception of justice—Mann used a 10-syllable word: *Studierstubengerechtigkeitsbegriff*—can clothe with reality.[24]

West German revisionist efforts might perhaps enjoy a greater prospect of success if more attention were paid to the question of how to achieve just and effective protection for the *legal rights of minorities* in the East. It must be assumed for this purpose that Germans from the West would again be free and willing to migrate in large numbers to the former German East and to neighboring countries east of Germany. Instead of such studies, unlimited legal expertise, motivated by touching love of homeland, is dedicated to justifying a right to homeland (*Heimatrecht*) not hitherto recognized by international law. Outside Germany it has not been forgotten that after 1933 this legal principle was regarded as nonexistent for and inapplicable to *non*-Germans, who were the victims of actual or planned expulsions and mass resettlements. With all due respect and admiration for the efforts of champions of a right to homeland, there is—if I am not very much mistaken—no prospect that this ideal will achieve recognition as a positive legal norm of international law, as long as this so-called right to homeland is regarded abroad as a political instrument for territorial revision in favor of Germany, and not as a means of helping to realize the idea of humanity, so often scorned and trampled upon in our generation.

A feature of America's picture of Germany is the firm belief that during the Eisenhower-Dulles era consideration for Adenauer paralyzed American moves toward a diplomatic initiative in Europe. When it comes to writing the history of German-American relationships in the Adenauer era, one of the most difficult, but also most rewarding, themes will be to bring into evidence what has been called Bonn's invisible veto over Washington. Only then will it be possible to state

---

[23] Draft instrument entitled "Unconditional Surrender of Germany," July 25, 1944, *Foreign Relations of the United States, The Conferences at Malta and Yalta, 1945* (Washington, Government Printing Office, 1955), p. 114.

[24] *Stuttgarter Zeitung*, January 26, 1957.

with certainty whether at any time American assurances to the Soviet Union—intended to facilitate her retreat and to reduce the dependence of the satellites on the Soviet Union—were withheld because of requests or suggestions from Bonn. (In view of the different dimensions of power concerned, it is impossible to speak of pressure.) Only such research will establish with certainty whether the Federal Chancellor discouraged constructive American ideas for conversations with the Russians. We will then also be in a position to evaluate the truth of Fritz R. Allemann's incisive, if not delusive, characterization of German-American relations during the last few years: that thinking and action on the shores of the Potomac are dynamic and follow the maxim that it is better to do something risky than nothing—while on the banks of the Rhine they are static and follow the argument that it is better to do *nothing* than something risky.[25]

No American has produced a more penetrating analysis of the European situation resulting from the war, and of American-Soviet relations in particular, than George Frost Kennan. Kennan's thoughts, presented since the end of the 1940's with the objectivity of an historian and the responsibility of a diplomat, have been regarded as highly significant, not only in politically interested circles in America and Western Europe, but even in the Kremlin. A knowledge of the essence of Kennan's arguments may be taken for granted. The lectures published under the title *American Diplomacy, 1900-1950*,[26] have assumed revolutionary importance for the historical and political observation and analysis of the forces behind the excessively moralistic ostensible motives and the exaggerated legalism of American foreign policy during the first half of this century. Care should be taken, however, not to overlook the empirical element in American politics. According to Henry A. Kissinger, "our empiricism dooms us to an essentially reactive policy that improvises a counter to every Soviet move."[27]

For some years, a variety of neutralization and disengagement plans have been advanced as possible ways of averting a collision by separating the Eastern and Western power blocs. The present discussion must be limited to a few American contributions to the history of the disengagement idea. In connection with all these proposals, the

---

25 Fritz René Allemann, *Zwischen Stabilität und Krise: Etappen der deutschen Politik 1955-1963* (Munich, Piper Verlag, 1963), p. 237.

26 Chicago, University of Chicago Press, 1951.

27 Henry A. Kissinger, "Reflections on American Diplomacy," *Foreign Affairs*, Vol. XXXV, No. 1 (October, 1956), p. 40. (A German translation appeared in *Aussenpolitik*, Vol. VIII, No. 1, January, 1957.)

essential question for us is the determination of the relationship between disengagement and German reunification. Opinions are diametrically opposed on the questions as to whether disengagement is likely to lead automatically to reunification (an improbable proposition) and whether reunification must be regarded as a precondition for disengagement.

Kennan declared in 1958 that the withdrawal of Russian troops from Central and Eastern Europe was far preferable in principle to the organization of a new German army. He recommended that the military bipolarity of the world be overcome through creation of a neutral zone, in which a reunited Germany would become an important factor. Kennan, at least at that time, regarded a neutralized Central Europe as a sheet anchor that could serve to prevent an armed conflict between the East and the West. He was skeptical of the proposition that the stationing of American troops in Germany constituted an indispensable pledge of United States military interest in Europe. Kennan felt that this commitment overstrained America by subjecting the nation to excessive and protracted demands, and that the strength and capacity of the European states were being underrated.[28] Kennan's proposals brought the Berlin question, the German and Central European questions, and American interests within an imposing structure of integrated thought. His opinions were, however, of such an unorthodox, uncomfortable, and unpopular nature that they were bound to arouse vigorous objections.

Former Secretary of State Dean Acheson described Kennan's ideas as "mystical."[29] In a declaration published by the nonpartisan American Council on Germany, leading American experts on Germany, including Professors Carl Joachim Friedrich, Hans Kohn, George N. Shuster, and James B. Conant, took a position in opposition to Kennan. Kennan's critics emphasized that failure to station missiles and atomic weapons in the European NATO states would make the world practically defenseless in the face of Soviet threats of attack. In this declaration, as well as in many Western statements both before and later,

[28] George Frost Kennan, *Russia, the Atom and the West* (New York, Harper, 1958)—the Reith lectures. See also James E. King, Jr. "Kennanism and Disengagement," *The New Republic*, Vol. 138, No. 14 (April 7, 1958), pp. 12-16.

[29] "Dean Acheson Scores Kennan Proposal to Withdraw US, British and USSR Troops from Europe," *New York Times*, January 12, 1958, pp. 1, 24-25. In this statement, Acheson accuses Kennan of "a rather mystical attitude" toward the realities of power relationships. See also Acheson's article criticizing Kennan: "The Illusion of Disengagement," *Foreign Affairs*, Vol. XXXVI, No. 3 (April 1958), pp. 371-82.

the entire argument was based on the self-evident assumption of the world-revolutionary drive of Communism. The subject of *German* expansion was hardly mentioned, even though Germany, during the First and Second World Wars, erected temporary military empires in the East, which are responsible for understandable security complexes among Germany's eastern neighbors. Although they are recognized in the United States, these complexes are not taken seriously enough in West Germany, where they are downgraded and held up to scorn.[30] There is a sound basis for the assertion that the need for security against Germany is still today one of the decisive elements of Soviet German policy.

If the terms "static" and "dynamic" are to be used with reference to the Russian policies of Bonn and Washington, it should then also be remembered that the policy of liberation for Eastern Europe proclaimed by John Foster Dulles was introduced as a dynamic American forward strategy directed at rolling back the Iron Curtain. Compared with this policy, Kennan's doctrine of containment must necessarily appear static, since it accepted a status quo based on the situation in the Soviet theater of operations at the end of the war and on the theory of spheres of responsibility transformed into spheres of influence.

Kennan has remained remarkably faithful to the disengagement idea. In a television appearance in August, 1963, he returned to the subject of a withdrawal of American and Russian troops from Central Europe.[31] It would not, he said, be necessary for the United States to withdraw all their troops. A compromise could be found, which would limit American troops to specific garrisons in Europe. The thing to be avoided was the demand for a unilateral withdrawal of Soviet troops from the former Soviet Zone—the usual form in which troop withdrawals had been proposed in the past. The United States should endeavor to reach an agreement with the Soviets, under which both sides would move their troops back from the Iron Curtain in Europe. A nonaggression treaty between NATO and the States of the Warsaw Pact should be concluded only if it did *not* result in recognition of the "German Democratic Republic."

The same line of disengagement advocated by Kennan in the early

[30] Senator Mike Mansfield said on the floor of the Senate on February 26, 1959: "It has long been a part of the policy of this Government to recognize that a peace treaty for Germany, which provides for the reasonable security needs of its neighbors, *including the Soviet Union*, is an essential to peace." *Congressional Record* (86th Congress, 1st Session), Vol. 105, Part 3, p. 3039. (Emphasis added.)

[31] *Die Welt* (Hamburg), August 20, 1963.

1950's was reflected in the cold war strategy proposed by Henry A. Kissinger. This called for a neutral belt consisting of a reunited Germany, Poland, Czechoslovakia, and Hungary, with German participation in an integrated European economic policy and with American forces stationed in the Benelux states (Belgium, Holland, and Luxembourg) as well as in France.[32]

The end of the Eisenhower era and the assumption of responsibility by the Democrats became the occasion for numerous trenchant statements on American foreign policy, particularly that relating to Europe. Considerable attention was paid an attempt by the Democratic Senator from Montana, Mike Mansfield, to introduce a new conception in the discussions on Germany, in order to move the negotiations with the Soviets on Berlin and Germany away from dead center. Mansfield considered the status quo of partition a greater danger than efforts to find a new formula for reunification.

In 1959 Mansfield rose twice in the Senate, on February 12[33] and February 26,[34] to analyze the German situation. His speeches attracted much attention. Following a precedent set by Secretary of State Dulles, he denied the proposition that free all-German elections were the only possible way to achieve German reunification. "Free elections," said Senator Mansfield, were an impractical slogan which ought to be discarded, as well as an excuse for inflexibility. He wished to treat the kind and quantity of German armament and of non-German military aid on German soil as a phase of the problem of German reunification, and thus subject to negotiation. His proposal was therefore "to thin out foreign forces in West Germany in return for a thinning out of Soviet forces in East Germany," so that the Russians would no longer be able to justify their continued presence under the pretext of American intractability.

To reduce tensions in Berlin, Senator Mansfield proposed continued presence of Western armed forces in Berlin, but simultaneously recommended replacing the thousands of Allied forces in Berlin with West German troops; this combined with supervision of the access routes by international teams and bringing about the unity and interim neutralization of all Berlin through United Nations concilia-

32 Henry A. Kissinger, *The Necessity for Choice: Prospects of American Foreign Policy* (New York, Harper, 1961), p. 161.

33 Senator Mike Mansfield, speech in the Senate, February 12, 1959, *Congressional Record* (86th Congress, 1st Session), Vol. 105, Part 2, pp. 2242-48, "The Coming Crisis in Germany."

34 Mansfield speech of February 26, *loc. cit.*, pp. 3036-39.

tion.[35] The Senator hoped that the microcosm of Berlin would provide guide lines for a solution which could then be applied to the larger problem of all-German unification.

Future negotiations concerning Berlin will take as their starting point the fact of Western Allied presence in Berlin, a position not to be shaken. They will have to concentrate on the problem of unimpeded access to Berlin. A way must be sought to find a new agreement on access and on the transit routes leading to Berlin—that is, an agreement which maintains the Western corridor into Berlin—even though historical experience suggests skepticism about the long-range durability of territorial corridors.

The basic position from which American representatives will start in negotiations on Berlin and the Berlin corridor was clearly defined by the Department of State on May 23, 1962, in the following words:

"The U.S. does not recognize the regime in Eastern Germany as either a state or a government. The U.S. considers that the area is under the effective control of the Soviet Union and that the East German regime is but a local instrument of the Soviet Government."[36]

No formula for settling the Berlin problem has yet come to my attention which would solve the dilemma faced by the Western powers; how to assure themselves free access to the enclave of West Berlin by land, while simultaneously ignoring the existence of the DDR. The American government has left no doubt that it is absolutely determined to maintain its position in West Berlin. It would therefore be unfortunate if Bonn's absolute commitment to the Hallstein Doctrine of nonrecognition of Pankow were used to block a new agreement on access routes to Berlin. Although Bonn could not forbid its American allies to negotiate such an agreement, the German leaders could make it extremely difficult for the Americans to conclude an understanding that would be as much in the interest of the Federal Republic as in that of America and Western Europe.

The fact that the DDR actually exercises unhindered powers of control such as belong only to a sovereign state, as seen in the matter of

35 *Ibid.*, p. 3039.

36 "Consuls: Power and Duties. Action on Behalf of East German Nationals. Letter of the Department of State dated May 23, 1962." *The American Journal of International Law*, Vol. 57, No. 2 (1963), p. 410.

access to Berlin, is denied by nobody, even though the legitimacy of this exercise of power may be challenged. For according to the stand-ards of the West, where free consent by the majority of the governed is the criterion for the legality and legitimacy of a government, the DDR is no state. It would appear, however, that West Germany is moving very slowly toward an appreciation of the fact that to an in-creasing extent there is no longer any common international law for East and West, and that West European and American concepts of international law cannot be applied indiscriminately to the Commu-nist world of states.

Closely related to the Berlin and German questions are the prob-lems involving Eastern Europe, and American policies toward that region. There are detailed American studies of United States relation-ships with the nationalities of East Central Europe since the beginning of this century, of the circumstances under which the East European states fell under Communist rule after World War II, and of develop-ments since Stalin's death. In 1956, the Notre Dame Committee on International Relations published a collection of articles entitled *The Fate of East Central Europe,* with the significant subtitle "Hopes and Failures" (of American foreign policy). A companion volume entitled *East Central Europe and the World* appeared in 1962.

The Soviet control under which East Central Europe fell as a result of World War II signified an incisive change in the life of its peoples, who had hitherto been considered to belong to the West and the Medi-terranean area rather than the East. It meant, moreover, a shifting of political weights inasmuch as these countries with almost one hundred million inhabitants became the glacis of Soviet power in Europe, which could serve for defense just as well as for preparing an attack. Today, a decade after Stalin's death, we face the fact that the Soviet Union not only survived without permanent injury the severe crises that threatened its rule in Poland and Hungary in 1956, but has ac-tually succeeded in binding the satellite states closer to itself eco-nomically than ever before.

Professor Robert F. Byrnes of Indiana University has made an analysis of American and West European policies with respect to East Central Europe since Stalin. His conclusion, with which the present writer agrees, was the following:

"No Western policy towards East Central Europe and towards the Soviet Union can be successful until Western Europe and the Atlantic World have achieved a strength and unity which can serve as a magnet to pull East Central Europe free from Soviet control."[37]

To the prerequisite stated by Byrnes, a second should be added: an analogous political and ideological development in the East European region, without which a decisive step toward the West is unthinkable. A trend which not a few American scholars believe they have recognized is the metamorphosis of orthodox Communism of the Stalinist brand in Eastern Europe to a Marxist-Leninist reformism, the basic framework of a socialist welfare state having already been consolidated. Since the latter is characterized by a planned economy and the dominating role of the public sector, the restoration of an economic system similar to the Western model is out of the question.[38]

To make it easier for the West German government to establish diplomatic relations with the Eastern states, even under the Hallstein Doctrine, Brzezinski and Griffith have proposed that Bonn should distinguish between free and oppressed peoples. The Federal Government, they suggest, should make known that the Hallstein Doctrine applies only to free peoples who are able to make decisions for themselves, not to the oppressed peoples of the Soviet satellites. Should one of the free peoples decide to recognize the DDR, West Germany could then break off relations with that state immediately and, if appropriate, apply economic sanctions. So far as the Hallstein Doctrine is concerned, the distinction between free and oppressed peoples would afford the Bonn government greater flexibility in its relations with Eastern Europe.

An important aspect of the East European problem is that of American-Polish relations. America's attitude toward Poland is of immediate concern to the German Federal Government. Since the question of the German-Polish boundary, that is, of the Oder-Neisse Line, is the key problem in German-Polish relations, the American position on this question is one of the basic factors in American policy with respect to Poland. If one starts with the premise that a weakening of ties be-

[37] Robert F. Byrnes, "American and West European Policy toward East Central Europe since Stalin," in Stephen D. Kertesz, ed., *East Central Europe and the World* (Notre Dame, Indiana, Univ. of Notre Dame Press, 1962), p. 375.

[38] Zbigniew Brzezinski and William E. Griffith, "Peaceful Engagement in Eastern Europe," *Foreign Affairs*, Vol. XXXIX, No. 4 (July, 1961), pp. 642-54. German transl.: "Die Politik des friedlichen Engagement," *Ost-Probleme*, Vol. XIII, Nos. 18/19 (Sept. 9, 1961), pp. 602-07.

tween Warsaw and Moscow is in the interest of both Washington and Bonn as a prerequisite for a reunification of Germany, it follows that a policy should be advocated—as Americans are already doing—which reduces Polish fear of Germany. As seen from America, the Oder-Neisse Line has become consolidated as the *de facto* boundary, even though its questionable juridical status is fully recognized. The conviction is general that this boundary can no longer be changed in the foreseeable future except by violence. An official recognition of the Oder-Neisse Line by the United States is not, however, to be expected.

As long as the Communists believe (or pretend to believe) that the Americans intend to change the status quo and to transform the countries of East Central Europe into an anti-Soviet Western bridgehead—under German rule if possible—the task of American policy in this region may be defined as the undertaking of efforts to bring about such peaceful changes as will tend to remove the threat to the West from East Central Europe and to prevent the linkage of this area to the Soviet Union from becoming permanent.

How does the Kennedy Administration stand on the questions of Berlin, Germany, and Europe?

In a masterful speech in the Senate on June 14, 1960, containing a nine-point program which must serve as the standard of judgment on foreign policy for the future history of President Kennedy's first term, the Democratic presidential candidate said:

"We must look forward to a free Berlin, in a united Germany in a Europe, where tensions and armaments have been reduced—where perhaps the suggestions of General de Gaulle and Premier Adenauer requiring Soviet withdrawal behind the Urals can be accepted. Such a solution is far from reality today."[39]

The first half of President Kennedy's statement combines with admirable simplicity all the elements of that picture of Europe which shapes contemporary American policy in the struggle with the Soviet Union for Europe and the World: a free Berlin, a reunited Germany, a Europe that is more than just an idea, plus disarmament. Immediately afterwards, however, follows the remarkable utterance about the Urals, reflecting a strangely unrealistic conception of things. The geographical fact is not to be denied, that European Russia extends to the Urals. The geographic concept of a Europe extending to the Urals

[39] *Congressional Record* (86th Congress, 2d Session), Vol. 106, Part 10, p. 12525.

has, however, fallen into some discredit, since less than twenty-five years ago one of Hitler's proclaimed war aims was to drive the Russians behind the Ural Mountains. The Ural boundary was thus pushed into the twilight of a German geopolitical doctrine of pseudo-scientific character. To induce the Russians to retreat voluntarily behind the Urals can at no time be regarded as an object of a realistic French, German, or American peace policy, inasmuch as even the effort to obtain release and evacuation of Central Germany is meeting with insuperable obstacles. Mention of the Urals by Western statesmen at the height of the cold war is thus of historical significance only.

Since taking office, President Kennedy has frequently discussed the Berlin and German questions in speeches and addresses. The tenor of his remarks has always remained constant—in the sense of the first part of the quotation from his speech of June 14, 1960. At the time of his inauguration he was filled with optimism about these as well as other questions of foreign policy. It was his hope that firm and reasonable negotiations could induce the Soviet Union to cooperate and could lead to an accommodation which would simultaneously satisfy the recognized need of the Soviet Union for security and bring about a coexistence honestly respected by both sides. He was so bitterly disappointed by his meetings with Khrushchev in Vienna on June 3 and 4, 1961, that he described the parts of the talks concerning Germany and Berlin as the least encouraging.[40] The conversation with Khrushchev must have confirmed the President decisively in his image of Europe, according to which the efforts of Communists to force their political and economic system on other countries is the principal reason for the international tensions in today's world. The logical conclusion, which President Kennedy drew in his commencement address at the American University in Washington on June 10, 1963, was that peace would be far more firmly established if all nations would refrain from interfering with the self-determination of others.[41]

In his reply, circulated by TASS on June 15, 1963, Khrushchev ignored the conclusion drawn by Kennedy and denied that Communism was motivated by a desire to force its political and economic system on others. The fact to be recognized was rather that the capitalist

[40] In his address to the nation (New York Times, June 7, 1961, p. 16), President Kennedy noted that "Our most somber talks were on the subject of Germany and Berlin." See also, Public Papers of the Presidents of the United States, John F. Kennedy (January 20 to December 31, 1961) (Washington, Government Printing Office, 1962), p. 444.

[41] See New York Times, June 11, 1963, p. 16.

order was in the process of collapse because of the objective laws of historical development. Peaceful coexistence was possible between states with different social systems, but never peaceful coexistence in the field of ideology.

The principal difference between Kennedy's policy and that of his predecessor is that the present Administration has made clear its attitude of maintaining unequivocally the *theoretical* demand for the rights of self-determination for the German people and the peoples behind the Iron Curtain. It admits, however, that, at least for the present, there is no feasible way of realizing these demands and that it is consequently necessary as a *practical* matter to accept the fact of Communist authority in the countries concerned. Kennedy has expressed his conviction that two Germanies will continue to exist as long as the Soviet Union remains of the opinion that this is to its interest.

The Kennedy Administration bases its hopes for relaxation in the cold war on the assumption of a progressive internal liberalization in the countries behind the Iron Curtain. This is a matter of belief and trust; it would surely be an injustice to the Kennedy-Rusk-Mc-Namara government to consider it capable of, and to accuse it of, placing reckless and blind trust in its principal enemy, or to charge it with letting itself be lulled to sleep with superficial concessions and meaningless peace gestures. This is, however, what is involved when every American effort to analyze Soviet developments without blinkers and to take maximum advantage of such developments is denounced *a priori* on the German side as though it were treason against the West. In the June issue of the magazine *Der Europäische Osten* (The European East), published in Munich, the following may be read in the editorial by Edmund von Gordon:

"It seems almost as though opinion in the United States were beginning to succumb to a gigantic deception, in that serious credence is being given the misleading view that the liberalization in the Soviet Union is equivalent to a relaxation of expansionist policy on the part of the Kremlin."[42]

The article by Dr. Hans Lehmann, *"Mit den Sowjets oder mit Eu-*

42 [Edmund von] Go[rdon], "Ein Sendungsbewusstsein," *Der Europäische Osten*, Vol. IX, No. 99 (June, 1963), p. 321.

ropa?" ("With the Soviets or with Europe?"), is even more out-spoken:

> "Only a few years ago, the formula of the United States in dealing with the Soviets was: Refuse relaxation until Moscow restores to the Germans their freedom and their right to self-determination. . . . There must not be and cannot be relaxation so long as the right of self-determination is denied to the Germans in the Zone. The same demand applies to the right of self-determination of the Hungarians, Poles, Bulgarians and Czechs, and all other peoples whose right to live in freedom and to determine their own social order is now denied."[43]

What is advocated here, if I may say so, is an intensified form of the policy of liberation which was proclaimed a decade ago by Eisenhower and Dulles, and which proved a complete failure.

The naiveté which certain West German critics ascribe to American diplomats in the judgment of Eastern Europe and Russia is exceeded only by their own. The fact that Kennedy is surrounded by a brain trust does not protect him from occasional errors, but it does mean that his advisers undertake to develop long-range estimates in all basic questions, and that they consider all rational alternatives. There is no aspect of the Berlin or German question which has not been thoroughly discussed and considered during the last few years in Washington. The aggravation of differences between East and West is never even in the least degree denied or taken lightly in the White House.

The position of the United States in the struggle for Berlin has clearly deteriorated, since limitation of negotiations to the immediate "point of the needle" question of Berlin alone, in accordance with the ideas of Bonn, has deprived American diplomacy of necessary room to maneuver and trade in the negotiations. As a compensating factor, there has been a general strengthening of the American and Western position in the world balance of power. The American reaction to Soviet threats was to mount a prodigious military effort, so that today's America, Kennedy's America, is once more able to deal with the Soviets with the self-confidence and relaxation of a party of equal strength. The prediction made in 1942 by Nicholas John Spyk-

---

[43] Hans Lehmann, "Zwei verschiedene Strömungen in Amerika—Mit den Sowjets oder mit Europa?" *Ibid.,* Nos., 100-101 (July-Aug., 1963), pp. 390-98.

man has now come to pass, whereby the United States, after the war, would be forced to hold in check a Russia which had grown too strong.[44]

After Kennedy's visit in Germany—with its high points of the speech in St. Paul's Church in Frankfurt and the personal inspection of the Berlin Wall—as well as the tribute which the President paid to Chancellor Adenauer's historical achievement, Washington's criticism of Bonn and Bonn's criticism of Washington seemed to have been quieted, at least temporarily. The President's words—both the carefully prepared statements in exactly measured and meticulously polished language and the spontaneous and heartfelt outbursts which broke through the President's calculated reserve—aroused greatest enthusiasm on the part of the Germans.

Kennedy promised the Germans, including the people of Berlin, no miracle. He did not arouse expectations that American partnership would solve the urgent national questions of Europe, such as those of reunification and of Berlin, within a predictable or measurable time. Without waiting or patience, the President indicated, nothing could be accomplished. The object of American foreign policy, Kennedy stated, was to work toward closest cooperation of the United States with a Europe such as America hoped and wished for—"a fully cohesive Europe in equal partnership with the United States"—a united and strong Europe acting with a common will.

Here we have an idealized image: upgrading a Europe disunited today in many respects into a European world power—a Europe able to address itself to world problems as a full and equal partner. Washington has offered full partnership and equality of rights not to a single country of Europe, but only to a European union which would include as many free countries as possible. But Kennedy immediately added a note of reserve:

"It is not the task of Americans to prescribe to Europeans how these efforts are to be carried forward. It is the Europeans themselves who are building Europe."[45]

It is not unreasonable to surmise that this great European concep-

---

[44] Nicholas John Spykman, *America's Strategy in World Politics: The United States and the Balance of Power* (New York, Harcourt, Brace, 1942), pp. 466-67.

[45] Speech at the Paulskirche, Frankfurt, June 25, 1963; for text, see *New York Times*, June 26, p. 16.

tion of the American President exercised a decisive influence on the new program of the Pan-Europe Union of Germany. This program, which has far-reaching implications, was announced in July, 1963. Its Point Six states:

"The final goal of the Pan-Europe movement is the reunification of Europe through elimination of the Iron Curtain and the Berlin Wall. This greater Europe can only be established through friendly understanding between the NATO and the powers of the Warsaw Pact; with the addition of North America in the west and the Soviet Union in the east."[46]

America has now finally turned its back on isolationism. The advice and the warning in Washington's Farewell Address of September 19, 1796, the foreign policy creed of the United States for more than a century, now belong irrevocably to the past:

"It must be unwise in us to implicate ourselves, by artificial ties, in the ordinary vicissitudes of her [Europe's] politics, or the ordinary combinations and collisions of her friendships, or enmities."[47]

It was Carl Schurz, the great man of 1848, who formulated the relation of the United States to Germany and to Europe in words which today are still valid and may justly be termed classic: "American influence in Europe will be based on Germany, and Germany's position in the world will depend essentially upon America's success."

It may be assumed that President Kennedy abstracted his image of Europe and the European policy which he visualizes—with all its consequences and calculated risks—before he took his trip to Germany and formed for himself an image of Germany and of Berlin, which he then fitted into his picture of Europe.

In a time when countless Germans and Europeans take a skeptical view of postwar Europe, Hitler's inheritance, in a time of clashing social orders and irreconcilable ideologies, it is a good thing that the political leader of the American continent—the chief of a state that is now passing through a revolution, not entirely peaceful but gener-

---

[46] *Rheinischer Merkur,* July 12, 1963.

[47] *The Writings of George Washington* (John C. Fitzpatrick, editor), Vol. 35: March 10, 1796, to July 31, 1797 (Washington, Government Printing Office, 1940), p. 234.

ally nonviolent, for equal rights for all its citizens—takes up anew
the theme of a predecessor particularly unrecognized and maligned
in Germany, Woodrow Wilson, and says to the world:

"The United States has always represented the center of hope
for the people of the world. . . . I hope in the future we shall once
again provide the leadership and vision which will offer hope to
the world."[48]*

*P.S. These words are President Kennedy's legacy to our nation.
The manuscript of this article was made ready for print on November 22, 1963—the day when he died from an assassin's bullet in the
prime of his life.

[48] Speech of Senator John F. Kennedy, June 14, 1960, *Congressional Record* (86th Congress, 2d Session), Vol. 106, Part 10, p. 12529.

Index

Dr. David S. Collier is director of the Foundation for Foreign Affairs, Inc., and publisher of the quarterly review *Modern Age*.

Dr. Kurt Glaser is professor of government at Southern Illinois University.